T H I S
C A N ' T
W A I T

Talking With Your Kids About Sex

Scott Talley

HillCrest
PUBLISHING

THIS CAN'T WAIT: *Talking With Your Kids About Sex*

HillCrest
P U B L I S H I N G

1648 Campus Court
Abilene, TX   79601
www.hillcrestpublishing.com

Type Specifications: Headline set in Book Antiqua, Normal, 24 point, 90% width. Subhead set in Book Antiqua, Bold and Italics, 18 point. Body copy set in Book Antiqua, 12 point. Endnote set in Book Antiqua, 10 point.

Printed in the United States of America

ISBN 0-89112-435-7

Library of Congress Card Number 00-101046

1,2,3,4,5

PREFACE

In 1989 I wrote a book on how to help your children develop healthy sexual attitudes and how to talk with them about sex and sexuality. I wrote the book because during my many years of experience as a youth minister, I witnessed teens struggling with sexual temptation and sin. In the late eighties teen sexual activity and pregnancy reached record levels in this country. As a youth minister, I was on the front lines of a war we appeared to be losing. And so out of my experience and after many months of research, I wrote a book designed to help parents communicate and model godly sexual attitudes to their children and to help them become the primary sex educators of their children. I emphasized abstinence and sexual purity prior to marriage as God's will for His people. Many other educators, ministers, psychologists, and concerned adults were also writing and appealing to parents and teens to choose abstinence and sexual purity. And apparently the message was heard. Consider the following facts:

- Between 1991 and 1997, the share of the nation's teenagers who engaged in sexual activity declined 11 percent according to the Centers for Disease Control and Prevention. Last year, 48.4 percent of students in grades 9 through 12 were sexually active, compared with 54.1 percent in 1991.[1]

- On May 1, 1997, National Institute of Health Secretary Donna Shalala said, "both males and females increased in virginity, indicating a decline [in teen sexual activity] for the first time in more than two decades. In 1990 43 percent of teens indicated they were virgins. In 1995 that number increased to 48 percent."[2]
- Statistics from the Department of Health and Human Services show that births to teenagers fell 4 percent in 1997.
- A report from the Allan Guttmacher Institute finds that teen pregnancy dropped 4 percent in 1996 and fell 17 percent from its peak in 1990.[3]

Listen to what noted cultural critic Michael Medved says:

For parents the most important news is that this focused effort toward abstinence seems to have turned around the trends. For the first time in twenty-five years, the National Survey of Family growth, an in-depth federal study conducted every five years, showed a decrease in teenage sexuality. In statistics released in May 1997, 50 percent of teenage girls said they'd had intercourse at least once, down 5 percent from the 1990 survey. Previously, girls' sex rates had climbed every year since 1970.[4]

It does appear that sexual activity and pregnancy among teens is decreasing slightly. However, teen sexual activity remains high, and many educators, parents, and health officials still persist in the belief that teen sex is inevitable and uncontrollable. As a result, many of these authorities believe that teens should be taught about "safe sex" and condoms should be passed out at schools. Dr. Lloyd Kolbe, director of the CDC's Division of Adolescent and School Health, in reference to the decrease in teen sexual activity quoted earlier, says: "The findings give further evidence that teaching teenagers about *safe sex* hasn't resulted in more promiscuity."[5] Unfortunately, many parents, even Christian parents, believe Dr. Kolbe and the CDC's recommendations about teaching safe sex to their children. After all, the CDC is the premier health authority in the country. I, on the other hand, have seen too many emotional scars teens carried for years because of a teenage sexual encounter. I have counseled with many adults who cannot forgive themselves for past sexual sins. I have spent twenty-five years witnessing the consequences of sharing the ultimate and most intimate gift of sex before one is emotionally or psychologically ready. Many experts agree. Listen to what Derek C. Polonsky, M.D., an instructor in psychiatry at Harvard Medical School, says: "I don't know how to say it forcefully enough: Teens are not sufficiently developed emotionally to understand the deep levels of sharing required to have a sexually fulfilling relationship."[6] Many years of painful observation of teens and adults causes me to view the term "safe sex" as an oxymoron! Sexual encounters outside the will of God can never be referred to as safe. Even though sexual activity among teens is slightly declining, Christian parents must vigilantly combat the worldly idea of teaching "safe sex" and continue teaching their children a godly view of sexuality.

A few years of modestly declining sexual activity among teens does not erase the dramatic and harmful effects produced by three decades of sexual revolution in this country. This modern sexual revolution has encouraged and promoted the loosening of sexual morals and behaviors and contributed to a secular world-view that endorses sexual promiscuity. Unfortunately, this modern sexual revolution has also infected our Christian world. Many parents in our churches now routinely accept sexually provocative dress, language, and behavior from their children as a normal part of growing up. Dr. Archibald Hart, professor of Psychology at Fuller Theological Seminary, states the problem well when he says, "We believe that one of the most critical issues facing the church as we enter the twenty-first century is the whole issue of sexuality. We need to come to grips with our culture's portrayal of what constitutes normal human sexuality. We also have to open up a dialog in our churches about sexuality."[7] Dr. Hart goes on to say that he believes that our churches, more than any other social system, have kept society's nose to the grindstone when it comes to sexual morals and family values. But he believes that our churches must not become reticent about matters of sexuality because silence concerning sexuality will expose our children to sexual distortion, myth and confusion. As the new millennium approaches Christian parents must not become complacent and neglect to teach their children a godly view of human sexuality.

The Editors and Board of Directors at HillCrest Publishing also feel that our churches must articulate a godly, biblical view of human sexuality and prepare parents to be the primary sex educators of their children. Therefore, the editors encouraged me to write an updated and expanded version of my previous book. We feel an urgency to help churches equip parents in this vital area because many studies show that children whose parents talk to them about sexuality and maintain open communication with them about both the facts of life and the values of sex are more likely to postpone sexual activity. Our goal is provide a tool that will help and equip parents, grandparents, teachers, and other adults educate and train children to live godly lives of abstinence prior to marriage.

For the past year I have read and researched numerous books, articles, journals, and web sites in preparation for this new book. I have also interviewed youth ministers, psychologists, teachers, nurses, health care workers, parents, and teens. Much of the material from the previous book remains in this expanded version because it continues to be relevant and helpful. However, this amplified version contains an abundance of current and new material. For example, new statistics related to teen sexual activity, pregnancy, abortion and sexually transmitted diseases will be contrasted with the statistics from ten years ago. Also included will be the latest research concerning pornography and the internet and how to protect children from this new and dangerous phenomenon. Additionally, several sections of the former book have been increased to encompass new and pertinent information. These sections include: media influence, communicating with teens, peer pressure, abuse, dating alternatives, date rape, and many others. I attempted to place specific subject material in the book according to where it would most logically need to be discussed with children or where it would most naturally fit from an age appropriate standpoint. However, many subjects are not so easily categorized and specific material might need to be discussed earlier or later depending on your child.

Many of the subjects discussed in this book are controversial and arguable and dedicated Christian people hold differing opinions regarding many of these issues. This book presents a range of diverse and distinct opinions and beliefs held by Christians. When I am in agreement with a particular opinion, I will so state. In these debatable areas parents should consider all opinions and prayerfully decide what is best for their particular children in their specific situation.

It is my prayer that this book will help you maneuver through a very difficult part of parenthood — teaching your children the mysteries of human sexuality. Unraveling the mystery of sex and how it fits into a healthy, happy and godly life is one of a parent's biggest challenges. This book will provide you with information concerning how to teach children about this important area of life. It will help you and other adults know what to say, when to say it and how to say it. It will help you teach your children how to take control of such a significant part of their lives and in so doing, empower them to resist premature sexual activity.

At this point you may be asking yourself if you really can make a difference and be a positive influence on your children's sexual behavior. Absolutely! As a parent you are now and always will be the greatest influence on your child's developing sexuality. According to the Sexuality Information and Education Council of the United States (SIECUS) report: "54 percent of sexually active teens say they would like to talk to their parents about sex."[8] Parents have two very important reasons to teach their children about their developing sexuality. First, if you do not teach your children about sex, someone else most certainly will. Second, God has given you the responsibility to train and teach your children about their sexuality.

May God be with you as you teach, instruct, train and model godly sexuality to your children!

Scott Talley
June, 2000

[1] "Sexual Activity Among High School Students Decreasing," *Dallas Morning News*. 18 September 1998.

[2] David Lewis and Carley Dodd, *National Adolescent Survey*. 1998 Youth & Family Ministry Conference, Abilene Christian University, Abilene, TX.

[3] "Teen Pregnancy, Abortion Rates Fall," *Dallas Morning News*. 29 April, 1999.

[4] Michael Medved and Diane Medved. *Saving Childhood* (New York: Harper Collins, 1998), 220.

[5] "Sexual Activity Among High School Students Decreasing," *Dallas Morning News*. 18 September 1998.

[6] Kristine Napier, M.P.H., *The Power of Abstinence* (New York: Avon Books, 1996), 6.

[7] Archibald D. Hart, Catherine Hunt Weber, Debra L. Taylor, *Secrets of Eve*, (Nashville: Word, 1998), 6.

[8] Report of the Sexuality Information and Education Council of the United States. June/July 1994, 16.

Contents

CONTENTS

INTRODUCTION

During twenty-four years of youth ministry I have observed many changes in our society and culture. Values, beliefs, ideals and morals have all been redefined as a secular society gropes for its moorings. Churches and families have also been impacted by our rapidly changing moral environment. It is becoming increasingly difficult for families to develop moral sense in our swiftly changing world.

Nowhere is this more visible than in our society's preoccupation with sex. Madison Avenue advertisers use sex to sell everything from automobiles to children's clothes. It is impossible to escape almost daily exposures to media references to sex. This cultural preoccupation not only damages society as a whole, but especially harms children and adolescents. Young people between the ages of eleven and nineteen do not have sufficient emotional, physical and spiritual maturity necessary to deal with the complex issues of human sexuality. Our society's modern sexual revolution of the past three decades presents Christian parents with many challenges as they attempt to rear, in the words of Tipper Gore, "P.G. kids in an X-rated society."

It's A Different Ball Game — Teen Sexual Activity

As I noted in the preface, teen sexual activity over the past decade has slightly decreased. However, when at least 50 percent of high school students have engaged in sexual intercourse, a major problem exists. Our society continues to encourage sexual immorality with rather dramatic effects. Consider the most recent statistics:

- A 1992 survey conducted by the Center for Disease Control(CDC) found that 54 percent of high school students reported having sexual intercourse at least once in their lives.[1]
- According to the 1993 Youth Risk Behavior Survey conducted by the CDC, 53 percent of all high school students have had intercourse; 40 percent of ninth graders and 72 percent of twelfth graders.[2]
- In 1996, 73 percent of young men and 56 percent of young women had experienced sexual intercourse by their eighteenth birthday, up from 55 percent and 35 percent from 1970.[3]
- Every thirty seconds a teen gets pregnant (3000 yearly). America has the highest teen pregnancy rate of any developed nation. Since 1970 the non-marital teen pregnancy rate has risen 87 percent. [4]
- Among thirteen-year-old boys, 20 percent have touched a girl's breast and 54 percent of fourteen-year-old boys have engaged in breast play.[5]

One would hope that the behavior of Christian teens would follow a significantly different trend. But this is not the case. Several studies of teenagers in evangelical churches revealed that:

- Over 45 percent of regularly churched youth have had sex before completing high school.[6]
- Fondling breasts is considered to be morally acceptable at times by 32 percent of teens and

32 percent see fondling genitals as sometimes morally acceptable.[7]

- 22 percent of Church of Christ teens ages fifteen to nineteen were not virgins, and by age seventeen 36 percent had experienced either oral sex or intercourse. [According to a survey conducted in 1995 by the Center for Adolescent Studies at Abilene Christian University][8]
- Between 45 and 50 percent of evangelical Christian youth are involved in sexual activity. Studies generally show that the percentage of sexually active Christian youth is about ten to twelve points behind the percentage of all teens.

It should be noted, of course, that the accuracy of statistics is dependent on the size of the sample and the method of sampling, the instrument used to obtain the information and many other factors. For example, statistics indicating that 50 percent of all teens between the ages of fifteen and nineteen are sexually active are somewhat misleading. Parents of younger teens should know that not until age eighteen for women and seventeen for men do the actual figures reach 50 percent. There is good news, too, for kids who value church involvement. For instance, adolescents who consider youth ministry extremely helpful have an 80 percent virginity rate compared to a 58 percent rate among adolescents who consider youth ministry unhelpful.[9]

The majority of statistics I have cited, of course, indicate that sexual activity among teens remains very high. A decade of modestly declining sexual activity among teens does not alter that fact.

Why do such figures surprise us? For one thing, most parents of today's teenagers were reared in the

1960s, 1970s and early 1980s. It is very difficult for many of us to fully understand the ramifications of three decades of sexual revolution and the dramatic and harmful effects on the attitudes and behaviors of children and teens. One reason may be that we do not have contact with significant numbers of adolescents and we have limited access to their world. Another contributing factor is that we parents have a strong reluctance to believe that our children are involved in sexual misconduct. Sexual activity among our children is too emotionally painful for many Christian parents to contemplate; therefore, we simply ignore it. But this means ignoring many teens! Parents desperately need to understand that for teenagers, sexual pressure and temptation have increased drastically for three decades.

When I first began as a youth minister in the early '70s, comparatively little of my time was spent counseling teens regarding sexual misconduct. By the late '70s and early '80s, however, things were changing and far more of my time was being consumed by this. I answered the phone late one evening to hear the voice of one of the teenage girls in my youth group. She told me she had just returned from the clinic and was pregnant. She asked if I would accompany her to tell her parents. I was shocked, not only because this was my first experience of this kind, but also because this was "one of our own." This young lady came from a dedicated Christian family; both her mother and father were Sunday school teachers. This was a good girl! But she was pregnant! It is apparent that sexual misconduct, sometimes resulting in pregnancy, is occurring with alarming regularity among young people from all types of families.

Unfortunately, there have been many other troublesome encounters in subsequent years. An eighteen year old girl in my youth group approached me for help and informed me that she was pregnant, and that she planned to get an abortion because she did not feel that her parents would be supportive. She further informed me that I did not have her permission to tell her parents or anyone about her condition and decision. Since this girl was legally an adult, I was bound by law not to reveal her secret. I could only offer advice and love. This young lady, too, was a good Christian girl from a Christian family.

A personal example will help illustrate the harmful effects of sexual behavior in our society. Several years ago, when my son was about fourteen years old, I found him burning a picture of his most recent girlfriend. Most fourteen-year-olds change boyfriends and girlfriends about as often as they change clothes so I was not overly concerned about the change itself. But my son is not usually given to severe emotional reactions, so I went into his room and asked why he was so upset with this young lady.

He said, "I'm sorry I burned her picture, but I was very upset with her and it seemed like a good idea."

Then I asked him to tell me why he was so upset.

"Well, Dad," he said, "I found out that she went to an unchaperoned party this past weekend and had sex with a guy."

I cautioned him about unsubstantiated rumors and the need to protect the reputation of the young lady, but he interrupted me.

"Dad," he replied, "she admitted it!"

That experience allowed my son and me to have several very meaningful conversations about sex, temptation, parties, and many other subjects. But I was sad for him and for this fourteen-year-old girl who perhaps unknowingly had created a multitude of problems at such a tender age.

Frazier

For the past eight seasons one of the most popular and highly rated situation comedies on TV has been the NBC series "Frazier." Three times the star of the series, Kelsy Grammer, received an Emmy as the best actor in a television situation comedy. On the program, Frazier is a radio psychologist and much of the show revolves around his bumbling attempts to seduce women. During one episode, Frazier's old piano instructor called and wanted to drop by for a visit. Immediately, Frazier began to invent reasons why this woman could not come to his home. His father, with whom he shares an apartment, could not understand Frazier's reluctance to allow his old instructor to drop by for a simple visit. Finally, Frazier revealed the source of his hesitancy — he had lost his virginity to this woman at the age of sixteen and he feared she might embarrass him by revealing his secret. Frazier's embarrassment focused on the age difference between his instructor and himself. Not once during the entire program was the morality of premarital sex discussed. Sex between these two individuals was apparently viewed as a normal youthful encounter. It was portrayed as neither moral nor immoral.

The Frazier program is certainly not an aberration. On any night of the week the plot of many television situation comedies centers on either premarital or extramarital sex and blatantly depicts such activity as normal.

The way in which sexual morality is being eroded by the media, especially television, is alarming. For example, in the '50s when Lucille Ball on "I Love Lucy" was expecting a child, the word "pregnant" was not allowed on the air. In the '60s Rob and Laura on "The Dick Van Dyke Show" slept in twin beds. In a little over two decades television has shifted from depicting married couples in twin beds to openly encouraging extramarital sex as an acceptable part of growing up. Times have certainly changed! Consider the following:

- According to an extensive 1996 poll, just 38 percent of the Hollywood elite (producers, directors, and so on) were concerned about how TV depicted premarital sex, compared with 86 percent of the general public.[10]

- Prime-time network TV shows air as many as eight depictions of premarital sex for every one of sex between married couples. And when premarital sex is depicted, concern about consequences is raised in only 5 percent of cases. "What was once considered as deviant behavior is now treated as the norm."[11]

- Sexual content aired during prime time on television has quadrupled during the past twenty years.[12]

What Are We Telling Our Kids?

Much of the information and counseling given to adolescents regarding sexual activity emphasizes disease, pregnancy prevention and "safe sex." This information ignores what an increasing number of teens really want to hear. In fact, in one survey of teenage girls, 84 percent said that what they most wanted to learn from sex education was how to say no.[13] Family life pastor and educator Tim Smith says:

> In my work with teens and families I have noticed a change in the last few years. Teens and parents are thinking about values. Though our teenagers represent the younger end of what has been called Generation X, *Parade* magazine has called them Generation V for their desire for stronger moral values. According to the Mood of American Youth study, today's teens are neither as rebellious as adolescents in the 1970s nor as materialistic as those of the 1980s. What they want is not to change the world or to own a chunk of it, but to be happy. Among teen's greatest concerns — the decline in moral and social values.[14]

I agree with Tim Smith's statements. Today's teens do care more about morals and values. Certainly children and adolescents must be warned about the damaging physical consequences of sexual activity, but children also need and desire to be taught the truth that premarital sex violates and defiles the sanctity of God's laws. In other words, they should learn that sex outside of marriage is morally wrong. As Christian parents, do not be afraid to view the teaching of sexual morality as an end in itself.

Most Christian parents feel the need to teach their children to abstain from sexual activity. But they also need to teach them a healthy, wholesome, godly attitude toward their sexuality. We must teach our children the biblical view that embraces sexuality as a gift from God and help them see sexuality as a part of God's intention for creation. "This God-given sexuality includes sexual intercourse. Not only is intercourse a spiritual symbol of 'becoming one' but this idea is used throughout Scripture to symbolize the relationship of God to persons."[15]

Jump In With Both Feet!

Many aspects of sexuality will be discussed in this book. My objective is to equip parents with the knowledge and understanding children need in learning about human sexuality. Notice, I did not just say "sex," but "sexuality"; by the term sexuality I mean much more than just sex. Sexuality is much broader and encompasses everything that has to do with being male and female, including how we view our bodies and our relationships with each other, how we grow and change over the years, who we are as men and women, and of course, how we reproduce. Additionally, you will learn *how* and *when* to use the information. The topics covered include:

- Understanding and accepting your own sexuality
- Sources of our children's sexual information
- How to effectively communicate with our children and teens
- How to become an askable parent
- How to establish practical guidelines and limits
- Family structure and discipline
- When, where and how to talk to our children about sex (typical questions)
- Specific factual information appropriate for each age
- Specific age-related topics: puberty, menstruation, masturbation, contraception, dating, socially transmitted diseases, abortion, homosexuality, pornography, abuse

- At each age category, the effects of self-esteem, peer pressure, and stress on sexuality will be examined

It should also be noted that while subjects such as communication and discipline do not directly relate to sexuality, they promote a healthy family atmosphere without which instruction on sexual matters would be very difficult. This book is the result of research and study of competent authorities, both secular and Christian, in the field of sexuality and sex education, and twenty-five years of ministry with parents, and young people making decisions in a Christian framework about their own sexuality. Remember as you engage in this important and sometimes frightening task, that you occupy a unique position in the life of your child. Your relationship, based on your love and knowledge as a parent, enables you to communicate and teach your children a biblical view of sexuality better than anyone else. And if your children are to acquire a godly, moral understanding and appreciation for human sexuality...you must teach them!

---

[1] *Morbidity and Mortality Weekly Report,* vol. 40 nos. 51 and 52, U. S. Department of Health and Human Services, Public Health Service, Centers for Disease Control, January 2, 1982, 885-888.

[2] Kristine Napier, *The Power of Abstinence* (New York: Avon Books, 1996), 4.

[3] Linda and Richard Eyre, *How to Talk to Your Child About Sex* (New York: Golden Books, 1998), 181.

[4] The Alan Guttmacher Institute, *Sex and America's Teenager* (New York: The Alan Guttmacher Institute, 1994), 52.

[5] Josh McDowell and Dick Day, *Why Wait?* (San Bernandino: Here's Life Publishers, 1989), 23.

[6] Grace Ketterman, *Ketterman on Kids* (Wheaton: Harold Shaw Publishers, 1997), 231.

[7] John Nieder, *God, Sex and Your Children* (Nashville: Thomas Nelson Publishers, 1988), 19.

[8] David Lewis and Carley Dodd, *National Adolescent Survey.* 1998 Youth & Family Ministry Conference.

[9] David Lewis, Carly Dodd, and Darryl Tippens. *Shattering the Silence*, (Nashville: Christian Communication, 1989), 112.

[10] *U. S. News and World Report* 122 no. 19 (May 19, 1997): 56.

[11] Ibid, 56.

[12] *1996 Kaiser Foundation Survey on Teens and Sex.* Kaiser Family Foundation, Reuters, Dec. 12, 1996.

[13] John Leo, "Learning to Say No," *U.S. News and World Report* (June 20, 1994): 24.

[14] Tim Smith, *Almost Cool* (Chicago: Moody Press, 1997), 15-16.

[15] Archibald Hart, *The Sexual Man* (Dallas: Word Publishing, 1994), 167.

1

We're Gonna Talk
to Our Kids About What?

The mere thought of talking to their children about sex renders many parents totally speechless. Even the most confident, self-assured parents can shudder when contemplating a "facts-of-life" talk with their twelve-year- old son or daughter. But regardless of fear and sweaty palms, this is a task you cannot get out of. Most all parents need some motivation to push them through their discomfort in discussing sexual matters with their children. The typical Christian parent has wonderful intentions for teaching children traditional biblical and moral standards regarding sex. However, nearly all parents also have a great deal of trouble talking about sex with their children. Unfortunately, this discomfort causes most parents too wait too long and say too little! Stanton and Brenna Jones state in their book, *How & When to Tell Your Kids About Sex*, "The question is not whether you will provide sex education for your child. The question is: Will you do it carefully, thoughtfully, and in accordance with God's desires, or will you do it poorly through neglect, miscommunication, poor preparation, and bad timing? Parents *are* the principal sex educators; you will either have an anemic, unintentional, mixed-up, and hence negative impact, or a powerful, deliberate, clear, and positive impact."[1]

The Institute for Family Research and Education takes the same position. "Parents are the sex educators of their children whether they do it well or badly. Silence teaches no less eloquently than words."[2]

Parental Sexuality

Before leaping headlong into educating your children about sex, you should take time for some self-evaluation. Such evaluation is necessary because attitudes, values and beliefs concerning our own sexuality dramatically affect what we teach our children about sex. Perhaps a good starting place would be to simply ask yourself "Am I comfortable with my own sexuality?" Parents are often embarrassed or uncomfortable talking to their children about sex because they are not comfortable with their own sexuality. Former Surgeon General C. Everett Koop believes that the best thing parents can do for their children is to feel comfortable about their own sexuality.[3] Parents should also ask themselves how their attitudes about sexuality are played out in their marriage relationship. Is your sexual relationship satisfying? Can you talk about sexual matters with each other? Unhappy sexual attitudes and habits can affect not only what you teach, but also what you model. Remember that parents' behavior and attitudes toward sex and marriage teach children more than words. Children learn a great deal about sex and sexual matters by simply watching and observing their parents, so parents are teaching values and beliefs both verbally or nonverbally.

First of all, parents need to accept themselves and their mates physically. In other words, be comfortable with your body and appearance and the body and appearance of your mate. This will communicate physical acceptance to your children and make it easier for them to accept themselves physically.

Parents should communicate to their children that they love each other, not just platonically but sexually. Children should be taught that God created us as sexual beings, and that within the context of marriage sexual expressions are normal and healthy. Such communication is important because young people often grow up without an awareness that their parents are sexually attracted to each other. A survey among college students revealed that many of them could not imagine their parents having sex. Parents should let their children know in appropriate ways that they love each other and enjoy their sexual relationship. The more children see their parents treat sex as wholesome and normal as God intended, the more likely they will be to do the same.

Learning to handle emotions openly and positively can be helpful as parents attempt to model healthy, sexual attitudes. This is true because the interaction of our sexual attitudes and emotions is very important. Many people do not enjoy a good sex life because they have been conditioned to deny their emotions in every aspect of their lives. And when emotions are left unexpressed or misunderstood, they begin to create a barrier between partners. Many adults have developed a habit of protecting vulnerable feelings such as hurts, disappointments and loneliness with a facade of anger. Such a habit on the part of one or both spouses can interfere with positive sexual feelings and attitudes. Learning to communicate one's feelings openly and honestly not only contributes to solving marital problems, but also models positive, helpful attitudes to children. Of course, a complex subject like emotional openness should not be trivialized and learning it can be a long, difficult process. My point, however, is that your emotions can and do affect your sexuality as well as what you model before your children.

Our attitudes, values, and beliefs concerning sexuality are influenced by our past experiences. Childhood experiences and parental influence affect individuals well into their adult lives. We are all influenced by our past.

Sorting out values and feelings is an interesting process. It is also a sensitive and fragile task requiring honesty with yourself. Although this self-examination can be painful, getting in touch with your feelings and clarifying your values is both necessary and rewarding.

It may be helpful to think of the process as a "journey of exploration" into your inner self. Ideally, at the end of this imaginary journey you will have a clearer picture of your own feelings, values, and attitudes concerning sex. To begin this process let's take a journey. The purpose of this journey is to assist you, the parent, in clarifying and identifying your thoughts and feelings concerning sex. This journey may trigger deeply buried emotions and recollections of painful experiences, but by remembering and reliving these events of the past you will be better enabled to empathize with your children. In addition, from a practical standpoint, you may remember negative examples from your own childhood sex education experiences that can be avoided with your children.

It may be easier for you to take this journey if you can get someone to read the questions for you while you sit with your eyes closed. Whether you are reading the questions yourself or having them read to you, proceed slowly, taking time to collect all your thoughts after each question. Next, close your eyes and rummage through your thoughts. It will also be helpful to find a place where you are comfortable and where you will not be disturbed. Please remember that the purpose of this journey and these questions is to help you not only focus on your own values, feelings and attitudes, but also define your goals and objectives in teaching your children about sex.

The Journey

Close your eyes and think back to your childhood. Think back as far as you can.

- What were the attitudes regarding sexuality that were modeled by your parents in your home?
- What was the first question about sex you can remember asking your parents? How did they respond?
- Did any crucial experiences shape your feelings about sex in childhood? (abuse, rape, pornography)
- From what sources (parents, friends, books) did you first learn the basic facts about reproduction and intercourse?
- How did you feel upon acquiring this information?
- Were you ever punished or made to feel guilty or ashamed because of childhood curiosity about your own or a playmate's body ("playing doctor", or "physical exam")?

- Were you informed by your parents about menstruation, nocturnal emissions, and masturbation?
- How open and honest were your parents in discussing sex with you? Did either, or both, of your parents act embarrassed or angry when discussing sexual matters?
- As you entered your late teens did you have all the sexual information you needed or desired?
- As you entered adolescence how did you feel about your developing sexual desires, feelings, and longings?
- Was most of your sexual information about physical and/or biological aspects? Were you ever given information about the emotional, psychological and spiritual aspects of sex?
- How was love and affection shown or demonstrated by your parents (either to you or to each other)?

Open your eyes. What have you learned about yourself and your sexual attitudes?

As you continue in this evaluation process, it is important for you and your spouse to communicate with each other about sexual needs and problems. Such frank communication is important because if a husband and wife do not feel free to talk to each other about their sexuality, they will not feel free to talk about the subject with their children. To gain this comfort requires open, honest communication, not only between spouses, but also between parents and children. In the role as a modeling, teaching, parent, open and intimate communication with children is especially important. This personal touch in the area of parent-child communication is very effective because what children learn is as much caught as taught.

> If communication has been open with
> children and if the parents themselves believe
> that sex should be connected with love, then
> teens are less likely to be affected by what
> peers are doing.[4]

In other words, your influence can be dramatically
increased by close, intimate, communication.

Sometimes one or both partners in a marriage
may be troubled by persistent, ongoing sexual
problems. If this is your situation seek professional
help. Parents cannot offer their children appropriate
sex education if all their energy and attention is
consumed with their own sexual problems.

The focus of this book is not marital sexual
problems, and the preceding paragraphs are not
intended to be exhaustive or to provide all inclusive
suggestions. The focal points are that parents model
sexual attitudes and values to their children daily,
and parental goals for effective sex education can
best be accomplished by parents with healthy,
wholesome, positive attitudes regarding sexuality
in general and towards their own sexuality
specifically.

I gave you some questions to help you clarify
early influences on your sexual attitudes. Try the
same procedure with the questions that follow. They
will help you identify your feelings about your role
in your children's sexual education. Close your eyes
now and think about these questions:

- Do you have difficulty talking to your
  children about sex?
- Do you feel that you have adequate
  information to discuss sexual matters with
  your children? In other words, do you know
  how and when to talk to your children about
  sex?

- Are you afraid your child will ask about your own sexual experiences?
- Are you comfortable with your own sexuality?
- Do you feel you are an approachable and askable parent?
- Do you think your children really want to discuss sex with you?
- What are the sources of your children's sexual information?
- What kind of perspective about sexuality and relationships do you think your children are developing by watching your example?
- What are your major concerns and fears as you think about teaching your children about sex?

Open your eyes. How are you feeling about this after pondering these questions? A little nervous? During the next few chapters your courage and confidence will hopefully increase as you acquire helpful information that will improve your ability to talk to your children about sex.

Not All Bad News

Earlier I mentioned several disturbing facts regarding teenage sex and pregnancy. And even though for the past decade these statistics have improved slightly, teenage sexual activity remains high and continues to be a distressing and troublesome problem. However, not all the news is bad. A great deal of recent research is discovering that family closeness, openness, and religious training can have very beneficial effects not only on sexual practices of adolescents, but also on other deviant behavior. For example, Stanton L. Jones,

Ph.D. Chairman of the Department of Psychology at Wheaton College and clinical psychologist says:

> One study showed that teens who were involved in church were sexually active at about half the rate of those who were not. The general conclusion of research is that personal religious devotion is a strong protective influence against sexual experimentation. One major study showed clearly that "at-risk" behavior such as frequent alcohol use, theft, and drug use occurred at about half the rate among young people who were active in church as compared to those who were not. With regard to sex, 22 percent of those who were active in church were sexually active, as compared to 42 percent of those who were not active in church at all.[5]

Josh McDowell in his book *Why Wait* provides further evidence:

> A study of teenage sex-related values and behavior was done by sociologist Brent Miller at Utah State University and reported in *The Family's Role in Adolescent Sexual Behavior.* Miller discovered that the more openly parents discussed their sex-related values and beliefs with teens, the less their children displayed either negative sexual attitudes or promiscuous sexual behavior. He also shows that teens who learned sexual facts from parents were significantly less likely to be sexually active than those who first heard about sex from their friends.[6]

These researchers are telling parents that family closeness, as expressed through open, honest sex education, can promote abstinence from sexual activity. Also religious training and church involvement can reduce sexual activity among teens. This is good news!

Myths About Sex Education

Distinguishing between fact and fiction in areas of sex education can at times be extremely difficult. To a large extent this difficulty is compounded by the controversial nature of the subject. It is, however, very important for parents to be able to differentiate between facts and myths in the areas of sex education. With this in mind, pause in your reading and take this quick true/false test. After answering the questions, read on and discover the facts and the myths!

T / F **1.** In today's enlightened culture, adolescents already possess adequate sexual information.

T / F **2.** Most teenagers know more about sex than most of their parents.

T / F **3.** Sexual knowledge is harmful to children and adolescents.

T / F **4.** Children do not want to talk to their parents about sex.

T / F **5.** In order to effectively talk to children about sex, parents need specific, scientific, technical information.

T / F **6.** Parents must be completely comfortable about all aspects of sexuality in order to be effective with their children.

T / F **7.** It is possible to give a child too much information.

T / F **8.** Parental mistakes in sex education are irreversibly damaging to the child.

Hopefully, you answered false to all the above questions, since they represent some popularly held myths about sex education. Take for example, the first two questions. Research shockingly reveals that adolescents are actually ignorant about critical sexual issues. In an important Johns Hopkins study of adolescent girls, only 41 percent knew when in the menstrual cycle the risk of conception was greatest.[7] Granted, from their exposure to adult fare on television and in the printed media, today's children know a great deal more sex-related words than their parents and grandparents did at the same age, but David Elkind, in his insightful book *The Hurried Child* labels this phenomenon "pseudo-sophistication."

> Children today know more than they understand. They are able to talk about nuclear fission, tube worms at 20,000 fathoms, and the space shuttle; and they seem knowledgeable about sex and crime. But much of the knowledge is largely verbal. Adults, however, are often taken in by this pseudo-sophistication and treat children as if they were as knowledgeable as they sound. Ironically, the pseudo-sophistication, which is the effect of television hurrying children, encourages parents and adults to hurry them even more. But children who sound, behave, and look like adults still feel and think like children.[8]

Several years ago, a parent from my church called and related a shocking story that graphically illustrates the inadequacy of our children's sexual information. Her eighth grade daughter was at home ill and was watching one of the afternoon talk shows with her mother. The subject of the program that day centered around thirteen- and fourteen-year old girls becoming pregnant. At the conclusion of the program, the girl from our church, turned to her mother and said, "That show is ridiculous, everyone knows it is impossible to get pregnant before age fifteen because that's when you get a vagina!" Needless to say, the mother was shocked.

Today's youth simply do not know enough about sex. Furthermore, the facts they do possess are not clearly understood in the complex context of human sexuality. Children need help from their parents in order to give meaning and understanding to sexual words and sexual feelings.

Question 3 deals with whether or not sexual information is harmful to children and adolescents. Again, generally speaking, the answer is false. Information alone is not harmful. Those who subscribe to this myth hold the view that sexual knowledge in and of itself will promote sexual behavior or promiscuity. They believe that if adolescents understand and know about sexual matters, they will engage in sexual activity. Doug Goldsmith, Ph.D., executive director of the Children's Center in Salt Lake City, says: "Some parents believe that if they don't talk about sex openly, their kids won't do it. But often the reverse is true—if you *don't* talk about sex, kids will sometimes do it, largely because they are so curious. If parents are more open about the subject, kids often lose their intense obsession with sex because their parents already shed light on the subject."[9] After several years of searching, I have yet to find reputable evidence (books, journals, articles, personal interviews) documenting the notion that children have been motivated toward promiscuous behavior by age-appropriate information and facts alone. The evidence indicates that it is actually ignorance, not knowledge, that leads to promiscuous behavior.

Question 4 relates to children's desire to talk to their parents about sex. The belief that children do not want to talk to their parents about sex is another myth. Although this may be true to some extent as children reach adolescence, even then this reluctance usually occurs only briefly and is related to typical adolescent behavior. Most all children, especially pre-adolescents and older adolescents, welcome honest, frank discussions with their parents about sexual matters. We'll talk more about this later.

Question 5 applies to the parental myth of scientific or technical inadequacy. Some parents believe that they must be in command of specific, detailed sexual information in order to be helpful and effective communicators with their children. In fact, most parents have adequate knowledge to teach their children about sexual matters. It is not necessary to be an M.D., Ph.D. or clinical psychologist in order to communicate sexual information to your children. Christian parents do not have to be experts in the field of human sexuality to shape the character of their children. Teaching children about sex in a moral and biblical context is vitally important and should be part of the legacy of all Christian parents to their children. As parents you need not be hampered by inadequate knowledge, for the technical information you need can be easily and quickly learned.

Question 6 concerns the myth that parents must be thoroughly comfortable with all phases of sexuality in order to be effective teachers to their children. Because of the complexity of human sexuality, few parents feel totally comfortable addressing the subject But children will understand if parents admit uneasy feelings to their children and plunge ahead.

Question 7 and 8 again apply to the subject of sexual knowledge and information. As we previously stated, knowledge alone is usually not harmful to children. Therefore, if parents make a mistake it should be on the side of providing too much information and being too explicit. By explicit, I mean being clear, detailed, and direct. Typically, little damage is done by giving too much information if the information given is true, sensitively described, and offered in a loving spirit. Children simply absorb the information they are interested in and ignore or file away whatever they are not interested in.

Parents should be encouraged by the resilience and forgiving nature of children. Because children are so flexible and forgiving, mistakes you make during sex education are not fatal. The only response that may be disastrous and ruinous is not to respond at all.

It is extremely important that parents not be misled by sex education myths and then fail to provide adequate sexual information to their children. If our children are to have quality sex education given in a moral and spiritual context, it must be provided in the home. So, parents, sweep aside the fantasies and fears and plunge ahead.

Sex education must begin at a very young age and continue as your children grow. In reality, the sex education of children is an eighteen year course of love, insight, and example. Overwhelming evidence suggests that parents who put their minds to it, and who have confidence and the right tools, can effectively teach their children about human sexuality. Research also shows that parents exert the greatest influence on their children. George Barna of the Barna Research Group says:

They may not like to admit it openly, but teenagers do realize that they are greatly influenced by their family. In fact, when asked to describe the individuals who exert the greatest degree of influence upon them, family members lead the pack: mother, then father, with siblings not far behind.[10]

Our goal is to provide children with wholesome sex education based on God's principles and teachings. Dennis and Barbara Rainey in their book, *Parenting Today's Adolescents*, list four convictions parents should uphold as foundational when teaching their children about sex.

- Our children need to learn a godly perspective about sex, primarily from us.
- Sex education consists of more than an explanation of human reproduction.
- We must teach and model true biblical standards of purity and innocence.
- We need to create a home environment that provides love, security, and physical affection for our children.[11]

If you achieve these objectives, you will be promoting healthy sexual attitudes and preparing your children for long-term, godly marriages.

For Further Thought

1. Am I comfortable with my own sexuality? If not, why?

2. Do I accept my appearance, looks, and body, and do I accept my mate's appearance? Do I communicate acceptance?

3. Do I in an appropriate way convey to my children that I love and enjoy my mate sexually as well as platonically?

4. Do I openly and positively deal with and communicate emotions such as fear and anger? How do these emotions affect my sexuality?

5. What past experiences have influenced my sexual attitudes, values and beliefs?

6. Do I communicate my sexual needs and problems to my mate?

---

[1] Stanton L. and Brenna B. Jones, *How and When to Tell Your Kids About Sex* (Colorado Springs: Navpress, 1993), 30.

[2] Institute for Family Research and Education, *Community Sex Education Programs for Parents* (Syracuse: Institute for Family Research and Education), 3.

[3] McDowell, *Why Wait?* 385.

[4] Candyce Stapen, "Speaking Frankly Isn't Being Permissive," *USA Today,* September 3, 1986, National Edition, 6.

[5] Jones, *How and When to Tell Your Kids About Sex,* 25, 61.

[6] McDowell, *Why Wait?* 92-93.

[7] Institute for Family Research and Education, *Community Sex Education,* 44.

[8] David Elkind, *The Hurried Child* (Reading, MA: Addison-Wesley, 1981), 77.

[9] Laura Langford, *The Big Talk, Talking to Your Child About Sex and Dating* (New York: John Wiley & Sons, 1998), 42.

[10] George Barna, *Today's Teens: A Generation In Transition* (Glendale, CA: Barna Research Group, 1991), 8.

[11] Dennis and Barbara Rainey, *Parenting Today's Adolescents* (Nashville: Thomas Nelson, 1998), 69-75.

2
Where do They
Hear all This Stuff?

Several years ago, a friend of mine was driving home one night with his seven-year-old son. As they drove the boy asked if he could listen to the radio. The father turned on the radio and soon lost himself in his own thoughts. He was jerked back into reality by a remark from his son. The radio station was playing a popular teenage song of that day and the song contained the phrase "wild thing." The young boy proudly announced to his dad that he knew what "wild thing" really meant. His dad said, "Okay, son, tell me, what does it mean?" Becoming very quiet and mysterious, the seven-year-old confidently said, "'Wild thing' means sex!" The father was a bit stunned and paused a moment to collect his thoughts, but it was too late. His son had a follow-up question. "Dad," he said very seriously, "what is sex anyway?" My friend managed to compose himself and used this opportunity to teach an appropriate lesson on sex. As he was relating this humorous incident, he asked me a question. He said, "Where do they hear all this stuff?"

My friend's amusing tale caused me to pause and ask myself some very serious questions. First, what are the sources of our children's sexual information? Where do they get their information, and from whom? And then, how accurate is this information?

Remember our goal is to provide children with wholesome sex education based on God's principles and teachings. Most of us agree that sex education remains primarily the responsibility of the parents. If we as parents are to discharge our responsibility as the primary sex educators of our children, we must know the sources and accuracy of our children's sexual information. Knowing the sources will help us determine who or what is influencing our children. When parents know the specific source of information and misinformation then counteraction is easier. Balancing or canceling negative influences will prove much easier if the influences are identifiable. It is also very important for parents to know the accuracy of their children's sexual information. Because much of what children learn about sex is false and inaccurate, a substantial amount of parental sex education may involve correcting errors.

Who Is Teaching Our Kids

A 1987 Josh McDowell poll of teenagers revealed some rather startling statistics concerning sexual information:

- Only 32 percent of girls and 15 percent of boys were informed about sex by their parents.
- Fifty four percent of boys and 42 percent of girls learned about sex from friends their own age.
- Fifteen percent pieced together information they had learned from other sources.
- Fifty six percent of these young people acquired their sex knowledge between the sixth and ninth grades and 18 percent learned about sex before the fifth grade.

- Eighty eight percent of these young people felt they needed more information about sex than they had received from their parents.[1]

These general statistics are not very encouraging. They do, however, emphasize that it is crucial for parents to have additional knowledge concerning who is teaching our kids.

In 1981 Hershal D. Thornburg, of the Department of Educational Psychology at the University of Arizona, authored a study for the *Journal of Early Adolescence* titled "The Amount of Sex Information Learning Obtained During Early Adolescence." The purpose of this study was to investigate the sources, age, and accuracy of sex information when it was initially obtained by adolescents.

Thornburg's article contains some facts that may be very interesting and beneficial for parents.

- Peers are the single most often cited source of sex information (37.1 percent).
- There are two categories where peers contributed more than 50 percent of the total information — petting and homosexuality. Sexual intercourse was another highly ranked area. In the areas regarding actual sexual behavior, peers seem to contribute the most information.
- The second most cited source of sex information is literature, which includes the media (21.9 percent). Abortion and seminal emissions were the two concepts learned primarily from the media.
- Fathers rank very low as a source of sexual information (2.2 percent). In fact, they rank below information gained from school and experience.
- Mothers rank third as a source of sex information (17.4 percent).

47

Thornburg's research also showed that in some areas males and females are likely to seek out different sources to learn sexual concepts. Females, for example, are more dependent on their mothers for information. According to the study, they obtain three times more information from their mothers than do their male counterparts. Males on the other hand are clearly more dependent upon peers than are females. And females seem to be more dependent on literature and media than males. This information can be helpful to parents as they attempt to balance the effect of peers and the media.

Thornburg defines early adolescence as ages 10 to 15. His research shows that 99 percent of all sexual information is learned during these early adolescent years. More specifically, ages 12 and 13, approximately grades 7 and 8, are the peak ages at which sexual concepts are learned. Of course, any parent of a junior high student could probably have related the same information without doing any research. Junior high is a very stressful and difficult time for parents, and it is not easy on the kids either. Some areas of sex education are particularly appropriate for junior high adolescents, and we will discuss these in a later chapter.

The last part of Thornburg's article is related to the accuracy of initial sexual information. Twelve topics were evaluated as either being highly accurate, accurate, distorted, or highly distorted. Information regarding several items was ranked as highly accurate: abortion, conception, intercourse, menstruation, and venereal disease. The two subjects covered by the most reliable sources of information were conception and menstruation. In both cases the mother was the primary contributor. The areas which seem in need of more accurate information were: contraception, ejaculation, seminal emissions, homosexuality, and masturbation.

This should give you a good starting point in your attempt to provide accurate sexual facts and to correct false and incorrect information your child may have.

Thornburg's work on early adolescence reaches several conclusions which may provide beneficial information for parents. First, adolescents learn most information about sexual behavior from their peers. This has tremendous implications for parents as they try to teach their children about sexuality. Do you know your children's peers? Are their closest peers male or female? What values do these peers and their families hold? How much time does your child spend with these friends? Parents must evaluate the influence of their children's peers, since peers obviously play a major role in a child's sex education!

A second pertinent conclusion from this article concerns mothers and fathers and their respective roles. According to the data, mothers play an important role of giving information in the areas of conception, intercourse and menstruation. Fathers, regrettably, play virtually no role in providing sex information. Christian fathers have a God-given responsibility to provide leadership in the home. That responsibility means we must take an active role in our sons' and daughters' sex education.

Thornburg's work also concludes that females tend to seek out more reliable sources of information than do males. This phenomenon is in part explained by the "macho" image males are frequently taught to project. Boys do not cry, they do not appear to be weak, and they do not admit a lack of knowledge or ask questions. In addition, boys in early adolescence generally talk less about feelings and emotions than do girls of the same age. Whatever the reason, it is important for parents of boys to know that their sons are less likely than girls to seek out reliable sources of sexual information.

Finally, this work concludes that, while overall accuracy seems to be increasing, there are still some key areas, which seem to be subject to highly inaccurate information compared to other areas. These areas are: contraception, homosexuality, and masturbation. These areas of inaccuracy are centered on some of the most controversial aspects of human sexuality, but as Christian parents, we must be sure that our children are taught God's principles in all areas of sexuality.

Thornburg closes his article by saying:

Regardless of the findings of this and other studies about teenage sexual understanding, teens typically have learned only partial concepts and basically stand in need of increased or more complete information about human sexual behavior. Many are still quite naive, and the risk of naivety among many adolescents is too high for responsible adults.[2]

The research quoted above is from the early- and mid-eighties. For comparison, let me introduce current statistics, from the nineties, related to sources of sexual information:

- A *Time* survey in 1993 reported that when thirteen to fifteen-year-old teens were asked how they learned about sex, 67 percent had learned most from friends, school, and entertainment. Less than one-third listed parents as their primary source.[3]
- A 1995 Sexuality Information and Education Council of the United States Newsletter

stated: "The Commission recognizes that the mass media have become a major source of young people's information about sexuality."[4]

- A 1996 survey conducted by Archibald Hart found that women first learned about sexual intercourse from their friends and school. Parents ranked third.[5]

- About one-third of fifteen years olds say *neither* parent has talked to them about sex.[6]

- A 1998 survey by the Center for Adolescent Studies at Abilene Christian University found that the peer group ranked as the most influential educator about sexual matters.[7]

Statistics for sources of sexual information are slightly better in the nineties than the eighties. For example, fathers and mothers appear to be moving up the list as a source of sexual information for their children. However, most available research indicates that the majority of our pre-teens and teens are receiving their sexual information from their peers and the media.

Media Influence

Now, let's conduct an experiment. If you have teenagers between the ages of 13 and 15 answer the following questions:

1. How often do you yell at the top of your lungs, "turn off that TV or computer and go do your homework"?

2. Do you have to gently remind your teens to turn down the stereo or radio?

3. Do you feel like a chauffeur for the local movie theater, especially in the summer?

4. Have you read *Seventeen* or *Pre-Teen* magazine lately?

5. Are any of the radio selection knobs on your car radio set on your stations?

I had two teenage children — our daughter is currently twenty-eight and our son is twenty-four. During their teen years, my answers to the above questions, in order, are: 600, yes, yes, yes, no! It should come as no shock to parents of teens and pre-teens that the media has a tremendous effect on our children. Especially is this true with regard to sexual information.

The research just cited clearly demonstrates an increasing trend toward media influence as a prime source of sexual information for children of all ages. Michael Medved, noted media critic, details in his new book, *Saving Childhood,* the frightening potential of TV as a negative influence on our children:

> Parents concerned for their children must be constantly alert because the media's assault on innocence is ubiquitous and comes on several fronts. The average individual watches twenty-four hours of television per week. The average school child under twelve watches twenty-one hours, forty-nine minutes per week. Imagine: at the end of the usual life span, the average person will have endured more than ten uninterrupted *years* of television, day and night, with no breaks. The average child will see 8,000 murders and 100,000 other violent acts.[8]

Our society is permeated by sex, especially on television. A 1997 *Newsweek* study revealed that each year the average American teenager hears almost fifteen thousand sexual jokes, innuendoes, and other sexually suggestive references on TV. Of these, fewer than 170 present a message supporting responsible sexual behavior. [9] Tony Campolo, noted Christian lecturer and author, states that "television must be cited as a major factor contributing to the difficulty of modern parenting. This isn't surprising when we consider the fact that the average child watches five hours of television per day. Television dominates the consciousness of young people."[10] Apparently kids are hearing these media messages. Six out of ten kids (aged ten to sixteen) polled by the advocacy group Children Now said sex on TV sways kids to have sex at too young an age.[11] As parents we are aware of the negative effects of television, and we know that today's advertisers use sex to sell everything from toothpaste to cars. Equally alarming is the fact that now most American homes have cable television and children can have unrestricted viewing of R-rated movies.

If you are the parent of a teenager you no doubt have been subjected to a marathon of music. Adolescents love music. From grades 7 to 12 kids listen to an average of 10,500 hours of rock music. The total amount of time spent in school over a period of twelve years is just 500 hours more than the time spent listening to rock music.[12] Parents should be aware that today's rock music is very different from the rock music of the 1960s. Several years ago at church camp, I overheard kids listening to questionable music and I decided to inspect a cabin of eighth grade boys and check out their music. I confiscated 18 CDs from such groups as Smashing Pumpkins, Nine Inch Nails, and Marilyn Manson. After twenty-five years in youth ministry, I thought nothing would shock me. I was wrong! The lyrics on these CDs were offensive, vulgar, filthy, and completely repugnant and nauseating. For example, the title song on one of the CDs was called "Cluster F_____," and on the Nine Inch Nails CD, the F-word was used in nine of the fourteen songs. These CDs were confiscated at church camp from kids whose parents were deacons and church leaders. When I asked the boys to explain how and why they would own and listen to music so completely nasty and un-Christian, they replied, "Everyone listens to this kind of music and besides, we don't pay any attention to the words." I wondered how these adolescents could spend hours each day listening to music such as this and not be influenced. Apparently, their parents were unaware that their children were listening to this type of music.

And what about movies? It was recently estimated that the typical teenager sees about fifty R-rated movies per year. And the F-word is used twenty-two times per film in the average R-rated movie, which contains over ten profane references to God.[13] Of course, this is probably of small concern compared to the frequency of explicit and immoral sexual relationships depicted in these movies.

There can be no doubt that the mass media has a profound influence on our children's sex education and sexual attitudes. It is, and will continue to be, one of the primary sources of sexual information and attitudes for children, and is often at odds with the values Christian parents wish to communicate and teach to their children. The question is, how do we neutralize this massive media influence on our children?

What's A Parent To Do?

Neutralizing media influence is not an easy battle. I have fought and failed many times. When my son was a teenager he was a battle-scarred veteran of this combat. Every time I formulated a new tactic, he devised a scheme to defeat my strategy. One of his favorite arguments was based on his need for relaxation before encountering the dreaded nighttime nemesis called homework. He very carefully and logically explained that a few hours of television would provide him with the relaxation required to tackle his very draining homework assignment. I did manage to win that particular battle, but I was not sure who would win the war! In a more serious vein, let me suggest a few ways that parents might neutralize media influence.

Parents must watch and monitor carefully the messages given by television, music, and other media. Being aware of harmful messages early allows you to filter and screen out what is dangerous and destructive. You are then in a position to create a positive frame of reference with the right messages and thereby preempt negative information.

Parents should regulate both the quantity and quality of media exposure. We need to set realistic guidelines and limits governing TV, movies, music, and printed material. The key word here is "realistic." Some social and cultural critics suggest pulling the plug on TV entirely and simply throwing away the television set. If you can pull it off, great. But for many parents this does not seem realistic. In today's society, children are going to be exposed to the media. It would be unrealistic to try and stop all exposure to the media, especially TV. As parents, however, we need to regulate this exposure. We need to begin limiting and monitoring our children's exposure to media while they are young. I would suggest limiting TV to no more than thirty to ninety minutes per day or a certain number of hours per week. Programs should have the prior approval of parents. Also try to avoid exposing your small children to any media news that you cannot filter. I have found that many religious parents concentrate their regulation on the quality of the program but are not concerned about the amount of time their children spend exposed to the programs. It is necessary to limit the amount of time spent watching television for at least two reasons. First, much of the damaging influence of television comes from the commercials. These commercials often promote promiscuous sexual attitudes, to say nothing of the blatant materialism they portray. In addition, spending hours in front of a television promotes poor stewardship in children. As Christians we are to be good stewards of all that God has given us. One of his most precious gifts is our time. Television pulls children away from face-to-face interactions with people and substitutes a phony world on a screen. The problem is not just too much violence and sex on TV, it's too much TV — period. Consistent, realistic regulations of both quality and quantity should be our goal.

A positive strategy you can employ is to use exposure to the media (especially television and music) as opportunities to talk to your children. Sex education is an everyday, on-going process and part of the process involves taking advantage of our opportunities. Watching TV and listening to music with our children and then discussing the values and issues we have encountered provides an excellent opportunity to teach many lessons to our children. By asking questions during a program we can determine their level of understanding. Viewing TV together is an excellent non-threatening way to discuss many delicate topics, especially sexual matters. Understand, however, that I am not recommending viewing and listening to sexually explicit and filthy programs and lyrics.

Parents should avoid a double standard which allows them to watch many hours of TV per day, while at the same time trying to limit their children to one hour per day. We must hold ourselves accountable to the same standards as our children!

Another strategy is to be creative in providing alternatives to the media. Encourage reading, conversation, outdoor exercise, and many other activities. Also look for good media programming and encourage its viewing in place of questionable programming. Videotape wholesome programs for later viewing. In the area of music, good, contemporary Christian music of all types provides an excellent alternative to traditional rock music. Several years ago when my youth group traveled out of town for an event such as a mission trip, camp or retreat, most of the music played was non-Christian rock music. Today, thanks to the popularity and availability of many Christian groups, most of the music played on our youth trips is contemporary Christian music. Providing alternatives requires work, planning and creativity on the part of parents, but the benefits derived from wholesome alternatives make the effort worthwhile.

One of the best ways to replace our children's exposure to the media is to give them our time. Consider this statistic: most fathers spend only three minutes a day talking to their children.[14] Parents often use TV to get their children out of the way. They are too busy so they let the TV baby-sit. We cannot positively influence the sexual development of our children or neutralize media influence if we do not spend time with them. Furthermore, simply turning off the TV will do nothing to teach our values to our children. It may stop them from being exposed to negative, un-Christian values, but it will not teach them godly values. This requires spending time with them, for without a positive relationship it is impossible to have a positive influence on a young person's sexuality. The most effective way to counteract the negative influence of the media, is to replace the exposure to the media with time spent with you. Fortunately, given the choice, most children, especially pre-adolescents, will choose to spend time with a parent rather than with TV.

For Further Thought

1. What are the sources of my children's sexual information?
2. Am I a source of sexual information for my children?
3. Who are my children's closest friends (peers)? What are the values of these friends? How much time does my child spend with these friends?
4. How do I feel about contraception, homosexuality, and masturbation?
5. What are my children's favorite television programs and movies?
6. How much time per week do my children spend watching TV and listening to music?
7. What are my children's favorite musical groups? What are these groups' lyrics promoting?
8. What specific plans have I made to neutralize the effects of the media on my children?
9. How much time per week do I spend with my children?

Where do They Hear all This Stuff?

[1] Josh McDowell, *What I Wish My Parents Knew About My Sexuality* (San Bernardino: Here's Life Publishers, 1987), 55.

[2] Hershal D. Thornburg, " The Amount of Sex Information Learning Obtained During Early Adolescence," *Journal of Early Adolescence* 1.2 (1981), 171-174.

[3] Nancy Gibbs, " How Should We Teach Our Children About Sex?" *Time,* May 24, 1993, 61.

[4] SIECUS Report, Aug./July 1995, 7.

[5] Hart, et. al., *Secrets of Eve,* 228.

[6] Langford, *The Big Talk,* vii.

[7] Lewis and Dodd, *National Survey,* 39.

[8] Medved, *Saving Childhood,* 19, 27.

[9] Victor Strasburger, " Turning into Teenagers," *Newsweek,* May 19, 1997, 18.

[10] Tony Campolo, *Growing Up In America: A Sociology of Youth Ministry,* (Grand Rapids: Zondervan Publishing House, 1989), 74.

[11] Napier, *The Power of Abstinence,* 116.

[12] Stewart Pound, "What Entertainers are Doing to Our Kids," *U.S. News and World Report,* 28 October 1985, 46-49.

[13] J. Maxwell, "Media: The New Hollywood Watchdog." *Christianity Today,* April 27, 1992, 38-40.

[14] Smith, *Almost Cool,* 86.

3
Hey, Mom,
Can I Ask You Something?

Becoming Askable

My wife had volunteered our services. It was all settled; we were to have our four- year-old nephew stay with us for three glorious days. Jordan loves his Uncle Scott (that's me), and he jumped at the chance to stay at our house. He feels totally comfortable and at ease around our family.

Included in Jordan's three day stay was a Sunday, and we took Jordan to Sunday School and worship services. During the sermon, as our minister was attempting to emphasize a particular point, he shouted loudly and hit the pulpit. An uncomfortable congregational silence followed. Then Jordan turned to me, gestured toward the pulpit with his hand and shouted, "What's he mad about?"

Everyone, including the minister, heard Jordan's question. I was embarrassed and wanted to hide under a pew. Jordan, however, was totally innocent and was genuinely puzzled by the minister's behavior. He felt totally comfortable asking me this question. He trusted his Uncle Scott to provide an honest answer to his inquiry. I was a primary source of information for him.

In the last chapter we pointed out that parents should be more active as primary sources of information for their children. Most parents agree that they should be their child's primary source of information. The key issue then becomes, how do we effectively communicate with our children? Are we askable and approachable parents? Do our children, like Jordan, feel free to approach and ask us questions? And, if not, how can we become askable and approachable?

Becoming askable is very important because when parents are not askable, young people invariably get their sexual information — often misinformation — from other sources, especially friends. A tremendous amount of sex education occurs without parental consent in the lunchroom, the locker room, the bathroom, through graffiti, pornography, sex jokes, and the boasts and bravado of some of the young people presumed to be sexually active. Young people also receive a great deal of sexual information from movies and television, most of it of a sensationalistic and distorted nature. Children need their parents' rational perspective to help counterbalance the distorted images of sex all around them.

Young people not only need, but desire sincere communication with their parents. Evidence supports the fact that communication about sexual matters postpones sexual activity. According to several studies, children who talk with their parents about sex behave more responsibly by postponing sexual relationships. Communication with your child about sexual matters increases the likelihood that they will not engage in premarital sex.

Effective communication with our children is very important. Parents should strive to talk with their children rather than talking at their children. Parents who rarely confer with their children when they are young have the most difficulty talking with their children when they are teenagers. Communication about sex is not something limited to a single talk or an occasional talk at significant developmental stages in a child's life. Communication about sex should be an ongoing process. Becoming an askable parent starts long before the child goes to school. The parents who have discussed sexuality openly with their child can expect the teenager to show confidence later.[1]

Are You An Askable Parent?

If you wish to take the major responsibility for your children's sex education, you will almost certainly have to deal with a variety of questions and behavior, some of which may catch you by surprise or come at inopportune moments. You can also expect, on occasion, to be embarrassed by questions much like that of my nephew, Jordan. Conscientious parents are concerned about doing the "right" thing when, for example, a child asks a specific question about birth, or finds a magazine with photographs of naked people, or "plays doctor" with other children. But many people are somewhat uncomfortable about these things and other aspects of sexual curiosity. This is largely because their own parents did not provide them with effective models for dealing with such things.

By now you are perhaps thinking, "How do I know if I'm an askable and approachable parent?" The first thing parents must do is decide to become an askable person — someone your children can feel free to ask about anything. Next, we must develop a plan for answering questions long before the questions are asked. Determining our convictions is the first element of a good plan because, if we do not know what we believe, effectively teaching our children will be difficult. Pray and study the Scriptures to determine your convictions, and then decide and plan to be an askable and approachable parent.

Here is an exercise to help get you started and help you determine your askability. Relax: this is really not a test because there are no right or wrong answers, just your own honest responses. As a parent who reared two teenagers and a youth minister of many years, I can assure you these situations and statements are very typical. These or similar comments will occur at some point in the lives of most families.

Askable Parent Quiz[2]

As a parent, you want your answers to be both factual and age-appropriate. The more comfortable you feel in providing adequate answers, the more askable you will be. To test yourself on this quiz, consider the following situations that are typical of those most parents will face at one time or another. Circle the letter by the response that you think is best. The given responses are necessarily abbreviated; real-life exchanges are naturally more complex. At the end of the quiz, I'll give my opinion about the best answer to each question, although the absolutely "right" answer depends on the dynamics of the relationship between you and your child and the situation.

1. Your 4-year- old comes up to you and asks, "Where do babies come from?" What do you say?
   __ a. "When you get older, I'll tell you about that."
   __ b. "When a Mommy and a Daddy want a baby, and they love each other, they just have one."
   __ c. "God made a special place in Mommy's body where babies can grow."
2. Ten-year-old Doug comes home from the playground and asks his father what a rubber is. What should Doug's father say?
   __ a. "It's nothing that you should be concerned about at your age."
   __ b. "It's something used to keep the woman from getting pregnant."
   __ c. "It's something a man puts on his penis to keep the sperm from coming out during intercourse. It keeps the woman from getting pregnant. Rubbers also help prevent sexual diseases."
   __ d. "Why do you want to know? Where did you find out about it?"
3. Your six-year old asks, "Why do you and Daddy close the door when you go to sleep?" What do you answer?
   __ a. "Sometimes we want to be really loving together, and we just like to be alone."
   __ b. "That's not really your business, dear."
   __ c. "We don't want to be disturbed."
   __ d. "If you ever come in when the door is closed, you'll be sorry!"

4. Nine-year-old Ted asks his mother, "What are homosexuals?" What should his mother say?

___ a. "They're people who are attracted to their same sex instead of the opposite sex."

___ b. "They're very sick people, and you'll become one if you don't stop playing with girls so much."

___ c. "They're people who are attracted to their same sex the way your Dad and I are attracted to each other. The Bible says it's wrong to act on that kind of feeling."

___ d. "They're people who aren't normal, and the less said about them the better."

5. Your thirteen-year-old daughter asks if a male could ever urinate in the vagina during intercourse. What do you do?

___ a. You tell her you don't really know, and that she should ask her health teacher.

___ b. If you know, you tell her straight out that sexual function prevents the urinary function. If you don't know, you say you aren't sure, but that you'll help her find the answer.

___ c. You laugh and say, "That's ridiculous."

___ d. You try to hide your embarrassment and quickly change the subject.

6. Eight-year-old Kenny says, "I saw Tom and Sue kissing with their mouths open, and Joey calls that 'yukky' kissing.'" He asks, "Why is it yukky?" What do you answer?

___ a. "One name for it is 'French kissing.' A lot of people really in love don't find it yukky, but it sure could spread germs, couldn't it."

___ b. "It's totally disgusting, and I don't want to hear you talk about it."

___ c. "It's a kind of kissing reserved for grownups."

7. Your nine-year-old comes home from school and asks you the meaning of a couple of obscene words he saw painted on the wall. How do you respond?

___ a. "I don't know."

___ b. "They're bad words for sex and I don't ever want you to say them."

___ c. "They are not polite words, and we don't use them in this house."

___ d. "They're sex words people sometimes use when they're angry, or when they want to put someone down. The Bible says our speech ought to be pure, not dirty."

8 Your four-year-old comes to you and asks, "What's the difference between boys and girls?" What do you say?

___ a. "Oh, you know."

___ b. "God made girls' and boys' bodies different, so girls could be mommies and boys could be daddies. Girls have a vagina and boys have a penis."

___ c. "Girls cook and clean and boys go to work when they grow up."

9 Your eight-year-old daughter asks whether it hurts to have a baby. What do you say?

___ a. "Yes, it hurts for a while, but the doctor shows you special exercises and ways to breathe that help. And most women think it's worth it, since a baby is one of God's most precious gifts."

___ b. "You're too young to worry about that dear."

___ c. "No, no—it's a wonderful experience."

10. You discover that your four-year-old son has been "playing doctor" with your neighbor's five-year-old daughter — without clothes, of course. What do you do?

___ a. Say to your son, "Young man, around here we wear clothes when we play, don't we?" After the two are dressed and his friend has gone home, say, "Let's talk about what you learned when you were playing doctor."

___ b. Send the other child home with an "Are-you-going-to-get-it!" Then punish your child.

___ c. Say to both children, "This is not a nice thing to do. Do you want me to say you can't ever play together?"

11. Mother's five-year-old son asks, "Why do you have big breasts and I don't?" What should she say?

___ a. "Go ask your father."

___ b. "Just because I'm a girl and you're a boy."

___ c. "Because when mommies have babies they feed them milk from their breasts. That's the way God made us."

12. What do you tell a six-year-old who asks, "How do babies get inside a mommy's stomach?

___ a. "You'll learn soon enough. Have you practiced your letters today?"

___ b. "God made a man so he can plant sperm — or seed — in his wife's body through his penis, in a very loving way. The seed finds its way into the mommy's womb — not her stomach — where it looks for the mommy's egg. If it finds one, they come together, making a baby! It grows until it's ready to be born through the woman's vagina. Isn't that a wonderful plan?"

___ c. "By a man and woman loving each other."

Well, now—let's see how your answers compare with my opinion of the best answer to these questions. Remember, the "right" answer depends upon the situation and your relationship with your children. As parents our goal is to become approachable and askable. Therefore, our attitude as we answer these questions becomes almost as important as the facts themselves. We should calmly relate the facts in a loving manner. We should also take advantage of every opportunity to present sexual information in a moral and biblical context.

1. "Where do babies come from?" is a typical question often asked by children four or five years old. In my opinion "c" accurately answers the question and communicates openness and askability. This response factually answers the question without relating complicated details that could not be understood by a typical four-year-old. It also introduces God as a part of the process. Notice that this answer did not say that a baby is in Mommy's tummy, but in a "special place" for babies to grow. Babies do not grow in tummies, and even four-year-olds need accurate, age-appropriate information. Answer "b" responds vaguely to the question and would be confusing to a four-year-old. Answer "a" is the least desirable answer because it discourages natural curiosity and openness. By asking questions, children generally indicate their desire for information. Most children will not ask complicated questions beyond their ability to understand the answers. Becoming an askable parent means answering questions when they are asked.

2. Unfortunately in today's world most 10-year-olds probably know something about condoms. They may lack accurate, appropriate information, but most will have some knowledge. The question

may have been asked not only to gain information but also to test the father's openness and askability. Answers "a" and "d" are both objectionable because they indicate disapproval, and because they make no attempt to answer the question. Telling children they should not be concerned about an issue hinders communication and decreases the likelihood of future questions. Response "b" accurately answers the question, but, in my opinion, does not provide enough information. Answer "c" goes further and gives additional pertinent knowledge, so I believe it best answers the question. "C" also introduces the subject of sexual diseases. While most 10-year-olds are not ready for in-depth discussions on sexually transmitted diseases, introducing the subject can lead to such discussions in the future.

3. Closing the bedroom door may appear to contradict parental goals of openness and approachability, but a proper explanation can satisfy inquisitive minds without indicating to children that your mind is closed. The worst answer in this foursome is "d." Threatening or overreacting to genuine childhood curiosity squelches communication and guarantees that children will quickly learn that their parents are not askable. Responses "b" and "c" are technically accurate because there are times when parental affairs are not the children's business, and when you have a right not to be disturbed. But please remember that our goal is becoming askable in order to effectively teach our children about sex. Answer "c" subtly suggests parental lovemaking, without unduly revealing more than a six-year-old can comprehend. Its tone promotes openness.

4. Questions regarding homosexuality frighten most Christian parents. Consequently, we may be

tempted to answer questions dealing with this subject less candidly and openly. But inquiring children will ask about homosexuality. And if they sense a reluctance to discuss this or any subject, our approachability will suffer. We must try to remain composed and unruffled even when fielding questions that shock and startle us. Responses "b" and "d" reflect a lack of composure. Also, "d" discourages any dialogue on the subject. Such a reaction might prompt children to seek their information from non-Christian sources. Response "b" creates unnecessary alarm and fear in children. Answer "a," much like several of the answers to other questions, does not furnish enough information. When parents give short, abrupt answers, they can miss opportunities to teach and reinforce moral and biblical lessons. The best answer, "c", supplies factual data and moral teaching, without producing fear in the child. Additionally, "c" leaves the impression that you are open to discussing the subject further if the child wishes.

5. This question accurately identifies a common fact about early adolescents' sexual understanding. While they understand certain aspects of human sexuality, they often have many misconceptions and misunderstandings. It's not uncommon for them to be confused about bodily functions and the physical aspects of sexual intercourse. The two worst responses to this question are "c" and "d," since they will probably guarantee that future questions will not be directed to the parent. Answer "c" belittles and laughs at the adolescent. No one likes to be ridiculed, so this answer would also severely curtail future communication. While not as bad as "c," answer "d" would also diminish the probability of future conversations, especially regarding sexual

matters. If possible, parents need to project an attitude of happiness and fulfillment with regard to their own sexuality and marital sexual relationship. Such an attitude lived and modeled before our children will create an atmosphere in which wholesome, godly, sex education can be both taught and "caught."

Answer "a" is adequate, but does not go far enough and hints at a reluctance to discuss sexual matters. Answer "b," on the other hand, straightforwardly provides the facts if they are known. And if not, it admits a lack of knowledge, and promises to help the adolescent find the answer. Teenagers appreciate parents who readily admit that they do not have all the answers, and who willingly help in the search for correct information.

6. Eight-year-old boys probably find all kissing "yukky." But as we all know, that will rapidly change. Response "a" best answers Kenny's question. It furnishes sufficient data without giving more information than an eight-year-old needs or desires. Responses "b" and "c" are somewhat dishonest, because French kissing is neither totally disgusting nor reserved exclusively for grown-ups. Of course, as children approach adolescence certain warnings regarding French kissing should be provided.

7. Inevitably, our children will come into contact with filthy and obscene words. Such situations should be viewed as teachable moments which provide excellent opportunities to teach about the importance of pure speech. Answer "a" would be harmful because of its dishonesty. Answer "b" correctly identifies the words as bad, but it does not utilize the teachable opportunity and thus fails to move toward the goal of providing godly sex

education. Answer "c" makes no attempt to explain why words are not polite or why they should not be used. Children need and deserve such explanations in order to learn. Answer "d" directly and frankly labels the words as sex words and further explains why and how they are used. It also takes advantage of the teachable moment to explain why the words are inappropriate and to portray wholesome sexuality in a marital relationship.

8. At about four or five years of age, children begin to recognize and become curious about anatomical differences. This curiosity will inevitably lead to many questions relating to the physical differences between boys and girls. Response "a" evades the question and communicates an unwillingness to be bothered by questions. The probable effect of such evasiveness will be that in the future questions will not be asked. Not only does answer "c" seem flippant and frivolous, it also subtly promotes sexism. Answer "b" correctly assumes that by "differences" most four-year-olds are referring to physical differences. These differences are simply explained, using age-appropriate and correct terminology. Also, God receives the credit for the differences. By saying that God created these body parts, children are being taught that their entire body is godly and wholesome—a very important lesson for a four-year-old.

9. Preadolescent girls frequently ask questions about birth. They know that this experience may eventually occur in their life, and they are somewhat apprehensive. I feel that answer "b" patronizes even an eight-year-old. It also makes no attempt to answer the question. Dishonesty makes answer "c" totally undesirable. Above all, children need honest, accurate information, and if you fail to furnish

correct information they will eventually seek the facts elsewhere. Answer "a" acknowledges that childbirth involves pain, while at the same time explaining specific measures that make the pain bearable. The honesty and correctness of this answer addresses an eight-year-old girl's apprehension and fear. In the future this young lady will feel free to ask additional questions. By being truthful and honest, her parents have created an atmosphere of trust and openness.

10. "Playing doctor" or engaging in some such form of physical exploration naturally occurs around age four or five. Such play indicates a normal curiosity regarding anatomical differences and does not imply sexual perversion or homosexuality. Response "c" accuses and threatens in a very improper manner. These children were satisfying a natural childhood curiosity, not being immoral or perverted. An accusation of this nature would communicate to a young child that certain body parts are dirty or unclean. In order for healthy sexual adjustment to occur, children need to be taught that God created all of their body, including their genitals. By following up on the threat of response "b," a parent would be punishing a child for a natural inquisitiveness. This response also indicates a level of anger on the parent's part that would not be understood by the child. Response "b" also provides no explanation for the anger and furnishes no teaching to the child. Response "a" best deals with this normal, yet delicate situation. This reply informs the child that in polite society people stay dressed. But it also takes advantage of a teachable opportunity in a non-threatening and calm manner. Effective sex education utilizes such moments to provide facts and information at precisely the time
of greatest awareness and need.

11. Not only are five-year-olds interested in anatomical differences; in all areas of life they want to know "Why?" Parents need to keep in mind that by asking such questions children are not obsessed with sexual thoughts; they are simply asking logical questions in their attempt to learn. We should answer sexual questions as matter-of-factly as we would answer questions on any subject. Answer "a" evades the question and subtly communicates that boys should talk to their fathers and daughters to mothers. Both parents must be involved in the sex education of their children, and it is important that children feel comfortable asking either parent questions. Answer "b" simply states a known fact and does not really answer the child's inquiry. This young man knows boys and girls have different bodies; his real question relates to the function of female breasts. By answering with information contained in "c," parents communicate their understanding of the real question. This answer explains the function of female breasts, and attributes it all to God's plan.

12. However children phrase the question, "How do babies get inside of a mommy's tummy?", it often produces fear and anxiety in parents. Perhaps this is true because we realize that once this question has been asked the process of sex education has reached the point of no return. Also, any honest attempt to answer the question forces us to discuss sexual intercourse. Of course, the discussion must be age-appropriate, but it must be addressed. Response "a" totally dodges the question and attempts to change the subject. If they are repeatedly confronted with such parental avoidance, children will stop asking questions and will simply turn elsewhere for information. Answer "c" is unacceptable for the same reason. Answer "b" lovingly and in an age-

appropriate manner explains conception to a six-year-old. This answer corrects misunderstandings and furnishes uncomplicated information. It also correctly identifies and names body parts using the proper terms. Correct terminology helps avoid myths and misconceptions as children learn about sex. When simple age-appropriate sexual information is communicated in a calm, loving style, childhood curiosity is satisfied and facts are easily accepted.

The best answers to the above questions illustrate how parents can respond adequately to questions related to sex and sexual matters. When answering sexual questions, just remember to:

- furnish the information requested
- use age-appropriate language and concepts
- look for the implied or "real" question
- use proper terms, not slang or cute words
- provide information that leads to the next logical question

Many of the answers and concepts referred to in this quiz will be discussed in detail in the remaining pages of this book.

Communicating With Our Children

In one of Josh McDowell's books he relates this conversation from a teenage boy:

"Do you know what I am?" a teenager once asked. "I'm a comma." He said, "Whenever I talk to my dad, he stops talking and makes a comma. Then when I stop talking, he starts right up again as if I didn't say anything. I'm just a comma in the middle of his speeches."[3]

Many children feel exactly like this teenage boy.

They are crying out for a real conversation with a parent, a dialogue which involves not only the exchange of thoughts, but also feelings. They also want a talk that involves both listeners and talkers. Stephen Covey has written in his book, *First Things First*, "Seek first to understand, then to be understood."[4] Instead of demanding that our children understand us and see everything our way, it is helpful to take time to understand them. This doesn't mean that we become permissive parents or give up our God-given responsibility to properly rear our children. It does mean that we show respect, humility, and genuineness as we seek to understand our children. Communication is primarily seeking to be understood. If we can create an environment of understanding, our children will be more likely to talk with us. A slogan that I try to remember when I am seeking to understand children and teens is, "Connect first, direct second."[5] Here are a few principles which can help us communicate effectively with our children. This list is neither unique nor all-inclusive. It is simply several suggestions that will hopefully make communication with your children easier and more efficient.

1. *Remember that rules without relationships lead to rebellion.* Long before the rules are imposed, there needs to be a relationship. In my ministry I repeatedly witness a sad situation. A child does something morally or ethically wrong and the parent approaches me and says "How could this happen? We've clearly taught our child the biblical principles and rules governing that kind of behavior." In many, but not all, of these incidents the parents have emphasized rules over relationships. Sadly, parents can formulate many rules and regulations designed

to produce compliant, well-behaved children, but if they do not invest heavily in relationships with their children all of these rules will produce rebellion instead of response.

2. *Spend time with your children in their world.* As we stated earlier parents need to spend time doing things with their children. Perhaps go out to eat, just you and the one child. Other activities could include shopping, hunting, walking, or anything else you both enjoy. These unstressed, low-key times together help parents promote good, open communication on the feeling level. During this time with your child, constantly try to see things from your child's viewpoint. Make an attempt to see their world, because it's different from your adult world.

3. *Show trust in the comments or statements of your child.* Too many children, especially teenagers, say that living in their house is like serving a jail sentence, or being continually on trial. They feel like they are continually looked upon as guilty and have to prove their innocence. Many parents do look upon their children as guilty until proven innocent, instead of innocent until proven guilty. But we must be willing to trust, even when our trust is violated at times. If your child has violated your trust, you might try saying something like this: "Yes, I trust you to use your own best judgment, but I know from my own experiences that one person's best judgment may not include enough important facts or knowledge to be completely dependable. And sometimes it may need buttressing with some help from others — even parents. If it's important to you that we trust you to use your best judgment, will you trust us to use our best judgment in the questions we raise and the suggestions we make?" Parents, it is essential that you trust your child as much as possible.

4. *Be encouraging, positive, and non-critical with your children.* All humans need and respond to encouragement. Children especially need their parents to be positive and encouraging. Encouragement can make all the difference in the world. Look at the example of the Apostle Paul. After his conversion he was rejected by the Christians in Jerusalem because they were afraid of him (Acts 9). He was shuffled off to Tarsus and might have died there had not Barnabas looked him up and asked for his help (Acts 11). And from that point on, Barnabas, whose name means "Son of Encouragement," encouraged Paul and his encouragement helped Paul become a great man of God. Why is it that, even though as parents we are aware of the positive results encouragement has on our children, we often seem locked into a pattern of negative criticism toward them? When my son was about thirteen years old, he stung me with this question: "Dad, do I ever do anything right the first time?" I said, "Sure you do, Paul." He replied, "Then why don't you ever tell me?" He was right. As parents we feel responsible for our children's behavior and morality, so we criticize, nag, and fuss all the time. Please do not wait until you are stung by your son or daughter. Encourage your children often. Be positive and non-critical.

5. *Check your timing.* In any relationship dialogue will be enhanced if the timing is right. Love must be your guide as to when and where you share bad news or discuss a difficult subject with your child. For example, never embarrass your child in front of his peers or in any crowd. If correction is necessary it will wait until a more private moment. Parents, make sure your criticism or correction will have a positive, uplifting effect, rather than being a

negative put-down. Choose your time wisely and never burn bridges.

6. *Never assume.* I am, by nature, a very loud, demonstrative, excitable, and passionate person. I can very quickly become excited and passionate on a great many subjects. When this happens I usually get very loud and demonstrative. Because of this, many people assume I'm angry, when in reality I'm just fervent and enthusiastic. My daughter shares many of these same characteristics; growing up, she knew how to interpret her excitable father. So when I would go off like a rocket on some subject she would simply shrug and walk away. She instinctively knew that I was not angry, and knew especially that I was not angry with her. My son, on the other hand, was sensitive as a child, and he began at an early age to have very bad nightmares. We took him to a psychologist friend who told me that I was the primary cause of my son's nightmares. Apparently, when I became loud and demonstrative, my son believed I was angry, and he usually thought I was angry with him. Needless to say, I worked on correcting my behavior in a hurry. But my point is this: I assumed that because my wife and daughter understood the way Daddy was, my son and others also understood. We do our children a grave injustice when we make too many assumptions. Never assume your child has interpreted you accurately. All our relationships will become more harmonious and intimate when we stop assuming and start understanding and communicating.

7. *Give a little.* Learn the healthy art of compromise. As children grow older they want more freedom and input about the things that affect their lives. Parents need to understand this and learn the art of compromise as we pro-actively help our

children grow in responsibility and self-control.

Communication with teens can be especially difficult and challenging. As children approach their teen years, we often expect them to begin communicating like adults. But even though teens look like adults, they talk and listen in a way uniquely their own. As adults we communicate in logical, reasoned manner with an eye to the "bottom line" and specific agendas. Teens, on the other hand, say just what pops into their heads, and jump from topic to topic. Often they will talk just for the enjoyment of company with no particular purpose and with no fixed agenda. Teens do not share our adult need to fix things and find solutions to problems. For many parents, communicating with teens presents some unique challenges. Here are a few suggestions and hints that can help parents with the daunting challenge of communicating with their teens.

1. *Avoid preaching.* Talking with teens in a critical, disapproving tone will cause your teens to tune you out immediately and communication will fail. Tone is critically important when talking with teens because they already feel outgunned by their parents. Teens feel their parents have more poise, more experience, more communication skills, and a larger vocabulary. Most teens don't feel equipped to compete with their parents in conversation. It is best to talk with teens using a calm style avoiding any hint of a preachy tone.

2. *Remember what it was like being a teenager.* Often we forget what it was like to be a teen, and we begin to expect our teens to act and think like adults. In their book, *Raising Self-Reliant Children in a Self-Indulgent World,* Stephen Glenn and Jane Nelson, call this an "adultism."

An adultism occurs any time an adult forgets what it is like to be a child and then expects, demands, and requires of the child, who has never been an adult, to think, to act, understand, see, and do things as an adult. These unrealistic expectations from adults produce impotence, frustration, hostility, and aggression in young people.[6]

3. *Create an atmosphere of comfort, relaxation, and safety.* Have you ever noticed how teens seem to talk non-stop in a vehicle? On a van or bus full of teenagers there are numerous conversations going on at the same time. Teens will also talk with adults in a much more relaxed manner in a vehicle. They feel safer and less vulnerable when they do not have to make eye contact. Parents need to create safe, interruption-free locations to openly communicate with their teens. Take a car trip, a walk or bike ride in the park, or a hike. Go anywhere that will make your teen feel comfortable.

4. *Remember the 50/50 rule.* This rule is found in Tim Smith's book, *Almost Cool.* I highly recommend this book as a great resource for parents of teens. The 50/50 rule says that parents only talk 50 percent of the time and that we are responsible for 50 percent of the conversation with our teens. We must try and make the teen pick up the other 50 percent of the conversation. One way to do this is to spend more time listening than talking, and to realize that you have the authority and experience that can produce a strategy for talking with your teen. Relax and utilize the 50/50 rule.[7]

5. *Avoid words that end conversations and cause defensiveness.* A quick way to cause defensiveness in our teens and end communication is to continually use words and phrases such as: you should, you ought, you never, you always, and you better not.

Such language causes teens to feel angry, defensive and useless. It is much better to use language that communicates respect and indicates to your teen that you do not view them as totally one way or the other.

Here are some rules that are keys to effective communication in any situation. These rules apply to children and teen alike. Some of them are so obvious we tend to overlook them in dealing with our own children. Please don't!

- Remember that actions speak louder than words.
- Make your communication as positive as realistically possible.
- Test all your assumptions verbally.
- Recognize that each event can be seen from different points of view.
- Do not allow discussions to turn into destructive arguments.
- Be open and honest about your feelings.
- Do not use unfair communication techniques; do not engage in "dirty fighting."
- Realize that the *interpretation* others put on your words or actions is what is communicated, not necessarily what you *meant* by them.
- Accept all feelings and try to understand them; do not accept all actions, but try to understand them.
- Be tactful, considerate and courteous, and show respect for each family member.
- Do not use excuses and do not fall for excuses.
- Do not nag, yell or whine.
- Know when to use humor and when to be serious.
- Listen.
- Beware of playing destructive games.

Communication is essential to showing love. Children will not talk to parents about sex or anything else if parents are not askable and approachable. Becoming askable and approachable is a lifelong process. It must begin when our children are young and continue through the teen years. Parents must strive constantly to improve their communication skills, because they will never have a major influence on their child's sex education, or any other significant matter, unless and until the child feels comfortable, understood, and at ease discussing all matters with them. You may have all the necessary information regarding any subject, but unless there is a good relationship, your child will never ask for the information.

For Further Thought

1. What is my most frequent method of communicating with my children?
2. Am I afraid to become askable or approachable, and if so, why?
3. How much uninterrupted time do I spend with my children each week? How can I increase the figure?
4. What specific traits or characteristics of my children can I encourage?
5. In what specific ways can I improve my communication skills with my children?
6. What assumptions about my children do I make?
7. When and how do I make my children defensive?

[1] Sol Gordon and Craig W. Snyder, *Personal Issues In Human Sexuality,* (Boston: Allyn and Bacon, 1986), 165.

[2] Adapted from *Community Sex Education* (Syracuse: Institute for Family Research and Education), 58-63.

[3] McDowell, *What I Wish My Parents Knew about My Sexuality,* 143.

[4] Steven Covey, *First Things First* (New York: Simon and Schuster, 1994), 213.

[5] Smith, *Almost Cool,* 35.

[6] H. Stephen Glenn and Jane Nelson, *Raising Self-Reliant Children in a Self-Indulgent World,* (Rocklin, CA.: Primo, 1988), 90.

[7] Smith, *Almost Cool,* 82.

4

Boundaries, Guidelines, Fences, Cows, and Kids

We have talked about becoming askable — how we can cultivate attitudes that make us approachable. We have talked about methods of communicating effectively with our children. We have stressed the fact that in order to communicate with our children it is essential that we have strong relationships with them. Good relationships, however, depend upon rational, reasonable, firm guidelines, boundaries, and limits.

Children's security doesn't come from watered-down values instruction offered in schools. Kids need the consistency of limits set in their own homes, from the earliest years. Delineating rules strongly from the earliest ages — particularly rules emphasizing self-discipline and control — provides your children with two extremely worthwhile benefits: Knowing what is expected of them forms the security children need for innocence. Limits enforced and practiced from early ages pays off later, inoculating your kids with self-discipline against the social problems plaguing teens.[1]

Boundaries or guidelines within the family are like fences for cows or skin on the body. They have two purposes: to keep everything in that needs to be in, and to keep everything out that needs to be out. They can also act as a map for children, giving them direction in a society which presents a multitude of options. Giving children guidelines, therefore, helps them make wise decisions.

Parenting Styles — Do I Have to Choose?

Before we discuss how we can set reasonable guidelines and limits, we need to discuss briefly parental discipline styles. They can be divided broadly into three types based on two major factors: what the parents expect of their children and how they respond to their children emotionally.

1. Authoritarian or strict parental style. Christian and secular psychologists describe authoritarian parents as the kind who are usually long on use of the rod and short on use of dialogue. For the authoritarian, obedience is a virtue, and punishment for willfulness or disobedience is swift. Authoritarian parents insist that the child should take their word for what is right. They attempt to control and shape their children. Verbal give and take is not encouraged. The authoritarian parent is strong on control and discipline, but weak on support, or love. Morton Strommen in his fine book, Five Cries of Parents, quotes several studies that relate to authoritarian or autocratic parents:

Findings in Study of Generations show that parents who are autocratic in treatment of their children tend also to be law-oriented in their understanding of religion. This means they view Christianity as basically a set of rules and standards that must be obeyed. Such parents find it hard to forgive and hard to admit they are wrong. Their religion tends to be self-centered and self-serving. In comparisons between groups we found greater family disunity and more distance between parents and youth in the families of overly strict parents than any other group. We found the effect of over control on youth to be lower self-esteem and heightened feelings of self-condemnation. Another frequent outcome is parent-youth conflict, with life in the home becoming an ongoing power struggle. Adolescents raised under autocratic control are more likely to be characterized by the following behaviors: hostility to parents, age prejudice; antisocial activities (for example, lying, fighting, vandalism); feelings of social alienation; rejection of traditional moral standards; an inability to relate well to people.[2]

I fear that too many Christian parents fall into this category because for some time Christian parenting books overemphasized discipline and control. Authoritarian parents are usually the ones who "provoke their children to anger" (Eph. 6:4 *KJV*).

2. Permissive parental style. Permissive parents are at the opposite end of the scale. They are described as making few demands for obedient behavior, and they usually see themselves as merely resources to be used at the discretion of the child. These parents do not punish, and they allow the child to run their lives. They do not make an issue of rules or limits and they shun the use of power to control their children — instead they appeal to reason. Permissive parents are usually strong on support and love but weak on control. Children reared in permissive home environments often feel that their parents really do not care about them. Permissiveness causes teenagers to feel neglected or rejected. Stanton L. Jones Ph.D. says of children from permissive homes:

Long-term studies of the children of indulgent parents clearly suggest that these kids do not fare well — they have very positive self-esteem and feel good, but their behavior tends to be quite immature; they tend to be more impulsive, to show more signs of social irresponsibility than others, but not as much self-reliance; and interestingly they tend to show more aggression and hostility toward other kids.[3]

3. Authoritative parental style. The authoritative parent could be described as someone who exerts firm control, but who is at the same time willing to listen. Authoritative parents are inclined to explain their reasoning and their boundaries. They value both independence and internal disciplined conformity in their children. Authoritative parents are a comfortable mix — taking the strengths of the authoritarian and permissive parents and combining them into a system that is both high on support and love and high on control. Children from authoritative homes have the highest levels of self-esteem, self-reliance, and are usually better adjusted and more service oriented. When this parental style is applied, there is more family closeness, and the children are more committed to a religious faith.

Extremes Can Produce Negative Results

Both extreme styles of parenting (authoritarian and permissive) can produce at least two major problems in children. First, both approaches may create children with an inability to interact and relate with people. The child from the authoritarian home has been taught not to talk back or question, and just meet the standards. The permissively raised child has been taught that he will receive the necessary help to meet what few standards he wishes to attain. Neither child learns independence or autonomy. Therefore, both are ill-equipped to handle most of life's obstacles. The second problem is that extreme parental discipline styles customarily and typically produce deviant behavior in children, especially adolescents. As parents we should strive for a reasonable, balanced approach to discipline and boundaries. This is borne out by all my research and personal experience in many years of youth ministry. As parents we should strive for a reasonable, balanced approach to discipline and boundaries. We must develop a style that will not "provoke our children to anger," but at the same time will allow us to rear them "in the training and instruction of the Lord." (Eph. 6:4)

Guidelines and Principles for Establishing Practical Limits

Several years ago my fourteen-year-old son and I had just had disagreement number 642, but who is counting? Our latest argument concerned his being able to ride in a car alone with a fifteen-year-old. It seems that his friend had received a hardship driver's license and was able to drive at fifteen. Now it seems to me that at age sixteen, the legal age for a license in most states, a teenager is just barely mature enough for the awesome task of controlling two tons of steel speeding down a highway at seventy miles per hour. But to trust this tremendous responsibility to a newly-turned fifteen-year-old was more than I could imagine. So I refused my son permission to ride with his friend. And, as you may have guessed, my son wanted to discuss the matter!

His first tactic was to attempt a very convincing argument regarding his friend's overall maturity. My counter maneuver was brilliant—I agreed that his friend was indeed as mature as any fifteen-year-old. But my belief was that no fifteen-year-old on this planet was mature enough to drive. My son tenaciously regrouped—he was not yet ready to retreat. He then brought out the time-tested argument of all teenagers: "Everyone else can ride with him, you don't trust me", and one of my personal favorites, "You're too strict." After several more minutes of discussion, in exasperation I said, "Paul, I love you enough to set limits on your behavior." To which he replied, "If you didn't love me so much, I might have a lot more fun." And with that parting remark he rode off on his bicycle (not in his friend's car).

This incident emphasizes a parental dilemma—how to set reasonable, realistic boundaries and limits; and once these limits and rules are established, how to enforce them. Setting firm and loving limits that protect our children, while still granting them enough freedom to grow up responsibly, is critical. Setting reasonable boundaries and rules for our children is a day-by-day job, and there are times when we fail. But as conscientious Christian parents, we can succeed often enough to produce godly children. There are no answers or simple formulas, but here are some guidelines, suggestions, and hints that may help you. They are in no particular order of importance, but they are the result of research, personal experience in the youth ministry, and parenting two teenagers of my own.

1. *Establish clear standards and rules.* A clear definition of what is acceptable and what is

unacceptable behavior is a good starting point. Never assume your child knows what is expected. Children are not mind readers and they need rules explained and demonstrated. If appropriate, discuss the limits with your child before establishing a hard and fast rule. This will help with discipline later on, and can help in establishing a cooperative development of standards. You are not a policeman or a judge. You are a loving, caring parent, who wants to work with your child for his or her good. Never set a limit without giving a good reason. They may not agree, but they will at least understand your reasons. In seeking to determine where your standards will be set, it may be helpful to look at older Christian parents. Experienced veterans can be valuable resources as you attempt to avoid mistakes.

2. *Distinguish between biblical absolutes and your personal parental preferences.* God's word has some very specific absolutes. It is unconditionally wrong to steal, lie and commit adultery. In a world void of moral absolutes, where all issues are beginning to be seen as personal preferences and genetically inherited predispositions, it is vital we teach our children that Scripture says certain behaviors are sinful. But God, in his infinite wisdom, did not make absolutes in all areas of life. Parents must be very careful not to tell their children the Bible clearly supports their own position, unless there are Scriptures that clearly define the issue. We need to tell our children why we believe certain activities are sinful and wrong and regularly search the Scriptures with them. But they can read, and if we have been misquoting God, they will ultimately discover our secret.

3. *Know which battles to fight.* Time, strength, and

sanity prevent parents from dealing with every potential conflict that arises. Therefore, one of our hardest decisions as parents involves deciding which battles are important enough to fight. As every good general knows, it is possible to win a battle and lose the war, so we must prioritize and work on those areas of greatest importance. Let me illustrate. My daughter Stephanie has always been a delightful and compliant child. She came into the world that way. Her mother and I had very few major difficulties with her during her growing up years. She was responsible and obedient most of the time. So why, during most of her teen years, did this beautiful, sweet, responsible child insist on living in a garbage dump? I mean, her room was so dirty we were afraid there would be things growing under her bed! Her room looked even worse than her younger brother's. She had no need for a closet and a clothes chest, because all her clothes were on the floor. But my wife and I decided that this was not a battle worth fighting. Stephanie was required to clean before relatives and guests came for a visit, but on an ordinary, day-to-day basis we simply shut the door. And when she ran out of clean clothes, she knew how to wash.

4. *Be consistent and fair in defining and applying rules and discipline.* What parent has not heard this cry from their child, especially their teen — "That's not fair!" In my work with teens, I estimate I have heard those words at least several million times per year. And yes, I know life's not fair, but children need consistently defined rules and consequences. It is disturbing to a child to be confused regarding expectations. Children and adolescents look for consistent rules in families, schools and communities.

5. *Limit what you give to your child.* Today's children have too many things. They have their own TV, VCR, and computer in their room and don't have to share or do without anything. They wear designer clothes and shoes and have birthday parties at popular restaurants. Many children have it all, have done it all, and seen it all! Therefore, they are addicted to instant gratification. Much of the destructive behavior of adolescence is a result of children living in a world of instant gratification where they receive everything they want. Saying "no" to our children and setting limits on what we give them promotes self-restraint and teaches delayed gratification. Our homes are the best place for children to learn the value of money, saving, and working for things. Teaching our children good principles such as delayed gratification and responsibility will help them understand and apply these lessons to sex. We must set boundaries and differentiate between what our children need and what they want.

6. *Be flexible and ask for forgiveness when necessary.* As parents we need to be flexible when the situation warrants it, especially when we realize we have made a mistake or wrong decision. If your child constantly complains about unfairness, you may be wise to check your actions with another person. If you have been unfair, be flexible and change. Also be godly enough to ask for your child's forgiveness. When we parents admit mistakes we open the way for our children to share with us, and we demonstrate one of God's greatest principles.

7. *Avoid overprotection.* Well-meaning, religious parents often make the mistake of being excessively overprotective in the rules and guidelines they establish. These parents continue to do things for

their children long after their help has become unnecessary. They break one of the cardinal rules of effective parenting: the parent should not continue to do something for the child that the child can begin to do. Overprotective parents can be very loving, well-meaning people who simply have a difficult time letting go. Overprotective parents project their own insecurity and need for support onto their children. They gain a sense of security by exerting more control over their children's lives, which in turn fosters more dependency on the parent. Through this dynamic, insecure parents beget insecure children. The dangers of overprotective parental behavior are many. First, this behavior subtly communicates to the child that his parents feel he is incompetent. David Lewis, a former professor at Abilene Christian University, says, "overworrying produces overprotecting, which produces the message to your child that he is incompetent."[4] A second danger is that overprotectiveness may push children to rebellion, and rebellion can cause serious problems. For example, one of the major reasons for pregnancy in early adolescents (ages 13-15) is rebellion. Finally, children from overprotective environments are usually more susceptible to peer pressure.Many children allow their parents to wait on them and develop a very demanding attitude, growing angry quickly when things do not automatically go for them the way they wish. They have little personal courage, quickly give in to pressure and give up when faced with a difficult challenge. Deep within overprotected adolescents is an aching feeling of inadequacy and helplessness. They believe that they will never gain the genuine approval of others.[5] As we stated earlier when talking about unfairness, when children constantly complain about overprotectivness on the part of their parents, it may be well for parents to evaluate their behavior in this area. Because the dangers of overprotectiveness are so great, parents should continually monitor their behavior and attitudes.

8. *Use natural and logical consequences to discipline and to teach responsibility.* There are two categories of consequences: natural and logical. Natural consequences are the results of choices we make. If we touch a hot stove, we get burned; if we don't eat, we get hungry. A logical consequence is decided upon beforehand by the parent, with input from the child, and which allows a child to experience the effects of his behavior or unfilled responsibilities. Logical consequences also need to be related to behavior. Logical consequences are designed to teach an immediate lesson, and to demonstrate to children the connection between their actions and consequences. When logical consequences are used, the need to nag, remind, and gripe is eliminated. Parents simply allow the consequences of a child's action to take hold. For example, if your child chooses to sleep past breakfast time, he will not get to eat until lunch. The child is living with the results of his behavior. If the car is not washed by the appropriate time, it is logical that your son or daughter not be allowed to use the car for a specified time. When logical consequences are applied the focus is on the child's behavior, not on who is right. When teenagers are involved, it is essential that both parent and child together draft the possible consequences of misbehaving or failing to carry out their responsibilities. Consequences should be agreed upon in advance of problems or misbehaviors, because people often become more responsible when they are helped to recognize the

relationship between their behavior and the events that follow. Discipline or punishment that is not connected naturally or logically as a consequence to behavior often produces effects that damage the parent-child relationship rather than strengthening it or teaching responsibility. Parents who do not set up reasonable boundaries around their children's behavior, or who continually undermine their children's experiencing the consequences of their behavior, are teaching their children to disassociate their actions from any consequence that might occur from them.[6]

9. *Do not snowplow their road.* Most parents today do a beautiful job of snowplowing the roads for their children. We think we know what's best for our children, and because we know what's best for them we don't give them enough decision-making responsibility. Then, when our children reach age 18, we throw up our hands and lament the fact that they are irresponsible and cannot make decisions for themselves. As parents, we often don't understand who is to blame for their condition. We are! We snowplow the roads. Let me explain. All too often, we short circuit the system. We prevent the natural consequences of our children's actions from teaching them valuable lessons. We fix all their messes and failures. We intervene with teachers, employers, coaches, and other adults to prevent our children from suffering the consequences of their actions. As a result the lesson they learn is that their parents can remedy any negative consequences of their actions. This produces people who cannot make decisions and accept responsibility for the consequences of their decisions. Within reason, we need to allow the consequences of our children's actions to teach them responsibility. In other words,

don't short circuit the system or snowplow the roads. If you say something is going to happen in terms of discipline or consequences, be sure it happens. Do not rob your children of much-needed lessons by making repeated, empty, vain threats.

10. *Avoid unrealistic expectations.* Often when I counsel kids concerning parent-child conflicts, they cite unrealistic expectations as a major problem. Children, especially teens, feel tremendous pressure because of unduly high expectations placed on them by parents. The key word here is "unrealistic." It is both desirable and beneficial to have high expectations for our children especially with regard to moral standards. However, our standards and expectations for our children need to be realistic and attainable. Unrealistic expectations, and the accompanying pressure to achieve, rank high as a major cause of stress for children.

11. *Accept children where they are.* It is often tough to accept your own child where he is. We don't always have trouble accepting other people's children where they are, but we know how we want *our* children to be, and how we want them to think and act. We don't have to agree with the way our children are, but it is necessary that we care for them. If your child's feelings or opinions about anything happen to conflict with yours, try to recognize that he has a right to his feelings. Hear him out and accept him as he is, then go on from there. If he is immature in the way he thinks, your understanding him and accepting him will go a long way toward helping him sort out his feelings.

12. *Respect your child's privacy.* One complaint I often hear from adolescents is that parents do not respect their privacy. Children are people, and they should have a right to privacy. Are your children

required to knock before entering when your bedroom door is closed? Why should your children not be entitled to the same privacy? Your children are not allowed to listen in on your phone calls, so why should you listen to theirs? Your children are striving for independence, and it is desirable for this to take place under the protection of your love and in a safe atmosphere. Of course, there are situations when parents have been given "probable cause" or have a good reason to deny privacy temporarily. That is a different matter. But under ordinary circumstances parents should respect privacy.

13. *Handle problems and conflict in an open, positive way.* Parents cannot rear children in today's world without encountering problems and conflicts. Some of these problems are relatively minor, such as my fourteen-year-old wanting to ride in his fifteen-year-old friend's car. But ultimately parents will be confronted with problems and conflicts of a more serious nature. For example, how should parents handle their child's apparent rejection of family values? Even when hurt, afraid, angry, and disappointed, parents cannot panic in such a situation and allow communication to cease. When children, especially adolescents, know that their parents are attempting to understand and appreciate their feelings even if they do not sanction the behavior, a bond of closeness develops between parent and child.

14. *Never embarrass your child–discipline and correct in private.* Children of all ages detest public humiliation and embarrassment. When they are chewed out in front of their friends, it evokes a strong emotional response. At this age they are extremely concerned about the opinion of others, particularly their peers. Your child may need a good, old-

fashioned chewing out, but have the courtesy to perform this task in private.

15. *Do not use excessive amounts of unrealistic guilt.* When my daughter left for college, I felt as if I'd lost her! As I said goodbye to her at her dorm, hundreds of memories rushed through my mind: reading *Goodnight Moon* as she dozed on my lap, her first day of school, junior high school, her first date, her first car, her baptism, and many, many others. Leaving her at college was very traumatic, but I survived–barely! In the weeks leading up to her departure, I attempted to use what I thought was humor to alleviate some of my sadness and loss. I would say to her, "It's okay, just break your parent's heart and leave home, after we've taken care of you for eighteen years! But, don't worry about us, just go ahead and leave." My daughter, Stephanie, took some of this as it was intended—as good, natural humor and a release for her sentimental father. But after awhile she began to feel guilty. And even though it was not my intention, she began to be burdened by this unrealistic guilt. As parents we are sometimes very fearful that our children will not turn out right. This fear causes us to pile guilt on ourselves, and eventually we began to push some of that guilt onto our children. When guilt is heaped on our children, either purposely or inadvertently, the door to effective communication and input is closed. We can avoid this guilt by spending more time discussing and less time evaluating. We can also, at times, just keep our mouths closed!

16. *Share yourself and your feelings with your children.* One of the greatest gifts we can give our children is ourselves—not just our money, our support, our car, etc., but the sharing of our thoughts, problems, and feelings. This is difficult for most

parents because they do not want their children to know that they have problems and fears. But children will receive much comfort, encouragement and strength when they see that their parents are human and that they make mistakes, have problems, and face fears and uncertainties. Parents, share yourselves!

17. *Respect your child's choices, and let them fail if necessary.* It is very difficult for most parents to respect their child's choices. As their parents, we are obviously able to make much wiser choices for them. But as children grow into adolescence they need the experience of making choices and decisions. The time will come when we will not be constantly at their side, and they will need to function and make responsible choices without our help. How much better to allow our children the opportunity to practice making choices and even to fail while they are under our care and supervision than for them to have their first experience with failure in the outside world! Failure teaches children about the realities of life. There are real responsibilities in the world, and kids must learn how to handle them while they're still in the home. Home remains the safest place in the world to learn about the realities of life. But, if they don't learn that the real world has teeth and will bite, they will be unprepared to function effectively.

A Final Word and a Letter

All children need structure. They are not ready to be completely out in the world, and they need the firm but reasonable boundaries and guidelines that loving parents provide. Children, especially teenagers, will at times complain and resist rules, but they desperately need and even desire guidelines and restrictions. Parental limits give children a feeling of being loved and secure while at the same time providing a safe environment in which to learn about the real world. Hopefully, as parents we can establish firm, reasonable, flexible boundaries that communicate to our children both support and love.

Let me close this chapter by reprinting a letter that was written by a young man in his mid-twenties. He wrote this to his father several years ago. This letter very eloquently expresses most of the things I have attempted to convey in the last two chapters. If we, as fathers, receive letters such as this, we will have done our job very well.

> Dear Dad,
> Well, today is Father's Day, and it seemed like a good time to write this letter. I have intended to write for a couple of years, and now seems appropriate.
> I really wanted to let you know what a wonderful father you really are. I know I've said that to you, and I've said thank you, and I love you, and all those things many times before. But I've always wanted to tell you some reasons why, and let you know that when I say those things, they're a lot more than just words.
> When I was growing up, especially in high school and college, I would hear my friends and other kids talk about their parents. The way they talked of them was usually not good. They didn't get along with them; they thought they were mean, or weird, or stupid. I felt out of place, because I loved my parents, and thought they were great! In high school and then in college, other kids complained

about going on vacations with their parents, or doing things with them; but I enjoyed it! We had fun travelling to Tennessee, or to Florida, or driving across the country.

I realize a lot of the difference between you and those other fathers was the way discipline was handled. When you disciplined me, or wouldn't let me do something I wanted to do (or made me do something I didn't want to do), you always explained the reasons. You always treated me like an intelligent person who had a right to know the reasons for your actions, rather than just ordering me around. And most of the time, as much as I would have hated to admit it, I agreed with your reasons. Looking back now, I agree with all of them! And I remember one time when you got very angry with me for something that wasn't my fault, you came and apologized later for that. That meant very much to me then and now. I know of very few people who could bring themselves to do that.

One thing that has made me feel the best is the way you have supported me, especially through college and beyond. When I first began seriously considering music as a career, I never heard a negative word from you. It was always encouraging. You would caution me about certain things, certain decisions, but you never criticized my choice. And you even began to listen and study types of music that I know you didn't care for, just so you could offer me advice, and help me out. I didn't (and still don't) know any of my musician friends' parents who did that. There is no way I can ever tell you how much all your concern, advice, time and money has meant to me concerning my music.

I feel very good about myself. I look around at my family, my accomplishments, and the things I am able to do, and the things I own, and am amazed at how good everything is. And all of it is directly or indirectly because of you and your teaching. One of my most fervent prayers at this time is that I will someday be the kind of father you were to me. Well, I could go on forever, Dad. I know things are tough there now. I wish I could be there with you, like you helped me through some difficult times. But remember I think of you often, and say a prayer for you.

I love you.

For Further Thought

1. Analyze your parenting style — when are you authoritarian, permissive, authoritative? What patterns do you see emerging? How can you improve your parenting style?

2. Read Ephesians 5:1,21; 6:4. How are parents and children to submit to each other? How is your family accomplishing this?

3. Read Hebrews 12:5-11. What does this passage tell us about discipline and relationships?

4. What battles do you fight that might be better left unfought?

5. Read Ephesians 4:32. When was the last time you asked your child to forgive you?

6. What roads do you snowplow for your children? Devise a simple plan to avoid this in the future.

7. Read James 3:17. This verse is especially relevant to resolving conflicts and working out logical consequences.[7] Are these characteristics present when you resolve conflict and use logical consequences with your children?

8. Relate a time you used unrealistic guilt to motivate your child.

[1] Medved, *Saving Childhood*, 220.

[2] Morton P. Strommon and A. Irene Strommon, *Five Cries of Parents* (New York: Harper and Row, 1985), 88.

[3] Jones, *How & When to Tell Your Kids About Sex*, 33.

[4] David Lewis, "Counseling Adolescents in the Church," Abilene Christian University Graduate Course, Abilene, TX, June 1987.

[5] G. Keith Olson, *Counseling Teenagers* (Loveland, CO: Group Publishers, Inc., 1989), 65.

[6] F. Cline and J. Fog, *Parenting With Love and Logic* (Colorado Springs: NavPress, 1990), 95.

[7] Fritz Ridenour, *What Teenagers Wish Their Parents Knew About Kids* (Waco, TX: Word Books, 1982), 162.

5

I Don't Know How
to Handle a Sex Talk!

Guidelines for Talking About Sex

Talking to other people's children is what I have done for a living for over twenty-five years. As a youth minister, I've listened to every question, confession and story you can imagine. Most of the time I can calmly, rationally and factually discuss a wide range of issues and problems with any teen. And I am not easily intimidated by even the most threatening questions. I consider myself a tested veteran of many children and teenage wars. If all of this is true, then why did I feel so panicked by a single question asked by my son when he was eleven years old? To him it was a simple enough question—"Dad, exactly what is masturbation, and why do people do it?" I had placidly answered very similar questions in many different settings. So why was I so scared? My mind, in computer fashion, was recalling all the volumes of material I had read concerning the do's and don'ts of sex education. Even with all my experience, I still felt unprepared and awkward as I began answering the question. But I suppose my answer was satisfying because, at the conclusion of my answer, he said, "That's what I thought", and calmly walked off.

My experience was similar to that of many parents as they grapple with feelings of fear and uncertainty concerning sexual discussions with their children. Most parents feel woefully inadequate when it comes time to answer specific sexual questions from their children. And this sense of inadequacy is heightened at the prospect of engaging in a sexual talk or discussion. Many parents are afraid to talk with their children about sex because of embarrassment, lack of a specific plan, or ambiguity concerning their own sexual feelings and beliefs. But learning how to talk with our children about sex is very important. Candid discussions with parents contribute significantly to the development of healthy sexual attitudes and appear to help delay sexual activity. "Research has proven that parents talking to teens about sex makes a difference. Syracuse University's Institute for Family Research and Education found that teenagers whose parents discuss sex with them tend to delay first intercourse longer than their peers whose parents don't."[1] A leading child psychiatrist was asked "What is the best way to prepare maturing boys and girls concerning sexual matters?" The doctor's answer was interesting:

> The best way is an emotionally mature set of parents with a comfortable attitude about sex, and a willingness to answer the child's questions appropriately and honestly. Other approaches (such as school sex education courses) only try to make up for a lack of this and are only second best.[2]

Parents clearly are the key. By talking freely with our children about sex, we train them to be open about sexual matters. We also need to realize that most basic sexual information comes to youngsters from their parents. Children learn their deepest lessons by example, and their attitudes toward sex are not so much taught as caught. There are no strict rules or easy formulas to follow here, however. Parents need to equip their children with the sexual knowledge and attitudes that can enable them to make intelligent, godly decisions. To assist you in this formidable task, I have put together some tips and suggestions from several authoritative sources to help you handle sex talks with children. This information is more general than specific, and is concerned with the "how" of sex talks. The specific "what" information will be discussed later.

One word of caution before we begin. Please do not think the sex education of your children will be accomplished by a single, or even a few, talks or discussions. In order to teach our children effectively about sex, it is necessary to have many such talks in the approximately eighteen years they are at home. What an exciting prospect!

Here's What the Experts Say

1. *Establish the proper climate for sex education.* This involves several factors. First, create a loving atmosphere. Parents emit sex education messages to their children from the earliest days of their infancy. The way a baby is spoken to, held, cuddled, picked up, and tucked into bed all affect sex education. When these and other physical contacts are tender and pleasurable, the infant begins to understand how wonderful and comfortable it is to be close to another's body. Through this nonverbal communication the baby finds that relating to other people makes him feel good, happy and accepted. Such a loving atmosphere provides a wonderful

setting in which his development as a human being, including his sexual development, can take place.

Another condition of the climate we should aim for in the home is one in which children can see the object lesson of their parents' love for each other. Love is demonstrated in different ways by different families, but the important thing is that love be shown. A child learns a great deal by watching how his mother and father relate to one another. Children need to see devotion, concern, affection and enjoyment of one another's companionship, and sexual purity modeled on the biblical standards for sexuality. When children see their parents demonstrate affectionate emotions, it conveys to them the proper meaning of love and respect. And this is a crucial part of sex education.

A third factor helping create the appropriate climate is for the parent to be relaxed. In the words of Christian broadcaster and author, John Nieder:

> Embarrassment creates anxiety. And anxiety usually cripples communication. If you get uncomfortable talking about sex, you will make your child feel uneasy, and the tension may very well destroy her openness. Next time the topic of sex enters a conversation, make sure you smile ... even if your stomach growls, your blood pressure rises, or nausea begins to set it in.[3]

Fourth, parents can create a climate conducive to good sex education by speaking positively about sex. As we have already seen, a primary source of children's sexual information is the media. And the media portrays sex as wonderful and the supreme experience. If we then, as parents speak about sex only in negative terms, our children will begin to get the idea that to us, sex is evil and ungodly. Our children need sex portrayed as a positive, exciting, and wonderful gift from God that is to be enjoyed by married couples. They need to understand that God designed Adam and Eve's bodies, blessed their union, and said it was good (Gen. 1:31). Such a portrayal will balance the enjoyable nature of sex with God's perfect plan.

Openness, or "askability," is a fifth requirement for developing a positive climate for sex education. Children should be encouraged from the earliest years to feel at ease in talking with their parents about anything that concerns them. As a result, they develop confidence in their parents' openness.

When we attempt to understand our childrens' point of view and are willing to learn and grow with our children, we are prepared to share our thoughts and feelings sincerely with our children. In this atmosphere children will feel free to bring us their questions, doubts and problems without fear of censure and condemnation.

Remember my son's question concerning masturbation? The words I used to answer him were very important. But far more important was my reaction to his question. If I had lost my composure and overreacted with a stern warning, he would probably have concluded that I was either ignorant of the facts, or I was discouraging his openness. If we want our children to come to us, not to others with their sexual questions, we must not discourage their openness and turn them toward less reliable sources of information.

2. *Get an early start and be prepared.* Your children's world can turn sexual quickly. One day your child may have little curiosity about sex, the next day everyone in the class may be excited over something sexual. Menstruation, masturbation,

breasts, erections, dating, kissing, intercourse—all are issues that can be stressful to the adolescent encountering them close-up for the first time. If parents have prepared their children over several years, they have a good chance of taking such problems in stride. Your early teaching can stand your teens in good stead. But this preparation must be done while they are receptive to your leadership and before the inevitable periods when they are asserting their independence. There is no precise timetable governing what sexual facts should be furnished at what age. If, however, your child has not started asking sexual questions by age four or five, look for natural occasions to bring up the subject. The more natural you can make the discussions, the healthier your instructions will be. It is also important that you be prepared to have sexual discussions and conversations with your children. Buy age-appropriate books or videotapes that can assist your preparedness. And remember, you want to talk to your children before someone else does. Sex education must begin early!

3. *Look for teachable opportunities and take the initiative.* A good teacher does not see her task merely in terms of sitting and waiting until questions are asked. Rather, she tries to stimulate wonder and curiosity so that questions will be asked. A good teacher also knows that learning occurs gradually. As teachers of sex education in the home, we must also keep these things in mind. Some children are very inquisitive and ask questions; other children do not ask questions, or they stop talking as they grow older. Adolescents are likely to be shy about approaching parents with specific sexual questions. We are neglecting our responsibilities as parents if we say nothing. It is our responsibility to bring up

the subject. Do we allow our children to drift spiritually in the hope that someday they will ask about God or find God for themselves? As Christians, we actively share God and his Word with our children. We don't sit back and wait for them to take the initiative and ask us about God. Because of the importance of the issue, and our love for our children, we take the initiative. Why, then, should sex be a taboo subject? We must take the initiative in discussing sexual matters with our children. And if our children fail to ask questions regarding sexual matters, we as parents must be alert and search for opportunities for teaching.

Teachable moments abound in the daily lives of our children. Suppose your child comes home repeating an off-color joke. You could scold and scream, or you could use the occasion as a teachable moment and teach valuable lessons. You can also find opportunities for teaching while watching TV with your children. During a program about pregnancy, for example, parents can ask questions, to determine the level of the child's information. If their information is inadequate, then a golden opportunity to teach is available. There are many documentaries, as well as other programs, that feature sexual situations. Trainable opportunities can be discovered in many routine day-to-day situations, such as movies, music, advertisements, and books.

Parents should also be alert to teaching opportunities stemming from their child's physical experiences. As young pre-teens approach puberty the physical changes occurring in their bodies can be used to expand the child's sexual knowledge. Other natural occurrences in life can provide a good opportunity to discuss sexual issues. A new baby in the family or a litter of kittens can make a wonderful natural occasion for talking about sex. Sex education opportunities are endless, and we need to seize them and not feel that sex can only be talked about by prescheduled appointment with our children. When we calmly and lovingly use natural occurrences and situations as opportunities to discuss sex with our children, we are taking the initiative and keeping the door open for future communication. By taking the initiative, parents express concern, openness and availability.

4. *Repetition will be necessary.* Sometimes, because of a negative approach by adults, children (especially teenagers) block out sexual information because they are frightened by it. Their earliest memories of parents and other adults discussing sexuality may have led children to believe that sex is dirty, sinful and wrong. These children frequently repress sexual knowledge. Therefore, there may be a need to repeat previously discussed sexual information. In doing so, we need to reassure the child that the issues are complex and not easily understood, especially all at once. It is also true that when certain facts were initially discussed, the information was probably only partially understood. As the child grows older, the information will have more personal relevance, and will need to be discussed again. Remember one of our basic axioms: sex education is a gradual process and involves much repetition. Parents should not feel they failed to "get through" if a child repeats a question they thought they had explained earlier. The repetition probably means the child is ready for a deeper and broader look at the matter. Gradualness and repetition are the key.

5. *Accept your child's sexuality and earn his trust.* Parents need to communicate to their children that

they accept their emerging sexuality and that they will never use against them anything they reveal about their sexuality. Research indicates that adolescents deeply mistrust their parents with regard to sexual feelings. They fear that parents may use this information against them in some way. One teenager, serving on a panel at a meeting of the American Association of Sex Education, Counselors and Therapists, gave this advice to parents:

> You have to show your kid that he can trust you. You shouldn't throw in a person's face something he did or something he doesn't know. You shouldn't say, "Oh, daddy's little girl shouldn't know that."[4]

Many of the other youngsters on the panel wished that they could talk to their parents about sex, but felt they could not. One panelist said:

> The parent has to make the first move. You have to know that you'll be received, that your parents will accept you.[5]

The feelings of these panelists express both a desire to talk to their parents and also a fear or lack of trust toward parents. In order to remove their fears and establish trust, you must take your child's sexual concerns very seriously. Never make fun of any misinformation they may have, or areas of ignorance. Also, be aware of your child's self-consciousness and embarrassment regarding sexual issues. Under no circumstances should you joke about your child's sexuality. Remember that trust and acceptance are extremely important issues to children, especially adolescents.

6. *Keep it casual and conversational.* Lectures turn kids off and cause children to feel as though they are being spoken at, not to. Informal, casual, relaxed, spontaneous conversations are more effective with

sensitive issues such as sex. One way to keep it casual is to give children time to absorb new information and clarify new ideas. Be brief and leave the door open for additional conversations in the future.

You also need to be prepared for questions to come at odd moments. Children will often initiate conversations regarding sensitive topics when they feel comfortable and at ease, so such conversations may occur during routine family activities.

7. *Calmly and without panic answer your child's questions.* Take your child's questions at face value and answer them factually and calmly. After you have answered the questions, you may find it helpful to ask: "What aroused your interest?" But ask that only after you have factually answered the questions, and have resisted the impulse to jump to conclusions. For example, if your son asks if condoms are effective against venereal diseases, do not assume he is asking because he intends to test the product. Children are very curious and routinely file away all sorts of sexual information they never intend to use. If you make assumptions and jump to conclusions, it may have the effect of scaring off your child and causing him to stop asking questions and seeking advice.

When your child asks a question that is not clear, ask in a matter-of-fact way, "In what way?" or "How do you mean?" Follow-up questions like these will help you identify the real issues and prevent you from giving long, tedious explanations that are both unwanted and unnecessary. Give honest, calm answers to questions about sex. Never shame a child over sex!

8. *Retreat if you encounter resistance.* Parents' efforts to discuss sexual matters can be frustrated by their children. Your children may tell you they

already know all they need to know, or they may simply walk away. If this happens, rather than press the topic or pressure the child, just say, "OK, let's talk about this another time." When we try to force the issue, our children sometimes sense our tension and feel pressured. At this point they become even more reluctant to include us in their sex education. You may need to wait for a more appropriate time. It is never easy to guess the mood of an adolescent, but if you sense problems, trouble, stress, or loss of interest, simply wait for these things to pass and look for a more appropriate time. You also need to follow the child's timetable rather than your own. Your child may be worried about a particular stage of puberty, and until that pressing problem is solved, the youngster will probably not be ready to discuss another sexual topic.

You may also meet resistance if the child senses an invasion of privacy. Teenagers have an especially strong urge to protect their privacy, and they are likely to react defensively if they feel parents are meddling. Avoid being overly curious and resist the temptation to ask ill-timed, personal, sexual questions. Such embarrassing questions can cause teenagers to become uncommunicative, evasive, and silent. Parents who take intrusive behavior to the maximum limits may also face rebellion from their teens. This rebellion is an attempt on the part of adolescents to pursue their autonomy and to achieve independence. As I mentioned before, rebellion is one of the primary reasons for pregnancy in early adolescents, and a well-timed retreat by parents is sometimes in order.

9. *Use proper terms.* James Dobson, noted Christian psychologist, once remarked in a speech that when it comes to discussing sex, parents usually

use "sophisticated" language. He said, "for example, everyone knows that a boy has a 'thing-a-me-jig' and girls have a 'whats-ya-ma-call-it.'"[6] Unfortunately, when discussing sex with their children, some parents do not use correct terminology. We do not need to be unreasonably detailed in this regard, nor should parents cite every minute technical term and burden tiny children with the vocabulary of a physiology textbook. But correct terminology, commensurate with the child's vocabulary, should be used. After all, children learn "hand" and "nose," so why is it different for genitals? Why are we embarrassed to teach our children to say "penis" instead of "weenie"? When we give the correct names to parts and functions of the body, we aid our children in gaining accurate sexual information. This will also help them to share their feelings about sexuality. The use of correct terminology is important in avoiding inaccurate impressions and creating the idea that these parts are secretive or different. For example, a baby does not grow in a mother's tummy. Reproduction is not part of the stomach or digestive system. Children who have been told these inaccuracies sometimes keep these wrong impressions for years.

Most parents do not use proper terminology because they are embarrassed to do so. One leading psychologist advises parents to say the correct words out loud and listen to themselves. Doing this will help you become less sensitive. You should also refrain from using euphemisms, baby talk, or obscene language. It is really just as easy to use the correct term for a part of a baby as to refer to the part by either a cute or dirty word. Do not deprive your children of the necessary vocabulary to increase their knowledge and understanding. Correct terminology is a vital part of sex education. As a parent, you will need to know these facts, if you are to teach your children correctly. To help you, we have included a glossary of easily understandable terms concerning sexual anatomy and physiology at the end of this book.

10. *Be accurate and dispel myths.* This follows from the previous topic. Use accurate terminology and give accurate information. This includes dispelling myths. The sexual "knowledge" of adolescents often consists largely of myths and folklore...much of it hazardous. Some of the more common myths many young people believe are: females can become pregnant only while menstruating; venereal disease germs can be washed away; only a limited amount of semen can be produced by males over a lifetime (many boys worry that they have used up their supply by masturbating); females cannot get pregnant during their first intercourse; and many, many more. When you squelch myths, however, avoid putting down your child for believing the misinformation. Such treatment could make your children feel their concerns are unimportant.

In order for sex talks to be really useful, it is often necessary to be blunt and expose euphemisms. Make no bones about the reality behind a word. For example, abortion is often described as "termination of pregnancy." Let your child know that it involves the complete destruction of the fetus. You will be giving the child a reasonable basis for making a decision, and chances are they will appreciate your honesty. Parents who repeat myths, or who "protect" their children from hard sexual truths, confuse their children and risk discrediting themselves. It is just as much a mistake to distort facts in an attempt to influence your teenager's behavior. Your teen will stop listening to you if you pass on falsehoods, and your subsequent statements, however accurate, will be doubted. Sometimes, even with the best of intentions, parents start out with a credibility gap.

11. *Admit your discomfort in talking about sex and furnish other resources.* Personal discomfort concerning sexual matters prevents some parents from discussing sex with their children. Unfortunately many Christian parents come from restrictive backgrounds that cause them to be more liberated intellectually than emotionally. In other words, you can often say the right thing but you do not feel right saying it. And when this happens, body language, facial expressions, and tone of voice give you away. This kind of behavior gives children mixed messages and may prompt them to avoid the subject of sex when you are around.

You can overcome some of your difficulties by talking about sex education with other concerned adults. Conversations with your spouse, other family members, or a support group could help you become accustomed to talking about sexual matters. You can also become active in community organizations that deal with sexual issues, such as rape crisis programs, teen pregnancy clinics, or hospital VD clinics. Hopefully, discussing or working with sexual issues will help ease your inhibitions. No matter how hard they try, some parents cannot overcome their inhibitions. If this is the case, tell your children that you are not comfortable talking about sexual matters; being honest will help break the tension. If you are totally and completely uncomfortable with your ability to discuss sex with your children, take steps to acquire valuable aids that will help you teach your children. First, make information available to your children. Many good books and video programs are available that teach on an appropriate level. Encourage your children's exposure to these mediums. Second, there are many well-run, realistic sex education courses conducted by churches and other groups that emphasize abstinence. Help your youngster sign up for these courses. Third, and most important, find another sensitive adult who can act as a confidant, instructor and advisor for both you and your teen.

12. *Stress the uniqueness of the Christian message and turn to the Scriptures.* From an early age children need to be taught the biblical message concerning sex. Unless your children know the biblical position and proper context regarding sex, they may find themselves adrift in a sea of conflicting values. Children need to learn that God loves and cares for them, and that he understands the mysterious stirrings, worries and concerns that occur during adolescence. Children can gain a sense of wonder at God's marvelous creation in their bodies. They can learn that God provides guidelines, gives comfort, and has not abandoned them on a sea of sexual confusion.

In helping our children learn about sex with the gospel message as a frame of reference, we help them see the truth that God created sex, and the often unrecognized fact that God wants to guide and help us with this powerful and beautiful gift. In their book, *Parenting Today's Adolescents,* Dennis and Barbara Rainey list some major points from Scripture that need to be shared with children concerning God's view about sex: God created sex; sex is for procreation in marriage; sex is for intimacy in marriage; sex is for pleasure and enjoyment in marriage; and sex outside of marriage is sin.[7]

A reading of the Song of Solomon, as well as an understanding of the fourfold purpose of sex, will help young people establish a true picture of the biblical ideal for sex in marriage. God intended for married couples to fully enjoy sex. A healthy attitude toward sex, as well as clear statements and teachings, will help your children understand the proper biblical message concerning sex.

13. *Put sex in proper perspective.* Help your children see that sex is just one part of their lives, and that it is tied to all other feelings. This is often difficult because the media portrays sex as the greatest achievement of humankind. Based on the amount of time TV, movies, and the recording industry devote to talking about sex, it is easy to see why our children are confused. Adolescents, because of their lack of experience, often do not have a realistic perspective on life and tend to be uncertain in their expectations. As an adult and a parent, you have experienced life more fully. Use your experience and wisdom to help your children see that sex is only one part of a successful marriage. It is important, yes, but by no means is it the only consideration. There are other aspects to our human makeup. In fact, according to research done by Dr. Sol Gordon (one of the leading experts on sex education in the United States) sex ranks nine on a list of the ten most important characteristics of a mature marriage.

Sexual intercourse, as an aspect of our sexuality, is greatly overrated. If some people's public persona were to be believed, however, it would often appear that only nuclear war is a more important issue in our lives.

Here is Dr. Gordon's top ten most important characteristics of a mature marriage:

1. Love, caring, and intimacy together.
2. A sense of humor and playfulness.
3. Honest communication and interesting conversation.
4. A passionate source of mission and purpose.
5. Friends together and separately.
6. Commitment to one's own identity and ideals.
7. Tolerance of occasional craziness, irritableness, conflict, error.
8. Acceptance of each other's style.
9. Sexual fulfillment.
10. Sharing household responsibilities.[8]

A Final Word

Talking to children about sex is not easy for parents, so we have discussed the feelings of embarrassment, inadequacy and fear that cause us to approach the topic of sex cautiously. In spite of these misgivings, we can effectively communicate sexual information to our children. However, it simply is not necessary to feel entirely comfortable about sexuality in order to communicate effectively with your children.

These suggestions and tips will hopefully make sex talks more relaxed and helpful. Remember, however, there are no pat answers. How and when to tell your children about sex is a sensitive issue. In today's world, children are often aware of highly sophisticated sexual facts at an unusually tender age. But remember, each child is different in his sexual interest, awareness, and comprehension. It is best to think of starting sex education at the birth of your child and making it an ongoing lifetime process woven into the flow of our everyday lives.

For Further Thought

1. In your home, is love openly demonstrated between spouses? How can this be improved?
2. Are you relaxed and positive talking about sex?
3. List several teachable opportunities that you failed to recognize at the time. How could these occasions have been used as discussion starters?
4. Do you accept your child's sexuality? Does your child feel this acceptance?
5. Do your children trust you not to misuse your knowledge of their sexual feelings?
6. Anticipate several possible sexual questions that could cause you panic, and work out answers for these questions.
7. In discussions with your children, which sexual issues, terms, or situations, would cause you the most discomfort? Why?
8. Read Hebrews 13:4. See how many different teachings on sex you can find and think about how you would share them with your teenage son or daughter.
9. How would you have answered my son's question regarding masturbation?

---

[1] Napier, *The Power of Abstinence*, 102.

[2] Howard R. Lewis and Martha E. Lewis, *Parent's Guide to Teenage Sex and Pregnancy* (New York: St. Martins, 1980), 30.

[3] John Neider, *God, Sex, and Your Child* (Nashville: Thomas Nelson Publishers, 1988), 83.

[4] Lewis, *Parent's Guide*, 36-37.

[5] Lewis, *Parent's Guide*, 37.

[6] James Dobson, "Focus on the Family" Convention, San Antonio, TX, Sept. 1978.

[7] Rainey, *Parenting Today's Adolescents*, 87-88.

[8] Sol Gordon and Judith Gordon, *Raising a Child Conservatively in a Sexually Permissive World* (New York: Simon and Schuster, 1983), 45.

6

Babies, Preschoolers, and Sex

I was teaching a parenting class at church and after I had already responded to several questions during a question-and-answer period, a young mother at the back of the room shyly raised her hand and asked very sheepishly, "At what age do you suggest we begin sex education?"

The class laughed and assumed I was joking when I said, "Well, Mrs. Jones you had better hurry up and start because your children are ahead of you; they begin at birth."

I quickly explained that I was very serious. Sex education begins at birth! The world of infants is one composed almost entirely of the senses. Their world revolves around sounds, smells and temperature. Babies need and desire to be touched. Much nurturing takes place as a mother holds and feeds her child at her breast. Infants very quickly begin learning all about themselves and their world through observation and association. They observe the manner in which they are spoken to, held, hugged, kissed, and then they associate these actions with warmth and security. Since all of these sensual delights are primarily provided by their parents, babies very quickly begin to see themselves exactly the way their parents see them. So parents are influencing and teaching babies from the earliest moments of life. Babies begin learning about sexuality when they are born. There are many seemingly routine issues surrounding infants and young children that can have a profound effect on their sexual well-being. Sex education truly begins at birth, whether consciously or subconsciously.

Sex Education for Babies (Ages Birth-3 years)

Many things that we learn during infancy stay with us throughout our lives. One of the most important lessons is whether we perceive the world as hostile or friendly. An infant whose needs are regularly met views the world as a friendly, warm place. But an infant whose needs are not regularly met learns to view the world as a scary place where no one can be trusted. The perception of a friendly world is translated into trust and has an effect on how the infant learns to relate to others. As we stated, infants learn trust primarily through touch. The nurturing touch of mother and father, or the lack of it, lets babies know whether it is safe to reach out to others, or better to withdraw. So, parents educate their children through such actions as the way they hold them, the way they touch the baby's skin; the way they play with the baby; stroking, cuddling and holding him close.[1]

The way you handle your baby and your facial expressions while holding him reflect your opinion of your child. For example, if you react squeamishly or negatively to such normal tasks as changing diarrhea-filled diapers or medicating messy umbilical cords, what message is your baby receiving? Parents must be extremely careful not to grimace or use body language that communicates disgust during the physical care of their babies. Such behavior can negatively influence an infant with regard to his sexuality.

There are several specific aspects of an infant's physical sex education that are important. Some experiences critically affect an infant's acceptance of his body and his attitude toward body parts and functions. First, as we have already mentioned, parents should avoid reacting with displeasure or disgust toward normal body functions. One day, when our son was a few months old, I returned home after a hard day at the office and found my wife in her underwear, crying in the hallway outside our infant son's room. He had diarrhea and vomiting all day long, and he was having so many bowel movements and vomiting spells that he had soiled all of his mother's clothes. Every time she went in to change him, he would ruin another layer of clothing. It quickly became apparent that mother was out of clothes and patience. Now my wife, Linda, had the good judgment not to react in displeasure in our son's presence. She saved the disapproval, disgust and frustration for me! But suppose she had reacted negatively in his presence? Suppose she had either yelled at him, or simply cried from frustration. How would an infant understand such actions? He would probably be completely confused at this response to his perfectly natural body functions. Since the excretory and sexual organs are in such close proximity, it is difficult for an infant to distinguish between them. Therefore, when parents react with displeasure or seeming disapproval, the baby is learning that certain parts of his body are distasteful or even shameful. My wife's experience that day many years ago was not a pleasurable one, but it is vitally important that parents learn to attend to normal body functions with grace and dignity. If a child grows up believing parts of his body are shameful it will adversely affect his sexuality at a later date.

Parents also teach an infant to accept his body by the way they react to his self-discovery. Have you ever witnessed parents, grandparents, and other excited relatives gather around an infant's bed watching him identify or play with his ears, nose, or feet? They all respond as if he is the most intelligent baby in the world. Each time he correctly identifies a body part he is praised and affirmed. That is, until the little darling reaches for and discovers his or her genitals! Everyone starts acting very embarrassed and Junior's parents, usually in response to everyone's distress, either slap or pull his hand away from his genitals. How can an infant understand this reaction? He doesn't even know he has a penis! Once again, he is being taught that certain parts of his body are shameful or dirty. Parents must avoid such reactions because an infant can sense whether he is totally loved by his parents or if they are hesitant, withdrawn, or rejecting. Parents need to be aware that infants live in a God-given world of sensual delight. Marriage and family counselor Mary Ann Mayo says:

> The world of the normal infant includes orgasm, sometimes as a newborn, but always within the first year of life. Physically or emotionally deprived infants may rock, bang their heads, and excessively suck their thumbs, but they won't masturbate. It is the healthy child who involves himself or herself in genital play. The sad, emotionally, or physically deprived child does not bother.[2]

Allowing infants the freedom to explore their genitals should not be frightening to parents. It is simply one part of their learning experience. It will not become their major fascination. After awhile the baby's interest will center elsewhere. But your comfortable attitude regarding your child's genitals will have a calming effect and help him learn to accept his whole body. Disapproving messages, on the other hand, can program doubts and negative reactions into the child's earliest understanding of himself.

Another area of physical importance in an infant's sex education is correctly naming the body parts. This is closely associated with parental acceptance of self-discovery. When allowing your child to explore his genital area just as he does other parts of his body, you should correctly name and identify all body parts. This will help you become comfortable using the proper names, and it will communicate acceptance of the whole body since all parts have been named and treated in the same way.

Another area of importance involves toilet training. Be patient and unhurried with regard to your infant's toilet training. If toilet training is attempted before an infant has the ability to voluntarily control the muscles involved in these functions, he will not be able to respond. Most child development experts agree that such control is rarely possible before the age of two or three years. Of course, you will discover that all of your relatives and friends had their babies completely toilet trained by age six months, and they do not mind constantly reminding you of that fact! Many years ago, with our first child, my wife was determined not to allow others to influence her decision to wait until our daughter was truly ready for toilet training. She waited until Stephanie was about two and a half years old. This caused somewhat strained family relations as she was the first grandchild on either side of the family. All of our relatives thought we were going to cause great mental anguish to our daughter and that she would probably go off to kindergarten in a diaper. But my wife stuck to her guns and did not begin until about 30 months.

Now you must understand, my wife is a very well-read and extremely creative person, and she does not do many things in the conventional manner. Toilet training was no exception — she began training Stephanie by placing the potty-chair in front of the television during children's shows such as "Sesame Street." Well, it only took a few days to completely toilet train our daughter. Everything was great until we had a house full of relatives one day and Stephanie got the urge. You guessed it! She ran into the bathroom, grabbed her potty-chair, set it down in front of the television and proceeded to do her business. She emptied the room in a hurry, and we had some explaining to do. But by waiting until our daughter was ready, my wife had completed an often very traumatic event in less than a week.

Have you ever seen a diaper-clad child in kindergarten? Probably not, but you have known many children who still wet their beds or wet their clothes in school. They are possibly the ones who, through punishment and threats, were toilet trained by six months of age. Take your time in the toilet training of your child. By doing so you can avoid several potential emotional problems.

Hold, cuddle and physically touch your infant often. Babies show the most contentment when they are being held, rocked, or in some way snuggled closely. Some babies appear to need more caressing than others, but all infants respond positively to relaxed, repeated caressing. When our son was about a year old he went through a stage during which he very intensely needed to be held. He would not allow his mother or me to put him down for even an instant. Well, after a few days this grew rather old. Besides the physical weariness, we felt by holding him constantly we were going to spoil him. So we put him down. After all, we had read Dr. Spock and we knew he, as well as other experts, said that a child would only cry for about ten minutes before going to sleep or finding some other interest. Our son had not read Dr. Spock! He cried for two solid hours and then began vomiting. This went on for two days. By this time Linda was at the end of her rope. In desperation she called a friend, a slightly older woman with older children.

After listening to the problem, this wise pastor's wife responded by asking Linda a question: "If your son had any other need what would you do?"

Linda said, "I would attempt to meet it."

This discerning lady then said, "Well he has a need to be near you right now, so why not meet that need?"

She then loaned Linda a papoose-like back pack. For about a week Linda carried our son everywhere she went; after that he was OK. Now, I'm not a doctor or a psychologist, and I do not presume to know all of the psychological factors at work in this situation, but I know at least one thing — during that particular time in his young life, our son needed a tremendous amount of physical intimacy. And I'm not sure he was much different from other infants.

As parents, whatever we do that communicates a sense of warmth and love to our babies teaches them security and the enjoyment of physical intimacy. And security, warmth, and love will help lay a foundation of self-confidence in our children, a vital element in the development of healthy sexual attitudes.

Allow your infants and toddlers to enjoy and learn about their bodies and the closeness of others. One way to accomplish this is by joining a swimming class for infants and parents. In this atmosphere children will learn familiarity with their own bodies and the bodies of others. One of the best ways to help them achieve this bodily knowledge about themselves and others is to permit your young sons and daughters to bathe together. By bathing together children are not only learning about their own bodies but are also experiencing a natural lesson in the physical differences between males and females. In a non-threatening, playful way children notice that they have different parts. This possibly could be one of those opportunities for teaching we talked about earlier. Parents can casually use such moments to begin teaching young children that God made people different, and that these differences have reasons. Around the age of five or so your children will begin requesting that they be permitted to bathe alone—it is time for some privacy. But for your young children, bathing together can produce perfect teaching opportunities.

In our discussion on important areas concerning our infant's sex education, we have up to this point stressed the "shoulds." Let's look at one "should not." Parents should not allow infants and toddlers to sleep in their room or bed with them on a consistent or regular basis. This not only restrains the parent's lovemaking, but it quite possibly causes the young child to become upset because of his lack of knowledge or understanding regarding his parents behavior during lovemaking.

Sex Education for Preschoolers (Ages 2-5)

Physically speaking, the preschool years are years to continue building the concepts begun during the first year of your infant's life. It is important to continue using proper names for body parts, and to speak about human sexuality. Using proper terms will help children properly learn and identify body parts.

In the area of toilet training and personal hygiene be sure to explain the reason for washing hands after using the potty. Help your toddlers to understand they are wiping properly and washing their hands to avoid germs, not because that part of their body is shameful. This differentiation needs to be made so that the child will not think of sex organs as dirty.

It is essential during this critical stage that you continue appropriately touching your children. No one, male or female, ever outgrows the need to be touched. Continue to hug, hold and kiss your toddlers.

Preschool children can learn many negative emotions — shame, guilt, anger, and fear–from their parents, in the process of learning about sex. Conversely, positive attitudes are taught when parents have wholesome, healthy, godly attitudes and teach about sex in a consistent and responsible way. Such positive teaching creates a loving, trusting bond between parent and child, and contributes greatly to laying a strong foundation of self-esteem. This is a vitally important aspect of sex education, since self-esteem, or the lack of it, profoundly affects all areas of child and adolescent behavior. "Promiscuous and exploitative sexual behavior, premature parenthood and a range of self-damaging behavior, feed off poor self-esteem."[3]

It is therefore imperative that parents begin at birth to help children formulate a positive, healthy self-esteem. Much of this is accomplished by doing the things we have already talked about: holding, cuddling, stroking, developing close physical contact, using gentleness and sensitivity when toilet training, and reacting positively to innocent, normal childhood sexual curiosity about their bodies. Children should never be punished or scolded because of innocent sexual self-discoveries. When punishment and scolding are allowed to happen a whole range of negative emotional responses can occur: anger, withdrawal, fear, guilt—all adversely influencing self-esteem. Because of guilt and fear a child may learn to be dissatisfied with his body and become so disappointed that even as an adult, sexual pleasure is impossible. Early childhood problems in this area leave scars, and while they can be healed, they are much more easily prevented.

Mentally and intellectually, the young child's belief system mirrors that of his parents. Children tend to believe what their parents believe. What attitudes and beliefs concerning sexuality are we teaching our children? Dr. Grace Ketterman, noted Christian pediatrician and child psychiatrist, in her wonderful book, *How to Teach Your Child About Sex,* says that by school age there are five attitudes your child needs to understand if he is to be a sexually healthy person.[4]

Attitude 1: *He needs to know that he is a beautiful child and that his imperfections only add to his uniqueness as a masterpiece created by God and nurtured by you.*

A child's attitude toward her body is an important element in sexuality. If she feels that the sexual parts of her body are shameful and is embarrassed by them, later in life she may have inhibitions and misconceptions that can make a healthy sexual relationship difficult. Teach your child that her body is beautifully made by God. Repeatedly emphasize your unconditional love and your total and complete acceptance of your child. In this way your child develops a good body image and begins to accept herself.

Attitude 2: *He needs to understand that every other person is also intended to be beautiful and unique and, therefore, to be respected as he respects himself.*

The second part of our Lord's great commandment was to "love your neighbor as you love yourself." Once again, children will probably do no better and no worse in loving and appreciating others than their parents do. If we continually condemn, criticize and put others down, then our children will grow up with much the same attitude toward others. If we want our children to be understanding and compassionate toward others, then we must be their model.

Attitude 3: *He needs to know some of the physical differences between boys and girls and some facts about how babies are conceived and born.*

Many families do not have a vocabulary with which to discuss sexual issues. Children need to know the names of various parts of the body, as well as their functions. This can be accomplished, as we have already seen, by answering in a straightforward way the questions that naturally arise when swimming and bathing with members of the opposite sex. Obviously, the facts concerning conception that children need at this age are simple and basic. But this is the age to begin providing such knowledge.

Attitude 4: *He needs to have learned to respect the needs and feelings of others and to understand and resolve some of his own needs with the help of others.*

139

THIS CAN'T WAIT: *Talking With Your Kids About Sex*

Once again, parents are the key. When you show respect, not only for the needs and feelings of your children, but also for the needs and feelings of others, your children will observe and copy your behavior. Teach your child to respect the privacy of others and expect it in return. You need to teach children not only to respect, admire, and appreciate their own bodies, but to respect other's bodies and privacy as well.

Attitude 5: *He needs to know how to accept children of either sex as friends, and how to interact with them socially in a way that is comfortable for both.*

The term "friends" here refers to playmates, and not boyfriend/girlfriend type relationships. Looking back over twenty-four years in the youth ministry, one of the most disturbing trends I have observed is the growing tendency on the part of society to thrust young children into boy/girl relationships. Even some well-meaning parents try to push their children into such relationships at much too young an age. For twenty years I directed a summer church camp for children ranging in age from grade three to grade nine. One night during the week we have an old-fashioned campfire. It used to be that the older kids, grades six through nine, worried about taking a person of the opposite sex to our campfire. However, during the last several years I have observed even the third graders start getting anxious if they do not have someone to take to the campfire. I do my best to discourage this practice. There will be enough time for boy-girl relationships in the years ahead when the maturity level is high enough to handle such relationships. Parents, please let your small children be children and learn to cultivate simple friendship. Dr. Ketterman also feels very strongly about this subject. She says:

It has come to be considered cute to tease very young children about having "boyfriends" and "girlfriends." It always surprises me that five- and six-year-olds seem to understand this as having sexual implications. They will bristle in anger, or they may laugh with those who tease, but they get the message that maybe they are supposed to start such relationships early. Childhood is very short at best, and it is sad to see it abbreviated even more by such teasing, with its implications. For many reasons, I urge you to avoid such teasing and caution your family or relatives to respect this policy.[5]

In her new book, *Ketterman on Kids: Answers to the Questions Parents Ask Most,* Dr. Ketterman mentions several additional attitudes about sex that children should learn by the time they reach school age.[6]

1. *Open attitude toward sex.* Children need to have an open and honest attitude toward sex. That attitude comes from parents. If you have an attitude of shame and embarrassment when talking about sexuality, then your children cannot have an open, unashamed attitude. We must model a comfortable attitude about sexuality for our kids.

2. *Respect for oneself.* Your child deserves privacy and dignity with regard to her body. Her body is her own, and no one has the right to touch it without permission. Help your children distinguish between loving touches and touches that violate their privacy and lead to sexual abuse.

3. *Awe of God's creation.* Teach your children to approach the human body with awe for God's

creation. When children have been taught to appreciate and enjoy the natural wonders of God's creation, they will instinctively associate their bodies as a wonder of God. Sexuality and the human body are God's creations, and they were created to be good.

The phone rang late one afternoon The young mother on the other end of the line was very distressed. She was almost in tears and desperately wanted some advice. She had just found her daughter with their friend's son playing "doctor." That is to say, they were satisfying their natural curiosity concerning the bodies of the opposite sex. Now these children were only four and five, respectively, but this mother was convinced that they were both perverted and headed for a life of criminal sexual offenses. Her reaction was rather typical. Most parents are not prepared to handle this situation well and almost instinctively react very negatively. I very calmly tried to convince the mother that these children were quite normal, and that her reaction to this situation was the most critical issue at the moment. Fortunately, she called me before responding to her child or her friend's child. I say, fortunately, because her first reaction, as she explained, was to punish her child severely, take her friend's child home and demand that he be punished also. In addition, she planned to break off all contact with her close friend. I managed to soothe her fears by explaining that all children do some innocent experimenting at about this age, and that as long as she did not overreact it would cause no long term damage to either child. I suggested that the best solution would be to take the children aside for a little chat. During this chat she should explain to them that their curiosity was normal, but perhaps a better way to find out about the body of the opposite sex would be for their parents to share this information with them, perhaps from a good book. She could also explain that our bodies are personal and private, and we keep them private by wearing clothes when we play with others. I also cautioned this mother to calmly discuss the subject with the little boy's parents, taking care to explain what she had told both children. I assured her that most children outgrow such behavior after a short while, and that after the conclusion of this matter she would have successfully handled one of the biggest social aspects of her preschooler's sex education. I did not, however, have the heart to tell her that it gets worse in junior high! Let me offer some cautionary advice. While it is typical for children ages four to six to want to explore each other's bodies and play out sex games, if such activity involves behaviors such as humping (simulating intercourse), oral sex, or inserting objects, you should be concerned. Under these conditions, I recommend professional advice because these behaviors indicate knowledge and conduct beyond the norm.

Your preschooler also needs to learn several spiritual aspects of sexuality. As Christian parents, we have the opportunity to teach our children about their sexuality in a biblical framework. The main lesson preschool children need to learn is that God created them, loves them, and cares deeply about them. They also need to know that they are a gift from God and are therefore very special. An excellent scripture for children this age is Psalms 139:13-16. This very beautiful portion of God's word tells children that they were created and formed in their mother's womb. Using this verse has two very important effects — it helps parents lay the basis for self-esteem that can be built upon for years to come, and it serves as a perfect introduction to the explanation of pregnancy.

Where Did I Come From?

Often before age five a child will ask the question—"Where did I come from?" Grasp the opportunity when it comes and tell your preschooler the wonderful story of the creation of life. Of course, these facts should be very elementary and commensurate with a small child's vocabulary and emotional level. You might say something like this:

"God loves children very much and he wants them born into a family with a mommy and daddy. A baby needs a family to love him, talk to him, change his diaper and feed him. Little babies are totally helpless and the family is God's way of giving a baby a happy place to grow up and be loved."

"Inside a mother is a special place where babies grow. This place is like a tiny room and is call the womb or uterus. The baby started growing in this special place when a tiny egg from inside the mother is joined with a tiny object from the father called sperm. The egg and sperm are so small you cannot see them without a magnifying glass. After they get together they grow in the womb. After a few weeks the egg has grown into a small baby with tiny arms and legs. After about three months the baby has fingers and toes. The baby grows inside the mother's womb for about nine months and when the baby is ready to be born he weighs about six or seven pounds and is around 20 inches long. The mother's body tells her when it is time for the baby to be born by beginning to squeeze, like you would squeeze your fist. When this happens the mother goes to the hospital for the baby to be born. The mother is helped at the hospital by a doctor. The squeezing keeps on pushing the baby from mother's womb into another special place called the vagina. The vagina leads to the opening between the mother's legs which leads to the outside world. The opening slowly stretches to let the baby out. The Mother has some pain during the baby's birth, but the doctor helps and gives the mother some medicine to help her and make her feel better."

Be sure and tell this amazing story with joy and happiness. Your attitude will teach as much as the facts you teach. This simple, accurate description of conception and birth will adequately satisfy your preschooler's curiosity. There will probably not be a need to discuss intercourse at this point because preschoolers are rarely interested in such details. But they are very interested in "where they came from."

Typical Questions Asked by Preschoolers

It is difficult to anticipate with any accuracy exactly the questions preschoolers will ask. Some children ask the expected questions right on schedule. Others appear disinterested until much later. But if you are an askable parent, sooner or later your preschool children will ask a variety of questions. There are several questions that are frequently asked by children under six years of age. Generally speaking, the questions usually fall into two categories. At this age children are most concerned with body structure and function, and all matters relating to babies. It is okay to be very specific. Do not be afraid that you are furnishing too much information. If your children need the facts, you will have provided them, and if the information is over their heads, they will simply ignore it until a later date.

Children this age will ask about breasts, penises, belly buttons (umbilici), body hair, and vaginas. In general, your answers need to center around the differences between boys and girls, and why God designed them differently. Explain that God's plan was for boys and girls to be different so that they could grow up to have bodies of men and women and become fathers and mothers.

Here are some questions and possible answers:

Q. A little girl points to a penis and asks, "What's that, and why don't I have one?"

A. "It's a penis and little boys have penises for urination, and little girls have vulvas for the urine to get out of the body. God made boys and girls differently."

Q. "Why do mommies have big breasts and daddies don't?'

A. "Mommies breasts are bigger because God made mommies so they can make milk for babies."

Q. "Why is my penis not as big as daddy's?"

A. "As your entire body grows bigger, your penis will grow some too."

Q. "What's a vagina?"

A. "It's a special place a baby goes through to get out of the mother's body at birth."

As you can see, questions of this type can be endless. Hopefully, your children will ask these questions of you rather than relatives or strangers. When our son was about four years old, he approached his paternal grandfather and very matter-of-factly said: "Daddy Bill, do you have a penis or a vagina?" My dad paused only briefly and replied: "A penis." Paul then said, "I thought so," and walked away. Fortunately my father knew and approved of our open style with our children. I'm just thankful Paul did not ask his Sunday school teacher the question.

Preschoolers also ask many questions related to birth and babies, especially if their mother becomes pregnant during this inquisitive age.

Q. "Can boys have babies?"

A. "No, it takes a daddy and a mommy to make a baby, but babies grow in the mommy."

Q. "Does it hurt to have a baby?"

A. "There is some pain—but God made mommies' bodies special so that with a doctor's help it doesn't hurt too much."

Q. "Did you know that I would be a boy (girl) before I was born?"

A. "Doctors have a special way to tell, but we just wanted you."

Answering your preschoolers questions simply and truthfully will begin the sex education process in an excellent manner. It will also teach your young child that you are approachable and askable, thus laying the foundation for an open communicating relationship with the child. From the beginning we have emphasized sex education as an on-going process, beginning at the birth of your child. When you start this education at birth, you eliminate the pressure of finding and setting aside a special time for this purpose later. And by then the "stages" process becomes rather perfunctory. Starting early also lays the proper groundwork for better, more mature discussions as your child grows older. Your honest and open attitude with your preschooler will communicate your love and concern for him, and it will greatly increase the likelihood that your child will look to you for sexual information.

For Further Thought

1. What are your earliest recollections concerning your own sex education? Were your parents open and askable?

2. Which body parts are you the most uncomfortable naming correctly? How can you eliminate this uncomfortable feeling?

3. What type example are you providing concerning the recognition of the needs and feelings of others? What improvements can you make?

4. What are some specific ways you can avoid having your young children pushed into boy/girl relationships before they are ready?

5. Have you ever caught one of your children playing "doctor" with another child? Were you pleased with your reaction? If it happened again how would you react differently?

6. Read Genesis 2:15-25. What explanations and observations regarding reproduction can be made using this passage?

7. What sexual questions can you anticipate your preschoolers asking? How would you respond if your child asked you a question in front of someone visiting your home?

---

[1] Dorothy L. Williams, ed., *Yes You Can! A Guide for Sexuality Education that Affirms Abstinence Among Young Adolescents* (Minneapolis: Search Institute, 1987), 39.

[2] Mary Ann Mayo, *Parents Guide to Sex Education* (Grand Rapids: Zondervan, 1986), 124.

[3] Gordon, *Raising A Child Conservatively* , 27.

[4] Grace Ketterman, *How to Teach Your Children about Sex* (Old Tappan: Fleming H. Revell, 1981), 93-94.

[5] Ibid., 94.

[6] Ketterman, *Ketterman on Kids*, 227-224.

7
The Carefree Years

Early Elementary Years — Ages 6-9

For children, the early elementary school years (ages six through nine) are among the most carefree years of their lives. Physical growth has slowed considerably; parents provide most all needs and wants; parents can be trusted, and puberty is an unknown enemy. The developmentally hectic preschool years seem far behind. These years are an easygoing time between the avid curiosity of young childhood and the unpredictability of puberty. During these early elementary years it appears that sexual activity and interest is diminishing. This apparent disinterest in sex is caused in part because school considerably broadens their world. Elementary children now have many interests outside the home. Also, elementary age children are more easily embarrassed and therefore tend to conceal sexual activities and interests. Of course, appearances can be deceiving. Elementary children are still very concerned about their bodies and sexual matters. And many of the emotions, characteristics, habits and qualities learned during these seemingly dormant elementary years will have a significant impact on their adult sexuality. Parents should, therefore, remain active and aware as they look for opportunities to extend their children's sex education.

During this developmental stage children are much more comfortable with general rather than specific information. They are now able to express their feelings with words and can understand that a person does not act on every feeling. This new understanding reinforces competence and has long-term effect on sexual functioning. At this age children want honest, accurate, answers to their questions and do not appreciate lectures. During this period, furnish accurate, dependable information in the context of open discussions. You should also express opinions, communicate your values, and be receptive to the personal needs of your child. Such an atmosphere will promote healthy sexual growth.

Sexual Play (Playing Doctor) Is Winding Down

At the beginning of the elementary years, there may still be some mild sex play, such as "showing out" in school, but this type behavior is in the process of easing off. And by ages seven and eight, it has slowed almost to a stop. As children outgrow "playing doctor," curiosity about male/female body structure often manifests itself in looking at nude or semi-nude magazine or catalog pictures. If this happens, do not overreact, but use these incidents as an opportunity to teach self-respect as well as respect for others. Such feelings and behavior are a normal part of growing up sexually.

Dirty Words and Smutty Jokes Are Winding Up

Just in case you were feeling relieved about sexual play decreasing, I need to inform you that dirty words, smutty jokes and writing sex phrases are the next concern. Ain't kids great? Such behavior usually begins around six and starts with laughing or name-calling about bodily elimination. By age seven or eight, however, such behavior has increased and usually includes dirty or off-color jokes, writing sex words, calling other children sexual names (dick, prick, etc.), and attempting to peek at the opposite sex. As children grow a little older, this behavior escalates into swearing and using sex words and phrases.[1] How are we to react to such behavior? Should we grab the first bar of soap we see and begin washing out our child's mouth? It depends on what has been said and to whom.

Children should be taught that behavior such as name calling, telling dirty jokes, and publicly writing nasty words can cause hurt feelings and embarrassing situations. They should learn that above all, the feelings of others are always to be considered. They should also know that using shameful slang terms for very beautiful God-given activities is not right. But parents should also be careful not to overreact. Children at this age often use words without knowing their full meaning. In addition, the words may mean something different to your children than to you. For example, when I was about twelve years old, it was the custom of my group of friends to refer to other boys as "queers." One day I made the mistake of calling a boy a queer in the presence of my dad! He was not pleased, and asked how I knew that this boy was a homosexual. I was horrified. I barely knew what a homosexual was, and it was not my intention to accuse this boy of anything so serious. To my group of friends, queer simply meant odd or weird. When I explained to my dad he understood, but he told me that not everyone would see it that way. He suggested that if my friends and I were going to use such terms, we do so in private in order not to hurt anyone's feelings. More importantly, he did not overreact and have me shot.

I have tried to use the same approach with my son. I have explained to him that I know he will use certain words and terms while he is with his male friends, and that I will not overreact as long as he respects the feelings of others and avoids crude references to wholesome activities. I have also explained to him that ladies are not pleased with even the hint of crudity. Please do not misunderstand me. I am not suggesting that you should condone filthy, dirty language. I am merely suggesting that parents not overreact and that they gather all facts before harshly punishing their children. We need to distinguish between acceptable slang, proper terms, and filthy language. Not everyone has grown up learning proper terms and may use slang innocently. We must determine in our own minds what we believe to be acceptable, harmless slang and what constitutes dirty, filthy language. Unacceptable language, at this age, should be handled in a matter-of-fact way. Calm, rational, controlled behavior speaks loudly to our children and keeps the door of communication open, and you can always re-visit the issue if the situation warrants.

Male/Female Body Structure

During these early elementary years boys and girls begin to be more aware of and interested in male/female body structure. Children maintain their interest in the bodies of the opposite sex, even though they approach their physical natures differently.

The boys are very competitive and macho, and flex their scrawny muscles at each other. This competitive nature can lead to frequent fights and disagreements. As most mothers are no doubt aware, boys this age care little about appearance and see no need for daily showers and matching clothes. Boys of this age like an activity that has two essential ingredients — the activity must be physical and competitive.

Girls in this age group are vastly different from boys. They are very concerned with personal hygiene and matching outfits, including socks and hair ribbons. They compare hair, clothes, shoes and friends. They tend not to be as competitive as boys. (Whether the difference is cultural or biological is not certain.)

Even though elementary age boys and girls would never admit it, they maintain a high degree of interest in the body structure of the opposite sex. Their rising self-consciousness, which begins shortly after entering school, begins to prohibit "playing doctor." They become sensitive about exposing their bodies. As they move through the early elementary years their self-consciousness increases and may even develop to the extent that they do not want to be seen unclad by the opposite sex parent. They are also highly susceptible to embarrassment concerning their bodies. This self-consciousness and embarrassment, coupled with their high interest in the bodies of the opposite sex, partly explains the peeking at each other and the looking at magazines. They are still very curious and want to see opposite sex bodies; they just do not want their own bodies seen.

Be aware of this increasing sensitivity and self-consciousness. Opposite sex parents should respect the privacy of their newly shy child. Also understand that although these children do not want to expose their bodies, they may have no objection to everyone else in the family parading around partially clad. So if your family custom involves some nudity, do not change. I believe a certain amount of appropriate nudity is healthy. It teaches children that our bodies are not shameful or dirty.

Sex Roles and Identity

Just as the early elementary period is characterized by an increased awareness in male/female body structure, this period of development is also characterized by a dramatic increase in male/female role play and role definition or gender identity. Both sexes are becoming more conscious of what boys and girls are supposed to be and do. Therefore, it is extremely important for them to have sex roles and gender identity defined and described. It is by learning what males and females are and do that a child begins to develop his own personal gender identity. By gender identity, I am referring to a person's inner feelings by which a person can say "I feel like a male, or a female."[2] Sexual identity is very important as it defines sexual personhood for individuals.

During this early grade school period, children's awareness of what boys and girls are and do increases because of their exposure to television, radio, movies, printed media material, and by their observation of friends and family. Parents, however, should not depend on any of these, or other sources, to teach or define sex and gender roles for their children. You need only watch television for a brief period to realize that our world today does not hold godly values and teachings in very high esteem. It is important that parents be the dominant provider of sex role information. Parents also need to understand that children do not learn sex role information by means of a short talk or lecture on the subject, but they learn these lessons, as they learn many others, by watching, observing and emulating their parents. Because children are working hard to establish a sense of their own identity, they do not have to be purposely taught about their gender identity, but rather they absorb or catch their identity from parents. Since children this age identify most strongly with the parent of the same sex, it is extremely important for same sex parents to be their children's role models and spend time with them. By observing the same sex parents, children learn how this parent walks, talks, dresses, and even thinks. "It is vitally important for boys to identify with males and for girls to identify with females. Without such identification, children may later suffer sexual maladjustments."[3]

Parents should also attempt to break down sex role stereotypes, such as: "boys don't cry, they're tough", "girls do not participate in sports, it isn't ladylike", "act like a man and be tough." Extreme stereotyping can lead to sexism, dehumanizing treatment of individuals, and confusion about what it means to be male or female. Several negative consequences can result from confused or incomplete gender identification: sexual dysfunction, sexual promiscuity, sexual addiction, and possibly homosexuality. Parents can take several actions that will help their children develop positive sexual identity and gender identification. First, continually affirm their gender and sex. Praise them for being male and female. Second, same sex parents need to be constantly available to their children. The most important factor in encouraging positive gender and sexual identity is time spent with the same sex parent. And thirdly, inundate your children with unconditional love and affection.

One practical way parents can break down stereotyping is by having all family members participate in household chores. When women work outside the home, as many do, they are contributing in a financial way (traditionally a male role), and should not be required to do all the housework and cooking (traditionally a female role). In our home, for example, my schoolteacher wife is not responsible for all the household duties. When our children were home they cleaned their rooms — at least twice per year — and I was responsible for cleaning the remainder of the house. Cooking chores were shared by my wife, my daughter and me. My wife also did the laundry and supervised homework. In your household the allocation of household responsibilities may differ, but we were attempting to teach our children that everyone should contribute to our family and that stereotypical roles are not very important.

Please do not interpret any of the above discussions concerning sex role stereotyping as a suggestion that males and females have no differences and that we should adopt a unisex approach to life. I firmly believe God created males and females uniquely different, and that our children need to be taught the clear differences and distinctions between the sexes. I believe this can be done, however, in a nonexploitive manner.

Before leaving the subject of sex roles and the definition of these roles, a word concerning single parents is needed. It is extremely frightening to rear children alone, especially opposite sex children. Mothers, who constitute the majority of single parents, are very concerned with meeting the needs of their sons. If you are a single parent and the absent spouse cannot or will not fulfill your child's role model needs, you must find adequate substitute role models. You must encourage same sex adult relationships with your children. Young children need these type relationships in order to develop an understanding of themselves as total, sexual beings. Such role models can be found in Big Brother, Big Sister Clubs, Boy and Girl Scouts, and Little League. In both public and Sunday school, mothers can request their sons be assigned to classes taught by men.[4] Single mothers also worry about not understanding their son's emerging sexuality. They feel extremely inadequate in even knowing what to expect in terms of the sexual development of their sons. Space does not permit an extensive review of the subject in this work. However, in her book titled *Mothers and Sons,* Jean Lush provides a comprehensive list of the characteristics of a boy's sexual development. [5] This book and *Single Mothers Raising Sons* by Bobbie Reed, are excellent resources for single mothers.

Boys and Girls

At about age seven or eight, children seem to have an instinctive awareness of their need to identify with same sex persons. Boys and girls begin increasingly to play separately. Boys gravitate toward select groups of peers and girls usually associate with one or two special friends. At this age the verbal banter between boys and girls begins. It is not uncommon for either sex to say that they "hate" boys or girls. Outwardly they appear to have no interest in the opposite sex; however, inwardly they are very much interested in sex and sexual matters. This is evidenced by their crushes on members of the opposite sex, and their admittance to having boyfriends and girlfriends. Sexual interest is also confirmed by their sexual discussions and teasing with their same sex peers. Boys, especially, engage in sexual discussions with their same sex friends. In general, girls talk much less about sexual matters with their girlfriends. This partly explains why boys this age may appear to be more knowledgeable than girls about sexual matters.

During this time of apparent separation of the sexes, parents need to avoid teasing about boyfriends and girlfriends. Children this age are very sensitive and easily embarrassed by such teasing because they really believe they are showing no interest in the opposite sex. So be respectful and understanding concerning their boy/girl behavior.

We have already discussed the importance of the same sex parent in defining sex and gender roles. Now the opposite sex parent receives equal billing. Opposite sex parents play a major role in helping their children develop comfortable and healthy attitudes toward children of the opposite sex. Children learn comfortable attitudes by observing how their parents relate to each other and by receiving love and acceptance from both parents. It then becomes easier for children to give and receive love and trust from members of the opposite sex. Opposite sex parents need to be involved in the lives of their children. Fathers need to take daughters shopping and spend time with them just as they spend time with their sons. Some of my fondest memories of my daughter's growing up years involve our semi-annual shopping trips to Dallas. I would take her and several of her friends to buy school clothes, and we would hit all the big malls and make a day of it. We started this practice when she was just in elementary school and continued right on through her high school years. Spending time with opposite sex children lays the proper foundation for your children's future relationships with the opposite sex, and it creates fond memories for Mom and Dad as well.

Increased Awareness of Pregnancy and Intercourse

At this age children begin associating pregnant women with babies, and their curiosity regarding pregnancy and birth increases. They often ask if the family is planning any new babies. They understand the process of pregnancy, but they become very curious about the father's role. This stage is characterized by many questions about the origin, growth and birth of babies. Some children begin to have curiosity concerning intercourse at this age while others are not curious until the later elementary school years. When to thoroughly discuss conception and intercourse is a matter of debate among educators, child development experts, and psychologists. Stan L. Jones, Professor of Psychology at Wheaton College and a practicing clinical psychologist, says: "We urge that children be told about sexual intercourse between ages five and seven, between their kindergarten and second-grade years."[6] Others say not before eight years of age, or between eight and ten years of age. There is no universally agreed upon age at which parents should talk to their children about sexual intercourse and conception. All of the experts I have researched, however, do agree that it should be done between the ages of five years of age and ten years of age. Parents should have laid the groundwork for a discussion regarding sexual intercourse during their earlier conversations regarding babies and anatomy. You need to be aware of your child's curiosity level regarding intercourse and look for signs that the time is right. During this inquisitive period you should thoroughly explain conception. Respond to questions and actively create opportunities to talk even when there are no questions. If a new baby is born into the family at this time an excellent opportunity for teaching exists. If not, consider visiting relatives or friends that have had babies recently. Such visits should provide excellent opportunities to teach these curious young minds. If however, your child has not asked by age ten, then you should take the initiative and explain sexual intercourse. There are several excellent books that will help you explain intercourse and conception. I highly recommend these books: *Before I Was Born,* by Carolyn Nystrom, for children ages five to eight. *In The Beginning,* by Mary Ann Mayo, for children ages four to seven. *Where Did I Come From?* by Peter Mayle, for children seven to nine.

Self-Esteem

Self-esteem is a much discussed concept these days. Once while teaching a parenting class to a group of junior high parents, I was asked by a father if I blamed poor self-esteem for all of life's problems. This man was attempting to be sarcastic, and my answer probably startled him a bit. I will endeavor to paraphrase my answer. I told him that during all of my study and research, low self-esteem was always listed among the characteristics or reasons given for any adolescent deviant behavior (chemical dependency, eating disorders, juvenile delinquency, and sexual experimentation). I further informed him that during many years in the youth ministry my own personal experience corroborated these findings. I am not saying that every child with a poor self-image will choose any of these deviant behaviors, but when one looks at any list of probable causes for all adolescent behavioral problems, a poor self-image is on every list! By poor self-image I mean self-esteem that is unusually low. All adolescents suffer from a slightly poor self-image during the transitional years of puberty. I have already said a great deal about building a positive and strong self-esteem in our children. However, because of the importance of self-esteem and due to the teachable nature of children during early elementary years, it is appropriate that we discuss it in more detail.

Children of early elementary age are hero worshipers. Boys know the names and year's statistics of many pro quarterbacks or point guards. And girls know many details about favorite actors and actresses. As children grow older their focus can become a favorite teacher, coach, or pastor. Such hero worship helps children begin to select desirable traits they wish to acquire. The self-ideal then is centered on the question, "Who or what do I want to become?" After determining a self-ideal, most adolescents consider a self-concept, their perception of what they are really like.[7] What children think of themselves is crucially important and their relationships will depend upon a healthy self-esteem. Children tend to view others as they view themselves. And more importantly, they will view themselves exactly as they are viewed by their parents. Parents are the prime creators of self-esteem in children. We can create either positive or negative self-images in our children.

In *Depression Hits Every Family,* Dr. Grace Ketterman lists twelve rules for building self-esteem in children. I have seen no better or more comprehensive list:

1. Develop an inner sense of unconditional acceptance of your child.
2. Practice communicating acceptance by listening, touching and spending time with them.
3. Explore their talents and interests.
4. Assign responsibilities to them.
5. Accept their friends.
6. Respect their ideas.
7. Respect and love their other parent.
8. Practice positive training and discipline.
9. Consistently express your approval and pleasure.
10. Teach and demonstrate forgiveness.
11. Teach your child to revel in all beauty.
12. Realize that your child has a mission in life.[8]

Take seriously your role as the principal provider of your child's self-esteem, especially early in their lives.

Self-Esteem Plus Character and Morality

In the 1980s, psychologists and educators enthusiastically embraced the idea that enhancing self-esteem would bring happiness and success. Research indicated that people who did best in life also felt good about themselves, so it was assumed that the reverse must be true. High self-esteem was equated with high achievement and healthy attitudes and behaviors. If people could only be encouraged to develop a good self-esteem, students would learn better, employees would work harder, and everyone's conduct would be above reproach. Well, certainly self-esteem is clearly important in a child's life, but a mountain of new research is beginning to show that self-esteem alone is not a predictor of success, achievement, or improved behavior. "Research now indicates that self-esteem is not, itself, a predictor of success. In fact, studies of gang members reveal that they have very high levels of self-esteem, while some people who do great things suffer from feelings of worthlessness. According to an expert at Stanford University, 'self-esteem affects neither personal goals nor performance.'"[9] Dr. James Dobson on his national radio program revealed similar findings. His research group studied prisoners at several different penitentiaries and found many hardened criminals had very high self-esteem. The results of this research startled many experts. So, what are we to make of this latest research? Have people like myself missed the point by emphasizing self-esteem? Yes and no!

Let me explain. Self-esteem is very important in the life of a child, but mountains of data show that by the time children get to school, their self-esteem is pretty much established. The problem has developed because much of our society, including schools, psychologists, and many parents, have bought into the secular myth that morality and values are relative. Most of the institutions in secular society believe that self-esteem takes precedence over moral and ethical values. There is no definition or sense of right and wrong. Right and wrong become defined by what will not bruise the self-esteem of the child, and as a result, kids today get away with behavior that a few decades ago would have been seen as wrong and resulted in instant discipline. When a society has no strict standards of right and wrong, acceptable behaviors flow and bend with available excuses. In other words, a child is not responsible for his behavior; he is merely acting out because of divorced parents, or single parents, or poverty, or any number of bad situations in his life. It seems that in society today, if we can find an external cause to blame for poor performance or bad behavior, then we tolerate the behavior and provide support and assistance in order to help the child cope. I am most assuredly not saying that bad experiences and dysfunctional families do not contribute to many childhood problems. I have spent a lifetime helping children and teens cope with problems caused by alcoholic parents, abuse, and many other deviant forms of behavior. But when children are taught that right and wrong depend on external causes and that one's definition of morals depends simply on viewpoint, then our society has done children a disservice. Kids raised with the idea that their feelings are always right (positive self-esteem) and that feelings excuse behavior end up as selfish, arrogant, and rude. Ironically, they may have great self-esteem!

We must teach our children self-esteem based on godly standards of morality and on a character rooted in the will of God. All throughout Scripture, God encourages us to examine ourselves based on the realistic standard of his Word. His Word teaches that there are moral standards and proper values based on right and wrong. When we glorify self-esteem over morals, values, and character, our children are simply learning to be rude, undisciplined, and arrogant. We must teach self-esteem in the godly context of character formation. That is, we teach our children that people really feel good about themselves when their character reflects godly standards. Godly self-esteem is based on character, morality, and a sense of right and wrong. A clinical psychologist friend of mine told me that teaching self-esteem apart from character formation, morals, and values based on a biblical sense of right and wrong produces kids that may feel really good about themselves, but who are narcissistic.

We as Christians must avoid the temptation to rear our children with self-esteem based on secular values; rather, our children's self-esteem should be based on God's standards. Children must realize their great value to God as reflected by the great price paid to purchase their salvation. However, Jesus paid this price in order for them to glorify God, not themselves! A good, godly self-esteem is important to our children and the absence of self-esteem can cause many problems in their lives. But a false sense of self-esteem based on worldly, secular values is even more damaging. As with all things, secular, worldly values can make a good thing like healthy self-esteem produce deadly results.

Sexual Abuse and Molestation

After spending almost three decades working with teenagers, I feel shockproof. However, one trend I have been observing over the past several years is both shocking and disturbing. I am amazed and saddened by the increased number of child abuse or molestation cases that I uncover while counseling and working with children and young people. Our attitude toward sexual abuse has traditionally been that these things only happen to deranged or deprived people. But abuse is occurring with alarming regularity across all walks of life. Consider these statistics and facts:

- There were 200,000 new cases of child abuse cases in children under 12, and over one million teen female victims of sex abuse in 1993.[10]
- Some estimates are that one in ten kids experience some significant unwanted sexual activity.
- It is believed that most sexual abuse offenders are family members or friends.
- According to the National Study on the Sexuality of Christian Women in 1996, 50 percent of the respondents reported that they had experienced unwanted sexual touch. 10 percent were molested as preschoolers; 23 percent during grade school; and 15 percent during their teens.[11]

Our focus in this book is on how to talk to and help our children. Therefore we must give consideration to preparing our children in the event someone tries to molest or abuse them. Hopefully, we can prepare our children in such a manner that they will be able to prevent such abuse, and if necessary successfully recover from such an occurrence. And like the other areas we've discussed, talking with our children about abuse is not a one-time discussion.

First, it is important to know that children are most often abused by a relative or friend that is known to them. Usually both the parent and child have a certain amount of trust for the person. Of course, there are the cases of total strangers abducting and abusing children, but these cases represent only about 25 percent of the offenders.

Secondly, if child molestation does occur, parents should not blame or accuse the child in any way. The child has experienced enough pain and trauma. Not only is it damaging to the child to be accused or blamed, it is totally absurd because children (especially small children) do not have enough understanding of sexual matters to have contributed in any way to the situation. Parents only make things worse when they make a child feel guilty and pile more shame on the child. Abused children do not need to be made to feel that the abuse is their fault. They need us to communicate to them just the opposite: "It is not your fault!" Victims of child abuse are never at fault. In the event of abuse, parents should remain calm and cool and immediately seek professional help.

The best way to prevent the abuse of our children is to prepare them with beliefs, skills, and a supportive environment. In order to prepare your child (boys need equal preparation) for any eventuality, the following items should be covered:

1. Warn your child specifically about molestation, describing some detail. The object is not to scare them, but to help them see the seriousness of the situation. Try to walk the fine line of warning without worrying.
2. Help them develop a plan. This plan should include details for escape, phone number and specific things to say. And if all else fails, to simply scream.
3. Tell them that their body is private and no one has a right to touch any part of their body or genitals.

4. Explain to them that, while not everyone is evil, some people are bad. Further explain that they do not have to talk to those type people.
5. Tell them they can trust their feelings. When someone makes them feel uncomfortable, they can trust their feelings and leave.
6. Tell them they must never keep it secret when someone looks at or touches their body or genitals. They can and should tell you everything. Even if they were threatened and they promised not to tell!
7. Tell them they have every right to say "no," and teach them to assertively say "no" in appropriate situations.

Child abuse hotlines and abuse centers exist in every state. A major nationwide provider of such services is Parent's Anonymous (PA): 1-800-421-0353, in California 1-800-352-0386.

Parents, remember: how well a child adapts after a crisis such as sexual abuse depends on how well *you* respond to the situation!

Typical Questions Asked by Early Elementary Children

In the early elementary school grades, children's questions about reproduction continue to focus on the baby's origin, growth inside the mother, and entrance into the world. At this age children are very interested in the differences between males and females. Obviously the depth of this interest is greater than during the preschool years. Here are some of the most frequently asked questions and possible answers concerning male/female differences, and origin and growth of babies:

Q. "Do all women have babies?"

A. "No, only women who have had sexual intercourse."

Q. "Can boys and girls like Billy and I make a baby?" " Can I have a baby?"

A. Such a question is common during the early elementary years and usually indicates an incomplete understanding of the reproductive process. You should explain that women can only start having babies after they start to menstruate. Explain menstruation in simple terms if necessary. Also explain that God wants people to wait until they are married and old enough to care for a baby before they have one.

Q. "How does a baby get out of mommy's stomach?"

A. First of all, the baby is not in mommy's stomach. It stays in a special place called the uterus. When the baby is ready to be born it comes out through the vagina. The vagina stretches to allow the baby to come out. Explain that sometimes there are special problems and the doctor takes the baby by a special operation. A brief, simple, explanation of a caesarian section is in order.

Q. "How does a baby get started?" Or, "How does a daddy put his sperm into the mother?"

A. Of course, this is the dreaded "big" question. It will usually not be asked until around seven or eight. By this time children are ready for an honest, factual answer. Actually, straightforward honesty in answering this question, while embarrassing to the parent, is preferable to some of the wild, imaginative stories children create in their minds. Your children will appreciate the honesty, and they will be properly informed during the critical years of puberty. Answer like this:

"God designed the bodies of mothers and fathers to fit together in a special way. The Bible calls this "one flesh" because they join together. The father joins with the mother by placing his penis inside the mother's body in the vagina. This is called making love or intercourse. The sperm from the father's body joins with an egg from the mother's body and a baby is started."

Q. "Is intercourse or sex a sin?"

This, or a similar question could easily follow the above question. Simply say, "God created sex and he made men and women want to have intercourse so they could have children, and have fun together. God's word, the Bible, tells us that sex is supposed to be for married people. When unmarried people have sex, then it is a sin."

Q. "Do you and Daddy have sex?"

A. Probably a follow-up to the two previous questions. Answer: "Yes."

Q. "Do boys have periods?"

A. No, only girls. Boys go through other physical changes to prepare to them be fathers.

It would be impossible to discuss all the questions children this age could ask. Their little minds can think of millions of questions, all seemingly designed to make parents squirm. But when children have been openly, honestly and lovingly told about sexual matters since birth, they will accept this new information in a natural way. They will see this information as natural and loving, not dirty and shameful. Remember—your attitude is the key.

For Further Thought

1. Anticipate your responses to your eight-year-old when he says "Boy, that's lousy, it really sucks!"
2. Think about your family's practices concerning nudity. Are they appropriate? What are these practices communicating to the children?
3. What specific activities are done with your same sex children alone?
4. What sexual stereotypes bug you? Why?
5. What do you teach your children regarding the roles of males and females?
6. Fathers, what activities do you enjoy with your daughter? How often are these done? (Mothers - sons)
7. What specifically could you do to strengthen your child's self-esteem? What possible self-esteem needs of your children do you find hardest to meet?
8. Are your children learning moral standards and a sense of right and wrong along with their self-esteem?
9. Have you discussed sexual molestation with your children? Devise a plan for such a talk.
10. Does your early elementary (ages 6-9) age child understand intercourse? Think of opportunities to provide teaching on the subject.

---

[1] Williams, *Yes You Can!*, 107.

[2] Donald M. Joy, *Bonding* (Waco: Word Publishing, 1987), 127-128.

[3] Paul D. Meier, Frank B. Minirth, and Frank Wichern, *Introduction to Psychology and Counseling: Christian Perspectives as Application* (Grand Rapids: Baker Book House, 1982), 116.

[4] Bobbie Reed, *Single Mothers Raising Sons* (Nashville: Thomas Nelson Publishers, 1988), 135.

[5] Jean Lush, *Mothers and Sons* (Old Tappan: Fleming H. Revell, 1988), 75-79.

[6] Jones, *How and When to Tell Your Kids About Sex*, 30.

[7] Olson, *Counseling Teenagers*, 28.

[8] Grace Ketterman, *Depression Hits Every Family* (Nashville: Thomas Nelson, 1988), 168-170.

[9] *San Francisco Examiner*, May 7, 1998.

[10] David Lewis and Carley Dodd, *National Adolescent Survey.* 1998 Youth & Family Ministry Conference.

[11] Hart, et. al., *Secrets of Eve*, 6.

8

You're Preparing Me for What?

Preteen Years—Ages 10-12

To begin with, it sounds weird or strange. Say it out loud: puberty. See! It sounds like something you would step in and then say, "Oh, no, now I've got puberty all over my shoes." Well, it not only sounds weird, most of the time it is!

For several years, I was invited to the local Christian school to show a film about puberty and sexuality, and then to answer questions from several classes of fifth-grade boys. This enlightening event followed a study of James Dobson's *Preparing for Adolescence*. After these young men are successfully taught this course about puberty by their female teachers, they are rewarded by watching a film and having their questions answered by me! I don't think I was invited to this film screening and hot seat session because I'm an expert—the school just figured I was the only one dumb enough to answer sex questions from fifth-grade boys for an hour.

Several years ago, a smallish-looking fifth-grader, after completing the course and watching the film, had apparently heard enough about puberty. He raised his hand in response to my invitation for questions and said, "Mr. Talley, this puferty (that's right, "puferty") thing has got me kinda scared. Isn't there something we could take?" Well, what could I say? Puferty–I mean, puberty–is pretty scary. I know many parents who would gladly pay huge sums of money for "something to take" when it comes time for their children to enter the mysterious world of puberty. Puberty, next to birth itself, is the most drastic change we experience in life, but unlike birth, we are actually aware of the exciting transition through which we pass.

Puberty can be a fearful experience even when young people are aware of what is happening. But children between the ages of ten and twelve typically do not have any conception of the tremendous changes that will shortly occur in their minds and bodies. Puberty is frightening at best, but if a child is totally unprepared for the traumatic events that accompany this developmental stage, major physical and emotional problems may be expected. Parents should take the lead, before puberty begins, to positively introduce their children to the wonderful and exciting changes that will soon occur in their bodies. This is no time for us to take it easy. We have a wonderful two-year window of opportunity in which to prepare our fifth and sixth graders for the tumultuous junior high years. Thus, our role during these preteen years (ages 10-12) is to thoroughly and adequately prepare our child for puberty and to maintain the positive, respectful, and beautiful attitude we have sought to establish about sexuality. These are critical years for teaching about sexuality because children are not yet emotionally or hormonally preoccupied with sex, so they can more objectively discuss the subject. After puberty begins, discussing sexuality feels much more awkward and personal and is more difficult. But if we have been engaged in preemptive discussions about sex with our children, we are establishing the direction of their thinking and reemphasizing healthy sexual attitudes. By the time a child finishes elementary school, the challenge has completely shifted from teaching him about sex to teaching him about how to view (and what to do with) sex. It's a question now of attitude and behavior rather than knowledge.[1]

At this point some of you are no doubt thinking that 10-, 11-, and 12-year-olds are too young for a discussion of puberty, and that there will be plenty of time as they grow older for such discussions. But because of better general health and nutrition, as well as several other reasons, young people are maturing physically at an earlier age. For example, just over 150 years ago, the average age of puberty in girls and boys was almost 17 and in the 1870s the average girl first menstruated when she was 16 or 17. Today, however, she is more likely to menstruate at 12 or 13. At this time in the United States, the average age for the onset of menstruation is under age 12. In 1870 the average age of puberty was 16.5. Today the average age for puberty is about 12.5.[2]

Some children, especially girls, begin the first physical signs of puberty as early as nine. In fact, 95 percent of all girls show at least one sign of puberty between the age of nine and thirteen and a half. Boys are beginning to go through puberty between the ages of 13 and 14. Live sperm can appear in a boy's semen as early as age 10. So it is important to begin preparing children for the changes of puberty much earlier than in years past. Of course, no two children will begin puberty at precisely the same age, so you need to be watchful and sensitively aware of your child's particular physical timetable.

Entering puberty at such early ages has tremendous implications for childrens' sex education. As previously, stated, it means that we must begin preparing children for puberty at much younger ages. But it also makes sex education and the development of healthy sexual attitudes vital because there is now a much longer period of time between the physical readiness for sex and the average age at which one marries and experiences sex. As the age of puberty has dropped, the period of waiting has increased. Several generations ago boys reached puberty at 18 or 19 and married not much later. But today, with the average age of marriage rising, boys who physically mature at 13 now typically do not marry until about 25. The length of time one must wait for sex has gone from one or two years to 12 or 13 years or longer. Sex education and healthy sexual attitudes are more important than ever for our children and we must begin before puberty laying the groundwork for godly sexual attitudes.

Before we proceed further, a definition of puberty is in order. Puberty may be defined as the process of reaching sexual maturity, or the age at which one becomes capable of sexual reproduction. A person's body experiences primary changes which are internal and involve the reproduction organs, and secondary, or external, changes which involve outward physical appearances. The only difference between prepubescent children is that girls may be slightly taller than boys; boys and girls tend to look much the same physically. But in puberty, this similarity is about to be radically altered.

Help! Something Is Happening to My Body!

During puberty children's bodies go through tremendous changes. These changes often begin occurring rapidly, and children do not have time to adjust to one change before they are attacked by another. Physically speaking, boys and girls mature into men and women before they leave junior high school. And the major physical changes that occur during puberty have a tremendous impact on a child's emotions.

Female puberty

Girls typically go through the changes of puberty a year or two before boys. For girls the physical changes that frequently cause the most concern or misunderstanding are: noticeable changes in height, weight, thighs, and hips; appearance and development of breasts; menstruation, and body shape.

For girls, signs of approaching puberty are the noticeable acceleration in both height and weight gain, and a widening of the hips. Growth in height usually begins the process, and as early as nine or ten years old, girls usually begin to outgrow boys. Girls' growth spurts usually start about two years before boys'. On the average, growth in height for girls begins at age ten and one-half and is usually over by age 14. As this growth spurt begins, the girl usually experiences a widening of the hips and a gain of body fat. This results in her becoming rounder and softer, and she may become very concerned about her shape and figure. A study at Princeton University indicated that "at puberty," girls satisfaction with their bodies drops sharply.[3] Other physical changes include growth of pubic hair, a slight deepening of the voice, and increased activity in the sweat glands.

The appearance of breasts is usually the first sign that puberty is in high gear. Breast development usually begins between the ages of eight and 13 and is normally over between the ages of 15 and 18. It is unfortunate that our society is preoccupied with breasts and equates sexual desirability, and even femininity, with large breasts. Because of this fetish, many girls with small breasts suffer real mental anguish because they believe they compare unfavorably with other girls and thus boys will not like them. This extraordinary sensitivity to breast development is one of the most traumatic worries of puberty for girls.

Another problem associated with breast development occurs when girls' breasts develop early. When young girls develop large breasts, they may become the target of comments and stares from older boys and men, as well as teasing and harassment from other girls. Such attention from older boys can cause some major problems. It can cause fear and trauma, or it can encourage early sexual experimentation and promiscuity. Remember that physical maturity does not signal emotional maturity and breast size has no relation to a young girl's ability to relate maturely to older boys. If your daughter's physical time clock races ahead of her emotional/judgmental/cognitive time clock, do not hesitate to slow the clock. Insist that your daughter be treated in a manner appropriate to her age, regardless of her physical endowments. When we talk about dating, we will discuss the effect of a girl's early physical development on older boys. However, for now let me say that at this age such contact with older boys should not be allowed!

Teenagers need to be reassured and taught to accept themselves just as they are. Use this time to reinforce the concept that what matters is who we are on the inside. We should uphold the godly values we have been building since birth, not validating the world's warped value system.

The most widely known and important aspect of puberty for girls is the onset of menstruation. This event usually occurs about a year to a year and a half after breast development and after the peak period of growth in height. As mentioned earlier, the average age for beginning menstruation is under 12 years, but it can occur any time between ages nine to 18 years. Every preteen girl needs to understand and be prepared for this very special event before it begins. Mothers need to watch their daughters for signs of physical change such as growth of pubic hair, rapid height gain, and breast development. These events usually precede menstruation by at least one year, and sometimes as much as three years.

In addition to observing your daughter's physical changes, it is important to at least introduce the topic of birth during the early elementary age years. Associating menstruation with matters related to babies and birth is natural, and by routinely discussing the topic at this time, a mother will be preventing complete surprise on her daughter's part in the event of an early beginning of menstruation. In any case, as soon as you first suspect that your daughter is approaching puberty, discuss menstruation with her and tell her exactly what to expect. Explain the process of menstruation thoroughly and provide complete, accurate information regarding menstrual care and personal hygiene. With today's modern advances producing thinner pads and smaller tampons, menstruation does not cause the discomfort of years past. Even the smallest girl should be able to wear tampons.

Menstrual cycles for young adolescent girls can vary and be irregular at times, and the length of periods and amount of flow varies with each individual. Young girls' periods can also be affected by stress, diet, illness and exercise. Of course, persistent problems with a girl's menstruation process should be quickly brought to the attention of a doctor. Physicians should be consulted if the hymen is completely closed, preventing the use of tampons, the menstrual cycle is still irregular two years after the first period, there is excessive bleeding with periods (soaking pads), there is bleeding between periods, or if the girl experiences excessive cramping or a tendency to faint during periods.[4]

Girls should also be prepared for the physical pain that can precede and continue through the period. This pain is usually the result of fluid retention by the body. The degree and length of pain varies with each girl. This swelling usually occurs about a week prior to the menstrual period, and will generally produce a feeling of physical heaviness and emotional tension. At the age of 10 to 12 the physical pain and discomfort of menstruation should not be overemphasized. However, young girls approaching puberty should be calmly counseled and advised concerning PMS (premenstrual syndrome) and the physical discomfort often associated with menstrual periods.

No matter how much preparation you have given your daughter, expect her to still be somewhat embarrassed during her first periods. At the start of menstruation a girl may worry that blood can soak through her clothing, or that the outline of her pad can be seen through her clothes. She may also fear a bad odor. All of these concerns are related primarily to the dreaded fear that somehow boys may know she is menstruating. Because they are concerned that boys may become aware of their condition, young girls may refuse to attend parties or other social activities. Mothers need to reassure their daughters that their periods are not so easily detectable. Girls should be encouraged to change pads and tampons frequently to eliminate any small possibility of staining. This should relieve her fears. Above all, a young girl experiencing menstrual periods for the first time needs calm reassurance that this strange, new, apparent inconvenience, is completely normal, healthy, and clean. It's a sign from God that she is becoming a woman. Some families celebrate a girl's first period as a time when she is passing from childhood to adulthood. Whether with a party, a card, or flowers — we should celebrate with our daughters and help them appreciate this marvelous gift from God. Your positive attitude will provide comfort and support, and will ensure your daughter's positive attitude concerning this new change in her body.

It is the opinion of most experts that boys need an understanding of the menstruation process. It is not inappropriate to discuss this process in mixed groups of males and females. But even if mixed group discussions seem inappropriate, boys need some teaching on this subject. Such teaching helps boys understand what is happening to young ladies and why. And it could help boys avoid embarrassing situations in future mixed-company events. I think it is important that boys be taught to respect the privacy of this occurrence, and to be respectful and not ridicule or make fun of girls during their periods. I often hear teenage boys and girls openly discussing menstruation, and I am amazed at their crudity and flippant attitude. It is not uncommon for boys to blame every single instance of anger, frustration and stress on menstruation. They say things like "she's on the rag, you better avoid her," or "it's the wrong time of the month, you better watch out." Teenage girls even join the seemingly harmless banter regarding menstruation. It is my opinion that such an attitude, while not intended to be harmful or degrading, is in most cases inappropriate and should be avoided. Boys, especially at this age, should be learning how to treat ladies. And I constantly told my son, "All women are ladies, whether they know it or not, and they should be treated in a dignified, kind manner." Harmful put-downs and the demeaning of female peers are not good preparation for being a thoughtful, loving, Christian husband.

At this time, parents need to also talk to their daughters about the additional differences between boys and girls. A girl needs to understand that boys are stimulated primarily by sight and the way girls look, walk, and handle themselves. Many young girls do not understand that their newly developing bodies attract the attention of boys. For this reason girls need to be taught to dress modestly and appropriately—a difficult task in today's culture. I am constantly amazed at the manner in which many Christian parents allow their daughters to dress in public. I have told teenage girls for many years that they should be careful with their advertising because someone just may answer the ad. Girls need to be taught that wearing skimpy, sexy clothing may attract the wrong kind of boys and give the wrong message. Girls should also be taught to be very cautious about how they touch boys and rub up against them. I remember once on a youth trip observing a very pretty and shapely fifteen-year-old girl sitting on a boy's lap on the bus. She was a very innocent and well-behaved young lady who had no idea what torture she was inflicting on this adolescent male. She had only sisters in her family and was not familiar with males. Please do not misunderstand me: I am in no way condoning any inappropriate advances or behavior from males. Nor am I blaming girls for rude, improper advances by oversexed adolescent males. My point is that we must teach our adolescent girls to dress and act in a manner fitting for Christian young ladies. A good time to stress this concept is prior to puberty.

Male puberty

Boys normally begin the changes of puberty about two years later than girls. Changes begin with a period of general physical development between the ages of 10 and 13. For boys the physical changes that cause the most worry and misunderstanding are lack of growth in height and weight, lack of body hair, the size of the penis, spontaneous erection, and wet dreams.

A boy's first worry related to puberty is that he is not growing as fast as the girls his age. Height is extremely important to boys because they consider it a visible sign of manhood and a way of attracting girls. On the average, boys' growth in height lags behind that of girls by about two years. Their growth spurt usually begins around age 12 (although it can begin as early as ten-and-a-half or as late as 17), is most rapid at age 14, and is usually concluded at age 16. For boys who grow tall rapidly, the problems of puberty are greatly diminished, but for the late developer, height can easily become the major concern of puberty. Boys who remain shorter than their peers during puberty are extremely self-conscious and need parental support and encouragement.

One of the most revealing signs of approaching puberty for boys is the appearance of pubic hair. For boys, pubic hair corresponds in significance to breast development for girls. Boys who acquire pubic hair early are the envy of their peers, and often show off this new growth by parading nude around the locker room. Conversely, boys who are late growing pubic hair will rarely even undress in front of their friends. Parents need to be as sympathetic and supportive toward boys who are late to grow pubic hair as they are toward girls who develop breasts late. Late development in either case can be very traumatic for adolescents. With the development of pubic hair comes other body hair, especially under the arms and on the face. And by about 16 or 17 boys gradually need to begin shaving. Other physical changes that occur during puberty are a deepening of the voice, increased activity of the sweat glands, growth and development of the muscle tissue, and acne.

A boy's testicles and penis begin growing at about age eleven-and-a-half or sometimes between the ages of 10 and thirteen-and-a-half. This growth continues for approximately three or four years. One of the greatest concerns for boys is the growth in the size of the penis. The penis grows rapidly about a year after the growth in the testicles has begun and pubic hair has appeared. This growth continues until ages thirteen-and-a-half to sixteen-and-a-half. The average penis size is between four and six inches in a flaccid state. Because there is so much erroneous and mythical information about penis size, let me quote an authority on the subject:

> The size and the shape of the penis are not related to a man's physique, race, virility, or ability to give or to receive pleasure. Like any organ, penises differ in size, but the differences tend to diminish in the erect state. The penis neither atrophies with lack of use or enlarges through frequent use.[5]

Parents should furnish their adolescent boys with such accurate information of this kind because they have many fears and worries concerning the size of the penis. Your awareness and understanding can be most beneficial.

Some time between the ages of 13 and 16 a boy's testicles can produce sperm (often earlier). A boy's penis is capable of erection since birth, but as a child his erections are most likely in response to rubbing or physical stimulation. Toward puberty, his penis is likely to become erect readily and frequently. This may occur spontaneously or in response to sexually provocative sights, sounds, smells, or fantasies. It can also occur for no particular reason. These physical changes and sexual feelings cause the dreaded unwanted or spontaneous erections. And the unwelcome erections seem always to occur at the most inopportune times; the resulting bulge in a boy's pants causes great embarrassment. Fathers should prepare their sons for such occurrences by explaining and warning them beforehand and providing warm, sensitive support and understanding.

Another possible traumatic occurrence for pubescent boys is their first ejaculation. This usually happens during sleep and is referred to as a nocturnal emission (wet dream). Prior to puberty, even when experiencing sexual dreams or fantasies, ejaculation was not possible. But following the physical changes of puberty, ejaculation is now possible and sometimes occurs during the sleeping hours. For the completely unprepared boy, much worry and guilt often accompanies his first wet dream. In addition to not understanding what has happened, he may experience guilt, somehow believing his lustful dreams are sinful. You should thoroughly prepare your prepubescent boys for this event, explaining that nocturnal emissions are the body's way of releasing sexual tensions and preparing for sexual intercourse during marriage. Your son should be told that this is all part of God's plan for his approaching manhood, and that he should not feel guilty.

Boys and girls should be told they will experience sexual feelings, desires, and passions during and after puberty and that at times these feelings can be mysterious and uncomfortable. Boys are especially prone to strong sexual feelings and urges because their pubescent bodies have twenty times more of the hormone testosterone than girls the same age. In fact, in boys, the first strong sexual feelings precede the onset of puberty by two years and continue throughout puberty. [6] The development of strong sexual feelings and sexual interest in girls can be troubling and produce anxiety in boys. They worry that they are not normal or that they are particularly sinful. Parents need to talk often about sexual feelings with boys before puberty and continue throughout the teen years. There is no completely effective way to eliminate or reduce sexual impulses and feelings in your child. But you can teach your child that these feelings are healthy and normal and show them how to control them. You can prepare your child in advance for what to expect and help him learn not to allow these feelings to control his life. First, children need to hear about the importance of self-control. They need to understand that in a world of instant gratification there are consequences. The only way to avoid consequences is to learn self-control. We need to help them learn self-control from their earliest years. Second, parents need to eliminate opportunities. When my son was in the eighth grade he asked if he could go to a friend's house and watch a movie with his friend and two young ladies. I said yes, and then later realized that I had not asked him if adults would be present and chaperone the movie watching. When I asked him if there would be adults there he said he was not sure. To make a long story short, Paul found out that the boy's parents would not be present. I then told him he could not go. He immediately said, "You don't trust me. I know how to act." I replied, "Yes, Paul, I do trust you—I trust you to behave like an eighth-grade boy in an unchaperoned situation." He was not happy, but I was eliminating the opportunity for sinful problems. Third, parents need to pray with their adolescents. Tell your child that he doesn't have to rely on his own abilities—he can rely on the power of God to help him resist and learn to control sexual feelings and desires.

Help Me! (What Parents Can Do)

Throughout our discussion on physical changes of puberty, we have alluded to the emotional concerns and worries of adolescents. It is very common for adolescents to compare themselves to their peers and to then be embarrassed and feel inferior. Girls compare their breasts and overall figures. Boys compare height, muscles, and penises. The reason that these comparisons are made is that physical appearances dramatically affect the social life of the adolescent. Beginning at puberty or about junior high age, a very inflexible social system emerges. Unfortunately this system has just two groups—popular and unpopular. Popular boys are the rapidly developed, athletic types. Popular girls are the pretty and full-figured ones. To be short, fat, flat-chested, plain, and non-athletic is to be permanently assigned to the unpopular group.[7] Is it any wonder that pubescent children attach so much importance to physical appearance? There are some things we can do to help our children overcome their fears and worries concerning their bodies and prepare them for the ups and downs of puberty. We can also help them start to understand and feel comfortable with their budding sexuality. The following suggestions can help our children through this difficult and exciting period in their lives.

1. *Prepare them adequately for puberty.* Your child is about to encounter a period of time when he is changing physically, emotionally, socially, mentally, and sexually. Our job is to get them ready for the dramatic changes of puberty. As fifth and sixth graders they are not expecting these changes, and they often feel confused and surprised with these rapid changes. They feel the most confusion about their sexual development and emerging sexual feelings. We must teach and guide them through these new and rapid changes. The key issue is: no surprises! When I was about 16 my younger sister began menstruation. I was the oldest child and was baby-sitting my sister and two younger brothers. My

sister was only about eleven-and-a-half. Consequently, she had not been prepared for the event. There we were! She was not sure if she was bleeding to death, and even though I knew what was happening, I was not able to explain adequately and show her how to take care of herself. Make sure you eliminate the possibility for surprises by preparing your children for all that lies ahead of them. To eliminate their fears of being left out of the puberty process, be sure you explain to your children that all people are different, and that physical development may be faster for some and slower for others. Assure them that their time is coming, and that they will experience puberty.

2. *Anticipate the changes and discuss them positively and lovingly.* As you prepare and discuss all the different changes of puberty, be positive and help your teen look forward to the future. Emphasize this period of their lives as an entry into the adult world. Make sure puberty and its changes are discussed often. Especially be accepting and affirming of changing emotions. During this time your child will display a wide range of emotions. One minute they are on top of the world, and just a few minutes later, they are in the depths of depression. Be loving and accepting of these emotional changes and make sure your own emotional condition remains upbeat. When you are relaxed and calm about puberty, your child will feel much better.

3. *Remember and relate your struggles through puberty.* Do you remember your own battle and struggles with puberty? Do you remember the embarrassment and the feelings of inferiority? Did you experience unwanted erections and guilt over sexual feelings? Share these struggles with your children. They need to understand that even though

you are now a confident, competent adult, you experienced the same struggles going through puberty as they are experiencing. By sharing your struggles with your children you are communicating three very needed messages. First, you are telling your children that they are completely normal. Everyone experiences these feelings of inferiority, embarrassment and guilt. Second, you are also communicating that you are aware of their concerns and that you are sensitive to their feelings and needs. Third, you are giving your children hope. You are saying to them, "Yes, it's a struggle, but you can and will survive." Your children see that, despite your struggles with puberty and all its accompanying problems, you developed into a mature, competent adult.

4. *Avoid embarrassing your children.* Pubescent children experience enough cruel jokes and put-downs from their peers, and they certainly do not need any embarrassing remarks from parents. Although they can usually survive being made fun of by peers, the ridicule of a parent has a particularly stinging effect. Especially avoid embarrassing them in front of their peers. Advice, correction, and sensitive suggestions should be made in private.

5. *Respect their privacy.* As children enter the years of puberty, privacy becomes very important for them. They suddenly begin locking the bedroom and bathroom doors. Respect this new need for additional privacy and encourage other family members to be sensitive to these needs. Respecting children's privacy also conveys to them that you are being responsive to their feelings. Of course, privacy has limitations. When our children have given us reason to question certain actions and behaviors, we may have to invade their privacy and snoop around.

For example, if our children are exhibiting strange or bizarre behaviors or attitudes, privacy issues need to be replaced with loving concern which may result in closer scrutiny of personal property.

6. *Distinguish between temptation and sin.* We have already mentioned the potential for guilt in adolescent boys over unwanted erections, wet dreams, and sexual thoughts. To keep your son's guilt from becoming unbearable, make a clear distinction between temptation and sin. When the Bible talks about lust, it is not talking about fleeting sexual thoughts. The word for lust used in this scripture is a very strong word meaning to "look at or stare at in order to lust." It does not mean just noticing that a person is sexually attractive and having momentary sexual thoughts. Adolescents should not feel guilty for having sexual thoughts or sexual arousal. God created humans as sexual beings capable of arousal. It is natural, therefore, that people will have sexual thoughts and become aroused. Sin occurs if we dwell on a matter and intentionally think about it repeatedly. Be sure that your sons can distinguish between temptation and sin. Being able to make this distinction will eliminate great amounts of unrealistic guilt for our sons.

7. *Recognize sexual pressure and help your child develop sexual and moral standards.* We must recognize when our children are encountering sexual pressure and use these times to help them develop sexual and moral standards. It is important to help your children establish biblical sexual and moral standards before they begin dating and confront sexual temptations. Instilling sexual and moral standards in your children takes time and effort and is a lifelong endeavor. If you help your children establish their own standards based on valid, biblical information,

while revealing your own strong feelings and beliefs, they will more likely adopt your beliefs as their own because they make sense. Even if your child does not apply the logic now, the information will make an impression, and chances are he will use it later if not now.[8]

8. *Understand your child's confusion.* As children approach adolescence and puberty they experience confusion and often feel socially inadequate. They don't quite know how and where they fit with other adolescents or with adults. Some days they feel and act like adults, and other days they feel and act like children. We must understand their bewilderment and help guide them through these perplexing times.

9. *Communicate unconditional love and forgiveness.* This has been mentioned previously, but as parents we cannot be told too often to communicate unconditional love and practice forgiveness. When our children know that they will always be loved no matter what, the burdens of puberty become bearable. What better way to enhance self-confidence and self-assurance than to say, "I will love you no matter what, and please forgive me." Always remember "love covers a multitude of sins."

Masturbation: Curse, Sin, or Gift?

One of the most traumatic physical sexual problems of childhood is masturbation. The very mention of the word causes some people to cringe and become emotionally upset. Masturbation is an issue that generates tremendous emotional energy and trauma. This is due to the many fears, prejudices, and myths surrounding this misunderstood and controversial subject. It is vitally important for parents to discuss masturbation with their children and not be guilty of silence on this subject. We should understand and discuss all aspects of masturbation including the psychological, emotional, and spiritual effects on children and teenagers. You should also know that highly respected Christian leaders have diverse opinions and beliefs concerning masturbation. I am not attempting to provide an authoritative answer regarding this very controversial subject. Rather, I will furnish you with accurate information and the opinion of a wide range of Christian ministers, writers, psychologists, and doctors. You must prayerfully decide what you believe and how to discuss this issue with your children.

First of all, let us properly define masturbation. It is easy to see why so many people have a very negative opinion of masturbation because the very word comes from a Latin phrase that means "to pollute with the hand." Masturbation is literally the act of stimulating one's own genitals by touching or caressing, usually to the point of orgasm or climax. During masturbation, sexual pleasure or sexual gratification is experienced alone, without a partner. Boys usually masturbate by holding the penis in the hand and moving it up and down until ejaculation. Girls in their early adolescent years typically do not have a strong need for genital sexual release, but when girls do masturbate it involves rubbing the vulva area, especially the clitoris. Surveys suggest that about 96 percent of males under twenty years of age masturbate. A 1994 survey of Christian men conducted by Dr. Archibald Hart and reported in *The Sexual Man* says that 95 percent of healthy males from good religious families admit to masturbating in their youth.[9] Masturbation has not been widespread among adolescent girls, but has become more common in recent years. Boys start masturbating earlier than girls, with 40 percent engaging in the practice by age thirteen. Some feel that much of the research is misleading because it generally asks, "Have you ever masturbated?" And when the respondent answers, "Yes," then he is figured in the high percentage. While this may be true, there can be no disputing that masturbation in adolescence is common, especially in males.

In the not too distant past, masturbation was universally regarded as filthy, offensive and physically, psychologically, and spiritually detrimental and damaging. Masturbation was said to cause insanity, deafness, blindness, and acne. Boys were told, "Your penis will fall off," "Hair will grow in the palms of your hands," "You will use up all your semen," and "Your face will become covered with zits." Girls were told that masturbation diminished their ability to bear children. In the 1920s and 30s children were severely punished, and in some cases fitted with specially designed chastity belts to prevent masturbation. Obviously, the practice of masturbation was frowned upon then.

Today, however, we live in a much more liberated and enlightened age. It is now admitted and recognized by all that masturbation is not physically harmful. As far as psychological harm is concerned, many psychologists and sex educators believe that the only harm caused by masturbation is the massive guilt that many young people have because of this practice. Many suggest that masturbation is one way adolescents can safely and harmlessly relieve their sexual tension. Others suggest that since adolescence has become a much longer period of time and since our society typically encourages later marriages long after the time of peak sexual intensity for males, masturbation is a natural consequence. Those taking this view believe that masturbation is a far better and a more acceptable outlet for sexual release than acts of promiscuity and fornication. Some Christian leaders agree and argue for tolerance as the most practical response to masturbation. On the other side of the coin, there are those in the Christian community who strongly believe that masturbation is harmful and sinful, or at the very least leads to sinful activities that diminish spirituality. Those accepting this view believe that masturbation is harmful because it originates in lust and fantasy, it becomes obsessive, it is self-pleasuring and selfish, and it causes homosexual tendencies.

As I said, Christian authors and ministers vary widely in their views on masturbation. There seems to be a range of opinion ranging from "masturbation is a sin in God's sight" to "masturbation is a gift of God." Let's examine the main viewpoints held by contemporary Christian writers, leaders, and professionals.

Among some Christian writers, ministers, and professionals there is the view that masturbation is sin. It is viewed as lust and fantasy and is therefore, sin. Often Genesis 38:6-10 and 1 Cor. 6:9 (KJV) are used as a biblical objections to masturbation. In Genesis, chapter 38, we find the story of Onan. Onan "spilled his semen on the ground." A careful reading of this passage, however, reveals that Onan's sin was not masturbation. He was simply practicing *coitus interruptus*. In other words, Onan withdrew before ejaculation. He violated a specific Hebrew law. His sin was his refusal to provide children for his dead brother as was commanded by Jewish law. In 1 Cor. 6:9 (KJV) the text refers to "abusers of themselves with mankind." Some believe that masturbation is self-abuse. A careful reading of this passage, however, in either a modern language translation or an original language text reveals this phrase to be referring to homosexual behavior. Many sincere Christians believe that masturbation can and often does lead to lust and fantasy or pornography. And since Jesus condemned lust (Matthew 5:28), masturbation is committing adultery in your heart and is therefore sin. Of course, much depends on one's definition of lust and what constitutes lust. However, for most males, masturbation generally does involve lust. It would seem that masturbation is not lust itself, but it ordinarily does involve lust and fantasy.

A second category of Christian professionals look upon masturbation as wrong because it can become compulsive and obsessive and focuses primarily on self. It betrays God's created natural intention and function for sex. Masturbation can become compulsive and obsessive especially when practiced by people with addictive patterns of behavior. These folks also believe that masturbation primarily focuses on self and that God created sex for marital intimacy. This is a valid point — there is already too much selfishness in our culture and anything that causes us to concentrate on ourselves rather than others is harmful.

In a third category are those Christians who suggest that masturbation may be a way of releasing sexual tensions. They suggest that masturbation may be a natural and easy way to compensate and avoid premarital or extra-marital sexual intercourse. Lewis Smedes, in *Sex for Christians,* says, "For most youngsters, masturbation is a passing phase of sexual release. They usually move beyond its secret aloneness into a search for intimacy with another person. Masturbation is the adolescent's answer to an obvious problem."[10]

These are some of today's prevailing views on masturbation. But as we have stressed before, parents must be very careful and selective about accepting or rejecting popularly held views on sexual matters. So what should we tell our children with regard to masturbation?

Before I make some suggestions regarding what children should be told about masturbation, let me first admit that I have mixed and conflicting feelings and beliefs on this issue. After many years of research and thought about this subject, I can neither regard masturbation as completely and fundamentally evil, nor as a blessing from God to be enjoyed with a completely clear conscience. For me, the critical issue is whether masturbation is practiced as a way of controlling sexual tension and therefore decreases sexual acting out or whether it leads one to become preoccupied with sex and results in more sexual acting out. At its worst, masturbation cultivates a selfish preoccupation with one's own pleasure and involves immoral fantasy or imagining degrading acts with others. It focuses one's energies and thoughts away from loving relationships with others and separates a person from God through guilt and shame. Conversely, masturbation at its least objectionable is a phase of adolescence that does not use mental images or immoral acts and that provides release from sexual tension and contributes to a person remaining chaste.

As we discuss what to tell our children about masturbation, let me ask you a question. How would you like your child to learn about masturbation? You have only two choices: either you tell them yourself or their peers will! It is much preferable that we

THIS CAN'T WAIT: *Talking With Your Kids About Sex*

thoroughly teach and prepare our children about this important subject. Discussions should begin before they reach puberty and encounter sexual tension.

Our discussion on masturbation, especially with males, needs to focus on the issue of self-control. Since a total ban on masturbation will probably never be successful or possible, self-control should be stressed. Our challenge is to teach self-control without creating too much guilt or shame. "Never shame a child over sex. Never punish a child for masturbating. Criticizing or humiliating a child over masturbation can permanently harm his or her sexuality."[11] Teaching about self-control is important because masturbation can become harmful or counterproductive when it is practiced compulsively or obsessively. The self-control we teach should emphasize two important elements: "Don't overdo it," and "Be careful about what and how you fantasize and lust." Also, any exposure of our children to pornography and erotic material should be eliminated.

When talking with our children about masturbation, some Christian leaders suggest a cautious approach. Such an approach is suggested because of the strong feelings of guilt and anxiety that masturbation produces in adolescents. Dr. James Dobson in *Preparing for Adolescence,* speaks to the adolescent from a Christian perspective:

> The subject of masturbation is a very controversial one. Christian people have different opinions about how God views this act. Unfortunately, I can't speak directly to God on this subject, since his Holy Word, the Bible, is silent at this point. I will tell you what I believe, although I certainly do not want to contradict what your parents or your pastor

believe. It is my opinion that masturbation is not much of an issue with God. It's a normal part of adolescence which involves no one else. It does not cause disease, it does not produce babies and Jesus did not mention it in the Bible. I'm not telling you to masturbate, and I hope you won't feel the need for it. But if you do, it is my opinion that you should not struggle with guilt over it.[12]

Linda and Richard Eyre in their book, *How to Talk to Your Child About Sex,* suggest answering a question about masturbation in this manner:

Everyone at least experiments with it. But it can be a problem if it becomes a habit or happens too often. If you use sex too much in a way that isn't best, it could get a little less unique or less exciting, and not as strong or special as if it were saved for the best time. Don't try to stop yourself from thinking about sex because you can't. But when sex comes into your mind, think about how beautiful and awesome it can be with the beautiful and special wife you'll have some day.[13]

In my opinion parents should copy both the style and content of both of these messages.

Masturbation will always be a controversial and debated subject. We must help our children pass through this difficult phase and on to a responsible heterosexual life. It is my view that most masturbation is a normal part of an adolescent's transitional behavior and as such, parents should avoid adding additional guilt to their child when dealing with this issue. As one psychologist said to me, "A good rule of thumb is not to excessively pressure boys ages 13 to 17 about masturbation because it is a normal part of growing up. Simply help them understand that if they think they are masturbating too much, they probably are." When abuses or excesses occur, parents should respond with a wholesome, loving attitude that will relieve guilt and promote healthy sexual attitudes.

Subjects That Should Be Discussed Prior to Puberty

In response to the question "What should I talk about when I discuss sex with my preteenager?", Dr. James Dobson gave the following list of subjects:

1. The role of intercourse in marriage.
2. Male and female anatomy and physiology.
3. Pregnancy and the birth process.
4. Nocturnal emissions (wet dreams).
5. Masturbation.
6. Guilt and sexual fantasy.
7. Menstruation.
8. Morality and responsibility in sex.
9. Venereal disease.
10. Secondary sex characteristics which will be brought about by glandular changes — pubic hair, general sexual development, increasing interest in sex, etc.[14]

The preteen years would also be a good time to either introduce or reemphasize the subjects of virginity, abstinence, and the physical and emotional dangers of sex. Most of these subjects have been (or will be) discussed in this book. The lone exception is venereal disease. Preteen children need to be introduced to the general topic of socially transmitted diseases (STD). Specific, detailed information regarding venereal disease should be handled during early adolescence (ages 13-15).

Final Word

Puberty represents one of the most stressful times of life. Even at its best it produces physical and emotional trauma. During this time children are experiencing mood swings and may exhibit antisocial behavior. Puberty is also a time of experimentation as teens try to figure out who they are and how they fit in. When children have been thoroughly and adequately prepared for this stressful and traumatic stage of life, they will adjust and mature in a much healthier manner. You need to lovingly provide your preteens with accurate information concerning all aspects of puberty. Of particular importance is parental acceptance of the confused feelings and emotions of adolescents during puberty. You need also to be generous with praise and encouragement and be available to listen when they are ready to talk. With accurate information and the loving acceptance of parents, most children can successfully weather this stormy period of their lives.

For Further Thought

1. What physical changes produced the most trauma during your puberty? Why?
2. What insecurities do you have today regarding your body and physical appearance? Why?
3. What preparation did you receive for either menstruation or nocturnal emissions? By whom? Was the preparation adequate?
4. What specific opportunities to praise and encourage your child are available during this time? Make specific plans to pursue these opportunities.
5. What personal struggles regarding puberty could you relate to your children? How would relating your specific struggles help your children?
6. During adolescence what were you taught regarding masturbation? Did you experience guilt over masturbation? How do you view masturbation now? What advice will you give your child? When would be a good time to discuss masturbation with your child?
7. What item from Dr. Dobson's list do you feel the least prepared to discuss with your child? Which item causes the greatest fear?

---

[1] Eyre, *How To Talk to Your Child About Sex*, 127.

[2] McDowell, *Why Wait*, 56.

[3] Anne McCammon, "Beating the Blues at Last," *New Woman*, February 1990, 64-69.

[4] Ketterman, How to Teach Your Children about Sex, 122.

[5] David Elkind, *All Grown Up and No Place to Go* (Reading, MA: Addison-Wesley, 1984), 56.

[6] Hart, *Sexual Man,* 39, 52.

[7] Wayne Rice, *Junior High Ministry* (Grand Rapids: Zonderman, 1987), 63.

[8] Langford, *The Big Talk*, 83-84.

[9] Hart, *Sexual Man*, 54-55.

[10] Lewis B. Smedes, *Sex for Christians* (Grand Rapids: Eerdmans Publishing, 1976), 161.

[11] Hart, *Sexual Man,* 193.

[12] James Dobson, *Preparing for Adolescence* (Ventura, CA: Regal, 1970), 86-87.

[13] Eyre, *How to Talk to Your Child About Sex*, 106-107.

[14] James Dobson, *Dr. Dobson Answers Your Questions* (Wheaton: Tyndale House, 1982), 93.

9
Help, We've Got a Teenager

Early Adolescence — Ages 13-15

Well, the last chapter was your basic training. Now you are ready for combat! Many parents dread and fear the approaching teen years, and they view the entire time as a massive inconvenience and struggle. And while it is true that the years of early adolescence can be one of the most dangerous phases of your child's life, these potentially troubling years need not be totally filled with problems and bad experiences. These years can be most rewarding for parents as they help their children navigate these troubled waters, and observe their maturing into adulthood. I thoroughly enjoyed the teen years with my children. Their early adolescent years were not problem free, but we have managed to keep growing and maturing. I challenge you to eagerly anticipate your children's teen years and look forward to the rewarding opportunity to help produce mature, godly adults.

Early adolescence is a relatively new concept in human development. The study of early adolescence has emerged because it is no longer viewed as an unimportant period of development. "Rather, due to increased development and sociological characteristics in individuals, it has become a dynamic, sometimes impacted, growth period which deserves more attention and concern in the future."[1] Up to this point in your children's lives they have been mostly under your control, now they will be experiencing increased freedom and more association with peers. For many, these junior high school years are a time when adolescents make major decisions about their lives. In order for our children to proceed down the right path and avoid disastrous decisions, we must maintain our involvement in their lives. And we must continually be engaged in addressing the important issues of adolescence. One of our primary goals during early adolescence is teaching and encouraging sexual restraint and responsibility.

Worries, Concerns, Pressures, and Developmental Tasks of Early Adolescence

Early adolescence typically is a time of fear, anxiety, emotional feelings, and rapid development. If you are to have a significant impact on the lives of your adolescents, you must be aware of the primary worries and the key developmental tasks that typify this age. In their book *Five Cries of Parents* Merton P. and A. Irene Strommen list typical worries of young adolescents, having compiled this information from a survey of over 9,000 adolescents. The worries listed range from the fear that their parents might die to the fear of being beaten up at school.

Many of the worries and anxieties center around physical and sexual concerns such as their looks and their physical development. Dr. Strommen in his survey, asks the question: "How often do you think about sex?" The percentage who said "often or very often" were:

7th Grade Boys 38%
7th Grade Girls 28%
8th Grade Boys 49%
8th Grade Girls 31%
9th Grade Boys 59%
9th Grade Girls .... 35%[2]

In a similar survey of teenage males in 1994, Dr. Archibald Hart found that 63 percent think about sex several times a day.[3] As these percentages indicate, young adolescents are concerned about sex a great deal of the time. Another related worry concerns the adolescent's feeling of being "in love." Dr. Strommen's research found that 50% of early adolescents (grades 7-9) say they are "in love with someone of the opposite sex."[4] It is very evident that sex and sexual matters constitute some of the biggest worries and concerns of early adolescents. Parents, remember our goal is to not only encourage sexual restraint and responsibility during adolescence, but also to help our children become sexually healthy adults. Research from the Center for Early Adolescence at the University of North Carolina has identified six key developmental tasks of adolescents. The pursuit of these developmental tasks answers three fundamental questions that adolescents ask themselves: "Am I normal?" "Am I competent? " "Am I loving and capable?" The Center's research affirms that becoming a sexually healthy adult involves development of these key tasks:

1. *Physical maturation.* Adolescents mature into adults biologically earlier than in years past.
2. *Sexual maturation.* Sexual maturity is also occurring at earlier ages than in the past.

3. *Independence.* Adolescents develop autonomy within the structure of the family. The parent-child relationship is transformed during adolescence as young people develop autonomy while developing the skills to maintain satisfying relationships.

4. *Conceptual identity.* Adolescents establish and place themselves in religious, cultural, moral, and political environments.

5. *Cognitive development.* Children and adolescents are concrete thinkers and focus on real objects, present actions, and immediate benefits. They have difficulty projecting themselves into the future. During adolescence, young people will develop a greater ability to think abstractly, plan for their future, and understand the impact of their current actions on their future lives and other people.

6. *Sexual self-concept.* During adolescence, young people tend to experience their first adult-like erotic feelings, and develop a strong sense of their own gender identity and sexual orientation.[5]

Parents need to understand the developmental tasks of their early adolescents, as well as their fears, concerns, and worries—especially the tremendous sexual pressures and concerns faced by teenagers. Parents who are aware of these sexual concerns and anxieties are better able to equip their young teens and help them successfully deal with sexual pressure. Remember, parents: you are the key. By providing information, love, acceptance and nurturing, you will be influencing your young adolescent tremendously and achieving your goal of teaching and encouraging sexual restraint and responsibility.

Dad, Mom, and Teen

As they did in the other developmental stages, early adolescents need strong relationships with their parents and positive role modeling from them. From their same sex parents, adolescents need to learn appropriate roles—how to be men or women. And in their relationships with the opposite sex parent, they prepare to relate to a future mate. So early adolescence is a time when children need their parents to make time for them and their activities. It is a tragic mistake for parents to believe the myth that teens no longer desire or need to spend time with their parents. While it is true teens are beginning to make strong peer relationships, it is not true that they do not want a relationship with their parents. Parents, your children need you during early adolescence! Rebellious children are usually those who are reacting to poor relationships, either between their parents and themselves, or between the parents. Most experts agree that rebellion is one of the primary causes of sexual promiscuity and experimentation by early adolescents. Some young women even become pregnant just to prove to their parents that they cannot be controlled. Strong family relationships are important and affect many areas of growth and maturity during early adolescence.

Early Physical Development and Hurrying Children

For several years many child development experts and cultural critics have been warning us that society is forcing our children to grow up too fast and pushing them into adult roles and behaviors before they are mature enough to handle adult-like pressures. In the mid eighties, David Elkind began sounding this warning in his wonderful book *The Hurried Child.* More recently, Michael and Diane Medved, commenting on this hurrying and rushing of children, have said: "The result is demonstrated in the wealth of research on the loss of the special set-aside time we understand as childhood."[6] In her bestselling book, *Reviving Ophelia,* Mary Pipher describes the world of teen and preadolescent girls who have been encouraged and pushed to grow up too fast. The book's title comes from a character in Shakespeare's *Hamlet* who, as a young woman, became obsessed with the desire to please. She was controlled by those who were trying to make her into the type person Hamlet should marry. She becomes a puppet, controlled by those who are using her for their ends. In her book, Pipher attributes the problem of many of today's adolescent girls to this same need to please and feel accepted. Our media-crazed, sexually oriented culture portrays women as thin, desirable and shapely, causing our young girls to become preoccupied with how they look and how they are perceived. They try to immediately skip from childhood to a media-created image of the perfect woman. And in so doing, they lose their innocence. We must protect and cherish our children's innocence and childhood because growing up too fast can contribute to many unwanted problems. For example, adolescents who go through puberty early are much more likely to become involved in premarital sex at an earlier age.

We have briefly discussed problems associated with the early development of certain physical characteristics. Early breast development usually causes girls to become the object of interest and attention from older boys. This is a potentially troublesome aspect of puberty. When young girls begin to receive attention from older boys, they are treading dangerous ground. In most cases these older boys are more experienced in terms of boy/girl relationships and can easily persuade younger girls to become more deeply involved in relationships than these girls desire or can maturely handle. For example, young girls may be persuaded by older boys to engage in sexual experimentation, which may lead to all types of sexually promiscuous behavior. Such behavior causes major guilt for a young girl who never intended to become involved in such activity. More than half of the fathers of babies born to eleven-to-fifteen-year-olds were over eighteen.[7]

Another problem of early physical development is that girls may learn to relate to males in an excessively sexual way, using their bodies as the primary medium. When this happens, personality development suffers. It appears to these young girls that being successful with boys depends on having a great figure, rather than developing personal relationship skills. I have seen young girls learn this lesson well and make it all the way through junior or senior high school using their bodies as the only means of relating to boys. Unfortunately, when social skills are needed later in life, they do not exist. For years I have cautioned parents about the problems associated with allowing early-developing young girls to associate with older boys. I have encouraged parents to watch these girls closely and to strictly regulate their dating and social activities, especially around older boys. This has been a soap box issue for me because I have seen the damage caused by older boy/younger girl relationships. And on an out-of-town youth activity, I tragically discovered that this issue can also relate to males. A physically mature 14-year-old boy in the group was being treated by older girls as if he were 17 or 18, as his physical appearance might have caused one to believe. This attention was relatively harmless until this boy was approached and enticed into a sexual situation. He was almost forced into sexual activity by a girl five years his elder. The effect on the boy was devastating, but fortunately he came to me for help. When I discussed this matter with an adolescent psychologist, I was told that such occurrences were increasing. The psychologist told me that the young man would experience the same feelings and emotions as a young girl who had been raped. In my counseling with this young man, this proved to be the case. He felt used, abused, and guilty of wrongdoing. The story has a happy ending, however. The psychologist was able to help the young man regain his confidence and deal with his feelings, and today he is doing fine. But the message to parents is clear. We must constantly be aware of the problems that may be caused by the rapid physical development of our young adolescents and strictly regulate and monitor their activities, especially those shared with older teens. I recommend that you completely restrict your child from unchaperoned activities involving older teens. In other words, junior high adolescents should not be allowed to "hang out" with high school adolescents on a regular basis. In situations where older and younger teens must be mixed, parents can volunteer to serve as chaperones. This issue is not lack of trust; young teens simply do not yet have the maturity to handle potentially damaging situations.

Appearance

During my twenty-five year career in youth ministry, I have organized and led countless youth trips. Each trip is uniquely distinct — different kids, different locations, different objectives. But one thing they all have in common is the questions asked by the kids concerning acceptable appearance: "Why can't we wear halter tops?" "Can we wear a two-piece swimsuit?", "Are these shorts too short?", "Can we wear our Marilyn Manson T-shirt if it's tucked in?", "Which body parts can I pierce and still go on the trip?" Of course, over the last twenty-five years clothing styles have changed several times, but regardless of what's currently "in," teens and preteens will attempt to wear the popular styles of the day. And unfortunately the popular styles of the day are designed to meet the demands of an image-conscious society. Our children are taught from an early age that appearance is everything. This message is especially emphasized to girls, who worry about clothes, makeup, skin, and hair. We must begin at an early age teaching our children about modesty in dress and appearance. We must help our children understand that appearance is ultimately a spiritual matter and that the way they dress says much about their values. Although boys need to learn how to present themselves appropriately, modesty in clothing is a particularly critical issue for girls. Because appearance is a form of advertising, when a girl dresses in a provocative manner she may be sending a message she didn't intend. There is a real danger in giving others the wrong impression and asking for trouble. Sex educator Teri Lester writes:

In a sense, clothes are the way we package ourselves. It's how we show who we are, what we think of ourselves. Usually, people put the most important aspect of a product on the package. If we see a package with chocolate on it, what do we expect to find inside? Chocolate, right? We are attracted to it if we like chocolate. If you dress in clothes that emphasize your sexuality, what does it say to others about your priorities? Who's going to be attracted to you? Are you interested in the kind of person who's focused on sex? Do you want to build a relationship with someone who's primarily interested in your body? What do your clothes say about you?[8]

We must explain to our girls that they have both a body and a soul. They can either draw attention to their bodies by the way they dress, or to their souls through their personality and behavior. We must tell our children that when in doubt, modesty is the best policy because appearance is a spiritual matter and reflects our morals and values.

Peer Pressure

When parents hear the words "peer pressure" they usually cringe. They fear they are losing control of their children to the child's peer group. During the years prior to adolescence, your child has been exposed to peer pressure. For example, as early as preschool, your child desired the latest popular toy — Barbie dolls, Power Rangers, or some other fad of the moment. But this form of peer pressure pales in comparison to the peer pressure of early adolescence. From the first day of middle or junior high school, the herd mentality takes control. Individuality is out — following the crowds is in! David Elkind writes, "The peer group is the most powerful component of the young adolescent's audience, and this is why young adolescents are so bent on conformity in dress, behavior, and language."[9] Research conducted by *Parade* magazine found that 83 percent of girls twelve to nineteen said that girls engage in sex because boys pressure them. In addition, 86 percent of the girls thought that boys pressured each other to have sex, and 70 percent said that girls pressure other girls.[10]

While it is true that during adolescence, especially early adolescence, peers do greatly influence our children, this influence need not always be negative, nor does it necessarily follow that it will totally replace parental influence. Research indicates that young adolescents are influenced more by their parents than peers. Leah Lefstein of the Center for Early Adolescence at the University of North Carolina says:

> Now you and I know the myth: young teenagers are the victims of the tyranny of the peer group. Quite the contrary! Researchers have discovered that young adolescents agree with their parents' view far more often than they disagree. The results of an American study tell us that young adolescents chose to accept the wishes of their parents more often than their peers on 14 of 18 questionnaire items, including church attendance, how late to stay out, opinions of people, and counsel on personal problems. Peers influenced the use of free time, parents were chosen for items involving the development of long-term values.[11]

This is especially true when parents have provided an honest, open and accepting atmosphere during the preteen years. However, peer influence is a major problem with regard to sexual matters, as well as potentially deviant behavioral areas. Unfortunately, the sexual activity of a teenager's peer group is an important factor that predicts sexual activity. One recent study found that the adolescent's perception of how much sexual activity was going on in his or her peer group was the single most powerful predictor of whether that child was sexually active himself or herself.[12] Research conducted by the Center for Adolescent Studies at Abilene Christian University found that pressure to have sex was ranked as the number one reason teenagers become sexually involved.[13] Today's teens are under tremendous peer pressure to begin sexual experiences very early. It is vital that we as parents take a vigilant role in preparing our children to combat the most harmful forms of peer pressure. How can we, as parents, offset the negative effects of peer pressure on our children? Let me offer the following suggestions:

1. *Promote positive self-esteem and self-respect.* A healthy, self-esteem and self-respect give adolescents the inner strength to resist negative peer pressure. When teenagers are caught in difficult situations, a strong sense of identity and a positive feeling of self-respect will help prevent them from succumbing to peer pressure. A young person with a healthy sense of identity will weigh the danger to his or her hard-won feelings of self-respect against the feelings associated with the loss of peer acceptance. When the teenager looks at the situation from this perspective, the choice is easier to make. Unfortunately, the reverse is also true. When

adolescents have a poor self-image for whatever reason, they often gravitate toward any activity that holds the promise of security within the peer group.

This point was tragically emphasized to me during a counseling session with a teenage girl. She had engaged in sexual intercourse with a young man she really loved, but he apparently was only interested in sex. When I asked her if she had not been afraid she would get pregnant, she said "No, I almost wish I had; then people would know that I had sex with someone, and they would know that at least one person loved me." This tragic statement is full of lessons for us as parents. This girl comes from a "good Christian home"; yet, she somehow failed to receive the affirmation necessary for a positive self-image. In her search for acceptance, love, and self-respect, she turned to sex. A healthy sense of identity and self-respect will help our children resist peer pressure. We must begin early communicating love, worthiness, and feelings of competence to our children.

2. *Influence your children by sharing your time.* Our children need to spend time with us. In this hectic world it is easy for parents and children to be insulated from one another. Do not allow this to happen. I have often heard and read about parents who attempt to defend their lack of time spent with their children by saying, "I spend quality time with my kids, even if I cannot spend a great quantity of time with them." This is just a conscience-soothing copout. Children need time, period. They need time with parents in order to discover parental beliefs, values and opinions. How can parents hope to offset the influence of peers if they do not spend enough time with their children to impart their beliefs? The only way we can know for sure what's influencing

our children is to be there while the influencing is happening. One effective way to counteract the influence of peer pressure is simply to spend time with your children and be a positive example.

3. *Set clear limits and expectations.* We must not be afraid to set clear limits and expectations. Earlier we discussed setting limits. Early adolescence is a time to re-emphasize limits and communicate expectations. It has often been my experience with teens that they will either live up to or down to your expectations. In other words, a teenager's conduct and behavior will often reflect our expectations. When we set and anticipate realistically high expectations our children will feel loved and secure and generally meet or exceed our expectations.

4. *Make home and family a safe refuge.* The teen world can often be a hostile environment for kids. Some adolescents are popular and accepted, but many struggle with feeling a lack of acceptance and exclusion. We must make the family a safe harbor in the adolescent storm. Our children need to feel loved, accepted, and needed at home. They need a place where they can experience belonging and feel secure in spite of what may be happening in the remainder of their world. Often while teaching teens, I will ask them if there is anything they could do that would make their parents stop loving them? They generally suggest several items of extreme behavior such as murder, rape, or other terrible crimes. But then most teens will stop and say, "No, my parents would be really hurt and angry if I did this or that, but they would still love me." Our children need to know that we will never stop loving them and that home is a safe secure place where they can escape all pressure, even peer pressure.

5. *Give children permission to blame you.* Offer yourself as a reason for avoiding peer pressure. Peer pressure is very intense during early adolescence and sometimes teens really don't want to do a certain thing, but they fear being ridiculed. Give your children permission to blame you when peer pressure becomes unbearable. Give them permission to say, "My parents would kill me if I did that," or "My mom would throw a big fit if I went there." During early adolescence, blaming parents can often help your children out of sticky situations.

6. *Help your children develop the self-discipline necessary to say no.* The ability to say no is a learned skill. It often takes a great deal of hard work to develop the strength to say no. My experience and research indicate that most teens want guidance and help in saying no to sexual pressure. Two out of every three urban junior high students surveyed by *Psychology Today* said their greatest need in sex education was to learn how to resist peer pressure to be sexually active. The overwhelming majority of teens polled by *USA Today* agreed they don't hear enough about saying no to sex.[14] Teenagers want to be taught how to say no to sexual pressure. Hopefully, we have been encouraging our children from an early age to respectfully speak their minds and stand up for what they believe. This helps our children develop the self-discipline necessary to say no. As children approach early adolescence, we must communicate that they have a right to say no—it's okay to say no and resist sexual pressure. We must also prepare our children in advance for the pressure of a sexual experience. You may be thinking, "But my child is not even interested in sex at this point!" Yes, but it is much better to prepare your children in advance because at some point, probably much

sooner than expected, they will face unwanted sexual pressure. Young girls especially need to be prepared with ways to respond to sexual advances because they are not developmentally mature enough to know how to handle these situations. However, they probably will not ask questions without some questioning. You must ask questions designed to get them to open up and discuss potential sexual situations. Ask them if anyone has ever tried to pressure them into having sex or doing anything sexual that they did not feel was right, and if so, how did they handle the situation? Ask about their feelings and how they might have handled the situation differently. Use these questions and your child's answers as an opportunity to specifically prepare them to avoid and manage sexual advances. In extreme cases, encourage your teen to verbally express anger or frustration when they are pressured. We must also make sure our children know how to rescue themselves from a bad situation. Tell them to say, "I demand that you take me home right now!" "If you do anything further, I will tell my father and he will call the police." Help your daughter do whatever is necessary to regain control. We must also teach our boys that it is wrong to manipulate and coerce someone into participating in sexual activity.

People have difficulty saying no in certain situations and areas of their lives. It is one thing to believe you should say no, but quite another thing to actually say no! You must help your children develop self-discipline, which leads to good self-worth and confidence. By teaching responsibility and decision making, and allowing the natural consequences of children's actions to occur, parents teach their children that actions have consequences, and that irresponsibility has a price. By learning these lessons, adolescents internalize and build their own control mechanisms. They learn not to follow every impulse and to exert self-control, which gives them the strength to say no.

7. *Help your children learn to choose friends carefully.* A normal part of early adolescent development is a movement away from parents and family towards peers. The young person begins looking primarily to their peers for acceptance and confirmation of personal worth. During early adolescence this transition is made primarily to groups of peers rather than to individual peers. Commitment to individual peers comes during late adolescence. This movement toward peers by adolescents is normal and represents a striving for autonomy and independence. Some teens, however, search for peer acceptance when they have not received approval from their parents. In their search for approval, teens may go along with the standards and behavior of the peer group. As a result, the selection of the peer group assumes tremendous importance. Fortunately, you are not helpless when it comes to whom your adolescent children select for friends. But much of what you can do to encourage your teenagers toward positive peers must be done prior to the early adolescent years and then reinforced throughout these years. Throughout the lives of your children, you must constantly monitor the friends they hang out with and watch for peer pressure. Encourage your children to invite their friends into your home as much as possible. Make your home the place to be for your children's friends. If you can, get to know the friends' parents and gain some idea of their values, beliefs, convictions. Also be especially careful about where

you allow your child to spend the night. Peer pressure can be strong in a home where values and morals do not conform to yours. When you sense a particular child is having a negative influence on you child, make it difficult for your child to spend time with that friend. And in extreme cases, declare certain friends off limits! Your child's friends are of the utmost importance. I have seen even good teenagers led astray in a short period of time because they did not choose their friends wisely.

However, parents should be encouraged because much research indicates that how a child selects a peer group is influenced by the strength of the relationship between the parent and the adolescent. In other words, you have the most powerful influence on your child's selection of friends. The child who has a strong relationship with his parents is going to tend to seek out a group of friends whose values and morals meet with his parent's approval. When we have a close relationship with our children, we are less likely to have to intervene in their selection of friends.

8. *Involve your children in a church youth group.* One way to ensure a positive peer influence for your children is to help them become involved in an active church youth group. When surrounded by peers who share their values, it is much easier for your children to resist negative peer pressure. If the youth group has effective leadership and is structured properly, all young people can find a measure of acceptance and friends who will support, encourage and love them. In fact, I believe that one of the most important functions of a youth group is to provide the kind of support that helps members discover and do God's will. Without such a group of caring Christian peers, youth have great difficulty surviving the stressful years of early adolescence.

In the summer months, many youth groups have active programs such as mission trips, camps, outreach and service projects, and youth rallies. At the end of the summer I always ask my youth group if it has been harder or easier to resist negative peer pressure during the summer. Almost all of them say it is easier. When I ask why, they say it's because they spent the entire summer with church friends working toward godly goals. They have been with like-minded people and have experienced the effects of positive peer pressure. Adolescent children need to be a part of an active church youth group — even if it means changing churches.

Dating

I still remember my daughter's first date — black Saturday! I was too consumed with my own anxiety to be much help with hers. Thankfully her mother was there to calm the fears and anxieties of father and daughter! This parental anxiety is produced by many factors. We begin to realize that our children are growing up and that someday they will leave and get married. Parental anxiety may be caused by memories of their own unpleasant dating experiences. Parents also experience anxiety because they fear they have not prepared their child properly for the dating experience. Dating can stir many emotions and be the source of many family problems and parent/child conflicts. Dating has also become a hotly debated topic among Christians. Christians see the problems of dating in a society obsessed and preoccupied with sex and sexual gratification. Some Christians suggest that dating should be avoided completely. This opinion has been expressed well in the best-selling book by Joshua Harris, *I Kissed Dating*

Goodbye. This book is well written and details many of the problems with a traditional approach to dating. Other Christians understand the problems of dating, but view a form of controlled dating as a more realistic approach than a total ban on dating (see *To Give Dating a Chance* by Jeremy Clark). I agree that dating as it has evolved in our society over the past twenty-five years has largely encouraged our children to grow up too fast and has promoted sexual experimentation. I would suggest major changes in the manner our children are allowed to date, but instead of an complete ban, I recommend a gradual or progressive approach to dating that encourages the establishment of wholesome dating practices focused on healthy relationships and activities. Parents need to study, pray, and establish their own convictions about dating and its surrounding issues.

At the beginning of the dating process parents typically make one of two mistakes. Either they are too restrictive, or they allow dating to begin too early. Overly restrictive parents typically had some negative experiences in their own dating that causes them to overreact and view the entire dating process in a negative light. Ordinarily these negative or unpleasant experiences were related to their own sexuality. It is important to avoid imposing unrealistic controls and restrictions on teenagers based on our own past mistakes and indiscretions. This only produces conflicts and confrontations with no winners.

Of all the questions I am regularly asked, one occurs repeatedly: "When should I allow my daughter to date?" I am continually amazed by the number of Christian parents (usually mothers) who encourage early dating or the parents who seem oblivious to the dangers of early dating. The question of when adolescents should start dating is a very serious one and has tremendous sexual implications. There is overwhelming evidence that early dating may lead to early sex. Research done by Brent C. Miller of Utah State University and Terrance O. Olsen of Brigham Young University strongly indicates a relationship between early dating and early sex. Their findings were:

> The younger a girl begins to date, the more likely she is to have sex before graduation from high school. Of girls who begin dating at twelve, 91% had sex before graduation — compared to 56% who dated at thirteen, 53% who dated at fourteen, 40% who dated at fifteen, and 20% who dated at sixteen.[15]

This research also found that adolescents who go steady in the ninth grade are more likely to have sex than adolescents who only date occasionally. Research conducted by the Center for Adolescent Studies at Abilene Christian University confirms that early dating promotes early sexual activity: the virginity rate for girls who started dating at age 13 was 79 percent; the virginity rate for girls who started dating at age 16 was 94 percent. Early dating can affect the sexual habits of adolescents. Even though many adolescents, especially girls, appear physically mature by age 13 or 14, they actually lack the wisdom, maturity and decision making abilities to successfully handle one-on-one dating relationships. For this reason, I recommend a more gradual or staged approach to the dating process (here the term dating means spending time with the opposite sex) First, "dating" could start with approved mixed or combined groups doing things away from home. Approved groups would include church youth groups and certain school groups and in most cases would be chaperoned by an adult. Such groups give boys and girls the opportunity to get to know one another within the context of common interests. This group approach avoids the possibility of young adolescents spending time alone. This form of group dating should begin at age 13 or 14, but no earlier than 13. The second stage could involve groups being allowed to participate in structured events such as sporting events, church activities, and movies. These group activities would not require the presence of an adult chaperone, but would require older siblings or parents to do the driving. During this stage, adolescents should be encouraged to avoid separating from the group to spend time alone. These unchaperoned group activities could begin at age 14 or 15. The third step could be double-dates in cars with approved couples. Allowing double-dating is a good step in moving toward solitary dating. This step might begin at 15 or 16. And finally, the last stage: solitary, single-car dating. Solitary dating should be allowed only in certain circumstances and should be limited by curfews and restrictions on activities. It is my belief that until adolescents reach age 16 or the last semester of their sophomore year in high school, they do not have sufficient maturity to deal with the pressures of solitary dating. Some adolescents do not reach this maturity level until they are at least 17. You must judge your child's readiness. Even when following a gradual or staged process as described above, parents should set limits, guidelines, and controls for dating, because even group dates can go amiss if adolescents make poor choices.

Purposes, Guidelines, Limits, and Controls for Dating

The beginning of solitary dating is a traumatic time for parents. They suddenly realize how little control they maintain over their dating adolescent. Well before the dating process begins parents should talk to their teenagers concerning certain aspects of this potentially volatile and tempting relationship. Start by asking questions designed to help your adolescent begin thinking about the purpose of dating. Ask your adolescent: Why do you want to date? What is the purpose of dating? Do your friends at school and church date? What do they do when they date? Do they have curfews? Do they hold hands, kiss, etc? Whom should you date? You can perhaps think of many more questions to ask. Asking questions such as these can be a great way to introduce a discussion on dating with your adolescent. Many teens begin dating because they believe it's the normal and popular thing to do. They have been lead to believe that romantic relationships are normal at an early age and that they must participate in the boy/girl game. The following suggestions, when applied to dating, will help your teenagers have healthy, fulfilling dating experiences which do not involve sexual activity.

1. *Help your child set realistic dating guidelines and goals.* The beginning of dating is an exciting and fun time in the life of most teenagers, but because of the potential problems and temptations associated with dating, teens should have certain limits and guidelines. You will need to help your teenager set realistic guidelines and goals based on the teen's own convictions and beliefs. As parents it may be possible to implement some guidelines and limits for dating,

but most guidelines will be enforceable only by the teens themselves. Teenagers need to be encouraged to set their own guidelines because parents will not be on dates to enforce the rules. If the teen is not self-motivated, the standards and rules you have imposed will not work. Parents should set certain basic rules such as curfews and which places are off limits, but the key here is flexibility. For example, assume that you have a rule that your daughter has an 11 o'clock curfew. What if her date to a football game started at eight o'clock and did not conclude until approximately 10:30? Let's say your daughter's date asked her to stop by the local burger barn for a bite after the game. Thirty minutes is not enough time to order, eat, pay the check, and drive home. Some flexibility is in order in this situation. Curfews for my daughter were always based upon where she was going, when the event started and ended, and what post event plans were involved. If she ran into time problems, she knew to call home. Flexibility and negotiation in the setting of all dating rules help convince teens that their opinions are valued and that they have a part in setting the limits. And when teenagers have participated in the development of guidelines and regulations, they will be far more likely to obey them. It is important also for you to clearly communicate your expectations concerning dating guidelines. At times, to refresh everyone's memory, it may be helpful for both you and your adolescent to have certain guidelines and expectations in writing.

In addition to guidelines and regulations, teens should be encouraged to think about dating goals. Typically, adolescents who are eagerly anticipating their first solitary date will not think about goals. You should suggest some goals and also have them write their own goals for discussion between you before they begin dating. Some possible questions might include: Why do I want to date? What do I hope to have happen? How can I give and receive acceptance? How do I get to know the other person? How can I have good, clean fun? How can I use this experience to fulfill God's will for my life? Helping your teenager internalize a set of realistic goals and standards will launch the dating experience in a fine way.

2. *Encourage your teenager to make* **specific** *plans for dates.* Many adolescents do not even know how to plan dates. And many get into sexual trouble because they have not made definite plans for the evening. When counseling with teenagers who have become involved sexually, I always ask when and where the sexual activity took place. Almost always it happened when they were just "messing around." They had no definite plans and as a result there was too much unstructured time. "Hanging out" is not a good plan. Creative, farsighted date planning helps teens avoid compromising situations. Plans should include specific activities at specific locations with specific beginning and ending times. Encourage your teenager to plan dates in advance, consistent with the guidelines and goals they have set, and keep you informed concerning these plans.

3. *Avoid unchaperoned parties and events.* Unchaperoned parties are not good for teenagers under any circumstances, but they pull in teenagers like a magnet. They are attractive first, because no adults are there; second, because there is no structure and third, because teens can do things normally reserved for adults, such as drinking and having sex. Alcohol consumption is one of the top risk factors for teen sexual involvement. While my children were

adolescents I had very few non-negotiable rules, but one of the rules was—absolutely no unchaperoned parties

4. *Encourage teens to date people who share their convictions.* Many Christians interpret 2 Corinthians 6:14-16 as prohibiting Christians from marrying nonbelievers, and many people extend this teaching to imply that adolescents should not date non-Christians. Whether or not you allow your children to date non-Christians is a private family matter. But I highly recommend that you strongly discourage your children from dating non-Christians. Why go out with someone who does not share your values? Teens need to understand that they must be careful, not only about their own lifestyles, but also about the lifestyles of those they date. If teens date others who share their convictions there will be a commitment to encourage and be accountable to each other. However, if the person they date has lower moral standards than theirs, they may find it easier to compromise their own convictions. Sexual pressures and temptations are difficult to overcome in the best of situations. These pressures are compounded by dating people with different standards and convictions. Our adolescents need to be trained to look for qualities and values that reflect the Christian standards of morality and character. Teens need to realize that the ultimate purpose of dating is to find someone to marry and they, in light of that purpose, need to be very discerning about those who they spend time with.

5. *Encourage teenagers to discuss sexual temptations, values, and limits openly and frankly.* In discussing sex with teenagers I regularly ask them what are some factors and reasons they have avoided sexual activity. Many teens tell me that one reason

they are able to avoid sexual misconduct is because they openly and frankly discuss their temptations, values and limits. Such talks, they say, are held with prospective dates, but are not limited to dates. These issues are openly discussed and prayed about by all in the group who share similar values. This is another example of positive peer pressure. These teens help one another by sharing their beliefs, talking about possible temptations, and then holding each other mutually accountable. Of course, it would be inappropriate to begin a relationship with a new friend by completely expressing your sexual temptations and limits, but teenagers need at least some friends with whom they can honestly and frankly discuss these things. Wise parents will tell their teens that such disclosure with the appropriate people is proper and desirable. Parents should make every attempt to see that their teenagers have an environment where such Christian friends are available.

6. *Help teenagers know how to set limits on expressing affection.* It is normal to want to express affection for someone you're dating. But there is a difference between appropriately expressing affection and arousing each other's sexual desire. When teens talk about their sexual temptations and values, they need to know in their own minds what their physical limitations are. In other words, in a physical relationship, how far is too far? Is holding hands okay? Is kissing okay? How about French kissing? How about petting and mutual masturbation? Today, sexual standards and expectations vary widely among teenagers. Teens need to be encouraged to avoid physical activities that cause sexual arousal to the point of losing control because crossing the line makes it very

difficult to stop. Teens need to ask themselves "Where is my line, the point beyond which I will not go?" When this is decided before the situation arises, it proves very helpful. Teens are going to have some physical contact as they go through the dating process. But they need to be encouraged to avoid physical activities that cause sexual arousal. Sexual arousal is meant to lead to intercourse, and once started, arousal can be very difficult to control. In order to avoid losing control, teens need to know their specific limits and avoid people and situations that attempt to stretch those limits. I often tell teens that they can do anything above the neck and below the knees. Another way to express limits is to observe the "underwear limit." Any area of a date's body that is covered by underwear–and that includes a girl's bra–is off-limits to touching. Touching these areas is called petting, and petting should be off-limits! Discuss with your teen, prior to dating, specific sexual activities and temptations and help them set rigid, godly limits.

7. *Encourage teens to avoid exposure to explicit media.* It is extremely hard to find movies that are not rated "R" and which are not loaded with explicit sexual scenes. Adolescents on a date should be urged not to expose themselves to explicit sexual situations as depicted by many movies and television. Limitations on these activities should be included in dating guidelines.

8. *Teach teens to avoid being alone for long periods of time with their dates.* Teenagers who are serious about setting physical limits will avoid spending large amounts of time alone. A lot of time together alone creates physical opportunities that most teens cannot handle. A good rule and guideline should be to avoid compromising situations. Parents typically

think of sex as taking place in the car, but that only accounts for 6.1 percent of the instances of intercourse between teenagers. Motels and hotels accounts for another 6.4 percent. Nearly 75 percent of the sexual activity occurs in homes. Twenty-five percent of it occurs in the girl's home, and 51.2 percent occurs in the boy's home.[16] Teens should be cautioned that any situation that could possibly cause them to be tempted should be avoided. No one should be allowed in the house when the parents are not at home. If teens are resolved not to have sex, they should never be in a home if a parent is not at home. In order to avoid these situations and places, teenagers need to think and plan ahead, and need to be keenly aware of their physical limitations. You can help teens escape chancy situations by forbidding them to be alone at either their or their date's home. Always make sure you are at home when your teen and a date will be there. It is not enough to have a sibling at the home; at least one parent needs to be present. Also suggest, and request, that after movies and other activities, your teen bring his or her date to your home. A prior agreement between the parents and their teen can allow for some privacy. Such an agreement helps avoid the likelihood of teens being alone in a car for long periods of time. Also do not be afraid to ask teens where they are going, when they will return and what activities they are planning. To provide help you need to be involved in the dating process.

9. *Encourage your teen to group-date.* Group-dating is preferable to single couple dating because it allows teenagers to be with the opposite sex in a relaxed yet controlled atmosphere. The pressure to become involved sexually is greatly reduced and the absence of this pressure forces them to focus on other

aspects of male/female relationships. Too often, teens do not learn to build and develop relationship skills. Group-dating provides an excellent opportunity for teenagers to develop necessary relationship skills without the added pressure of sexual activity. It also exposes teens to a broader spectrum of opposite-sex friends. Such exposure to many members of the opposite sex, with multiple relationships and experiences, will help later when teens become adults and begin looking for mates.

Many youth ministers encourage group dating. Activities are planned and structured to encourage boys and girls to participate in groups, rather than as couples. For example, in our youth program we never plan activities and say "bring a date." Teens are encouraged to bring a group of friends, and as a service, our older teens with cars invite the underclassmen to ride with them. In group-dating boys and girls are free to be themselves and to develop solid opposite-sex relationships.

10. *Discourage going steady.* This is much easier to say than accomplish, because our society encourages steady boy/girl relationships. Unfortunately, there is a connection between steady dating and sexual activity. Many studies indicate that steady dating increases the chances of pregnancy by about 100 percent.

In this context, of course, I am referring to teens who are old enough to single-car date and who will date only one person over an extended time period. I am not alluding to junior high adolescents who repeatedly say they are "going with" someone. During junior high "going steady" means that a boy and a girl might speak in the school halls and sit together in the cafeteria. Junior highers change these steady relationships about as often as they change clothes. Junior high relationships should largely be ignored, except when parents see a problem developing. You should begin in junior high, long before single dating age, educating and preparing your teen concerning steady dating relationships. And as has already been suggested, parents should encourage group dating as a way to avoid long-term exclusive dating relationships. Discouraging going steady is an uphill battle, but parents should create in their teens an awareness of the dangers involved and closely monitor any steady relationships. It is probably impossible to have a teenager pass completely through the dating phase of life and never have an exclusive relationship, but wise parents will continually caution (not nag!) their teens, and carefully oversee and observe their steady relationships in order to detect any troubling signs.

Date Rape

Many years ago, during the early years of my ministry, one of the girls in our youth group came to my office visibly upset. A boy from our youth group tried to force her to have sex. She was hurt and confused and did not know what to do. I was not much help because this was my first experience with someone trying to force another person to have sex. I thought this kind of thing only happened with criminals and deranged people. Unfortunately, over the next several years of my youth ministry, I had additional occasions to help girls in similar situations. Rape in general, and date rape in particular, are increasing in our society, and we must teach our adolescents how to avoid this very traumatic experience. Consider the following statistics:

- According to the U.S. Department of Justice, a rape occurs every seven minutes in the United States.[17]
- Eighty percent of rapes are committed by persons who know the victim. Half of the rapes occur on dates.[18]
- Every day in America, 5,000 women are assaulted by men they know.
- Rape is a tragedy of youth because 32 percent of all rapes occur when the victim is between the ages of 11 and 17.[19]
- Estimates of the frequency of date rape based on surveys of college women range from about four percent to 20 percent of women having been raped on a date.[20]

We must help our adolescents take steps to prevent date rape and, as parents, we must be prepared to be redemptive and helpful if our child experiences this fearful event. It is imperative that we have discussions with our adolescents when they are young enough to prepare in advance. Boys need to understand the seriousness of such behavior and girls need to be taught that certain actions can lead to serious consequences. We must teach our children how to prevent date rape and how to do everything in their power to avoid troublesome situations. In today's world boys are increasingly being pressured by girls, but mainly pressure and coercion are faced by girls. Our discussion will use females as examples.

Here are some things your child needs to know that may help avoid date rape. Although these suggestions apply primarily to girls, these items should be discussed with boys also.

- Never go out with someone of questionable character. Trust your feelings and stay away from people with bad reputations.

- Avoid secluded places such as isolated roads and empty houses.
- Clearly communicate your sexual limits and standards. Be very clear about what you don't want to do.
- Do not go to parties where the parents are not at home and do not go to parties in homes of people you don't know. If things get out of control at a party — leave or call your parents.
- Dress appropriately. Do not dress in a way that would invite sexual advances. Often sexual advances are made no matter how one dresses, but modest dress discourages sexual attention and is always a good policy.
- Avoid petting and never go beyond mild kissing. Generally a person can stop kissing with little trouble, but with petting the feelings become more intense and more difficult to stop.
- Avoid alcohol and drugs and the places where they are present. Alcohol and drugs are usually present in date rape situations and should be avoided altogether.
- Let your parents know when you are expected home or when you are leaving a particular event.
- Plan ahead for emergency situations. Have change for phone calls or cell-phones available and formulate a plan of escape in your mind.
- Do not date guys who are several years older than your present age.

Hopefully, by adhering to the above suggestions, date rape situations can be completely avoided. However, we should prepare our adolescent girls in the event they find themselves in a pressured situation. Tell your adolescent girls if they find themselves in a date rape situation, they should:

- Attempt to repulse pressure with words. Threaten to call police and humiliate the boy.
- Do not worry about making a scene — yell, scream, blow a whistle or anything that might distract the aggressor and break the spell.
- Be prepared to fight physically. Physical resistance is not advised against a stranger with a weapon; in date rape situations a slap or poke in the eye can cool off physical pressure.
- When pressured tell someone — parents, police, counselors.

If date rape occurs, we must be prepared to attend immediately to the physical and emotional needs of our daughter. We must offer total support and never blame her in any way for what happened. We should help her talk to the police and cooperate in their investigation. There are many potentially traumatic decisions that might need to be made, such as what to do to prevent pregnancy ("morning-after-pill") or how to respond to pregnancy, but the crucial issue for parents is to be loving, accepting, and non-threatening with your daughter. A teen who has experienced such a frightening event does not need the extra pressure of judgmental, unloving parents. Several years ago, one of the girls in our youth group was in tears as she came to see me. She had been dating a boy several years her elder and had accompanied him to his home after a date. Once there, he demanded sex. She attempted to resist but there was no one around, and she could not escape. She was raped! When she went home and told her parents, she was severely reprimanded for dating the boy in the first place and for going to his home.

All these accusations were true, but not helpful to a seventeen-year-old girl who has just been raped. Our adolescent girls who have experienced this great trauma need love, support, and good, Christian counseling to help them cope. Mostly, they need godly parents who model the love and gentleness of Jesus.

How Do Adolescents Think?

Many parents of early adolescents are so involved helping their children adjust to all of the physical changes of puberty that often the significant mental changes are completely overlooked. During early adolescence, or even as early as eleven or twelve years of age, youngsters develop a new thinking process. During the childhood years the thought process is dominated by concrete experiences, observations and facts. During early adolescence the thinking and reasoning process begins to change. Young people move from this concrete period and begin thinking abstractly. They are able to work with symbols and principles, and to develop formal reasoning and propositional thinking. Such new thinking processes allow the adolescent to imagine the future as well as contemplate the past. Dr. G. Keith Olson calls this new thinking process "if .... then." In other words, the teenager can imagine alternatives, anticipate consequences of choices, and systematically reason through problems and decisions. [21]

Often parents erroneously assume that stress, irritability, anger, and sullenness are solely the effects of rapid physical changes during adolescence. But in reality this new way of thinking has opened teenager's eyes to new ways of seeing themselves and others. Their newly discovered thinking process becomes the lens through which their physical bodies and appearance are viewed. This new view of themselves and others, coupled with their abstract thinking ability, enables them to go beyond the real and imagine the ideal. Adolescents often then compare the reality of the world around them to an ideal world of perfection. This idealism, while admirable, causes at least two problems.

First, adolescents just entering this stage become very critical of almost everything in their world—parents, church, society and friends. When criticism is directed toward parents, do not take it too seriously, but respond to it in such a way as to communicate to the child that part of growing up is accepting other people. You should also calmly express to the teen that you may be equally unhappy with them.

A second problem caused by this new thinking process and critical attitude is a self-centeredness which generally produces a self-criticism. Teens become consumed by thoughts concerning themselves and their appearance, and they assume everyone else focuses on them as well. They actually believe that when they enter a mall or a school cafeteria all eyes and thoughts are on them. Therefore, they must look and act appropriately or they will be forever embarrassed. When teenagers feel good about their appearance and behavior, they believe that others are also pleased with them. But when teens are filled with self-doubt and self-criticism, they believe others share their negative view of themselves.

As parents we can best help with egocentric self-consciousness in our teens by taking a moderate view of things. For example, do not totally accept or reject your teenagers' view of themselves, but try to express your opinion in a positive way that affirms them and at the same time helps them distinguish between their ideal egocentric world and the world of reality. There are other problems related to formal operational thinking in adolescents. These include having trouble making decisions, argumentativeness, and conflict between family and society. With patience, understanding, and love, you can effectively help your early adolescents cope with the trauma caused by their new thinking abilities. Remember that they are as unfamiliar with their new thinking abilities as they are with the rapid physical changes in their bodies.

This newly developed thinking ability provides parents with an excellent opportunity to teach specific lessons about God and his nature to adolescents. Learning about God and his grace, love, and forgiveness will help teenagers develop healthy attitudes for the future. Healthy attitudes toward God and his will are crucial for adolescents who are striving to live sexually pure lives because, as we have seen, commitment to God does help many teens avoid sexual activity. I would suggest that parents teach the following spiritual concepts and ideas to their early adolescent children:

1. *Define and develop values and moral standards.* Hopefully, we have been teaching our children godly values and morals from a young age, but the teen years offer an excellent time to reinforce these teachings. We live in a world where it is becoming increasingly obvious that there is something wrong with the values and morals of today's children. An October 1996 poll for the *Seattle Times* by Elway Research of Seattle found that 85 percent of respondents agreed or agreed strongly that "parents

today are not taking enough responsibility for teaching their children values and morals."[22] Much trauma during adolescence can be traced to confusion over values and moral standards. This is a time of questioning and offers many opportunities to clarify and strengthen values and standards. Be advised, however, that while adolescents do not respond to being told, they are usually open to being shown! They want to see their parents demonstrate their values and standards rather than merely discuss them. When your life reflects consistency with what you say, then your teen will be more likely to adopt the values and less likely to become confused. Stating values without demonstrating values is ineffective. Parents teach their values and morals to their children most powerfully by the values and morals they exhibit as parents. You need to know what you believe and clearly and explicitly communicate it to your adolescents. Children, especially adolescents, need to know that there are moral absolutes based on God's word and that these absolutes form the basis of our beliefs as Christians. It is also a good idea to establish discipline patterns related to values and morals. For example, my children know that I strongly value honesty. And when they have been dishonest or lied, I have not interfered or stopped the consequences of their behavior. Values and moral standards are taught and developed when consequences are allowed to discipline children in a natural way. You must also help your adolescents to use their values in decision making. They must be taught that good decision making involves asking questions concerning the moral implications of each decision. They must be taught to evaluate decisions on the basis of what would be pleasing to God.

You also communicate your values and morals in your praise. Do you praise your adolescent for making good grades or for behaving in a moral manner? Do you praise your adolescent for being popular or for being accepting of others; for being successful or demonstrating character and integrity? We need to intentionally teach, define, and model values and morals to our children. Teaching values and morals to children is tough, hard work. But kids need to learn values and morals from parents through years of explaining, correcting, enforcing, and modeling.

2. *God is loving, wise, and personal.* In the person of Jesus Christ, God becomes intimately involved in human life. Jesus was born and went through puberty and the teen years. He understands life from a teen's point of view. Early adolescents need to be made aware of the very personal and caring nature of God. They need to know that he actually involves himself with our problems and is concerned about all that affects his children. Such a view helps teens begin developing a personal relationship with a risen Lord. Too many teenagers are simply taught religious rules and traditions; when problems and temptations occur there is no identification with a personal Lord and Savior.

God gave the precious gift of his son to insure our forgiveness. The death, burial and resurrection of Jesus Christ confirm the Heavenly Father's intention of extending grace and forgiveness to his children. Jesus Christ is God's living proof that he is a personal, understanding and forgiving God. It is crucial for adolescents to understand the spiritual concepts of grace and forgiveness. Adolescence is a time of many temptations and trials, and most teenagers will be aware that they have stumbled and fallen short of God's standards. When failures do occur, however, teens need to understand that God's grace is unlimited, and he forgives penitent children. It has been my experience that many teenagers have great difficulty believing and accepting the grace and forgiveness of God. This is especially difficult when they have been involved in sexual sins. When parents have practiced and modeled forgiveness in the home, children have a much easier time understanding and accepting God's forgiveness. Adolescents need to know that sins and mistakes are not fatal.

3. *God considers them valuable, important and worthwhile.* Adolescents understand price tags. They generally believe that the higher the price, the more valuable the product. They should be taught that Christians are extremely valuable because of the exorbitant price tag. Christians were purchased with the precious blood of Jesus, therefore, they are of great value. Normal transitional adolescent feelings cause most teens to suffer from a poor self-image. One way to help our adolescent children to achieve a positive self-esteem is to remind them continually that they were purchased with the blood of Jesus, and that God loved them so much that he gave his son for them.

4. *Through Jesus and the Holy Spirit there is power to overcome sin.* Adolescents need to understand that God has not left his children powerless to defeat temptation and sin. Believers are indwelled by the Holy Spirit and Jesus has promised us help and power in our struggles. Adolescents can be comforted by knowing that God has made provisions to help them with struggles and sins.

5. *Our bodies are sacred and must not be abused.* In 1 Corinthians 3:16, 17 Christians are told, "You

yourselves are God's temple and that God's Spirit lives in you...God's temple is sacred." Early adolescents need to understand that their bodies should be properly cared for because they are sacred trusts from God. Abusing one's body with alcohol, drugs, and sex defiles the very temple of God and is sin!

6. *God's laws that forbid specific sins, including sexual sins, are for our protection.* Teenagers often see Christianity as merely a list of rules and regulations designed to prohibit their enjoyment and fun. You must communicate that God's laws are for protection and personal fulfillment. Teens need to be taught that following God's laws and principles insures ultimate happiness and peace. Help your adolescents understand that breaking God's spiritual laws produces unsatisfactory consequences. Often teenagers do not understand this concept because consequences are not always immediate or visible. It is up to you to teach teens the effects of violating God's spiritual laws, and to teach teens that happiness, peace, and personal satisfaction come from obeying God's laws.

For Further Thought

1. Were you an early or late physical developer during adolescence? Did your rate of development cause trauma? Why?
2. What self-esteem struggles did you have during adolescence?
3. Who are your teenager's best friends? How often are they in your home?
4. At what age did you begin dating? Was your first date a pleasant experience? Did you have specific goals and objectives for dating?
5. Have you discussed dating limits and guidelines with your teenager? If not, make specific plans to do so.
6. Make a list of reasonable dating guidelines to share with your teenager.
7. Read 2 Corinthians 6:14-15. How does this scripture relate to dating?
8. In your opinion, what amount of physical contact is acceptable on dates (holding hands, hugging, kissing, etc)? Discuss this with your teen.
9. Did you go steady during adolescence? For how long? Was this steady relationship a positive or negative experience?
10. Has your adolescent entered the "formal operations" thinking stage? What are some of the signs that have made you aware of this?
11. Has this new thinking process affected your child's spiritual beliefs?
12. Have you discussed your view of God or your theology with your adolescent? If so, does he comprehend your gospel?
13. Plan how to discuss the six spiritual concepts listed in this chapter with your adolescent.

[1] Thornburg, *Journal of Early Adolescence*, 171-172.

[2] Merton P. and Irene Strommen, *Five Cries of Parents* (New York: Harper and Row, 1985), 58.

[3] Hart, *Sexual Man*, 106.

[4] Strommen, *Five Cries of Parents*, 59.

[5] Scales, P. A. *Portrait of Young Adolescents in the 1990s: Implications for Healthy Growth and Development.* (Chapel Hill: Center for Early Adolescence, University of North Carolina at Chapel Hill, 1991), 8-9.

[6] Medved, *Saving Childhood*, 15.

[7] David Whitmore, "Was it Good for Us?" *U S News and World Report*, May 19, 1997, 56.

[8] Susan Browning Pogany, *Sex Smart: 501 Reasons to Hold Off on Sex* (Minneapolis: Fairview Press, 1998), 143-144.

[9] Medved, *Saving Childhood*, 140.

[10] Sey Chassler, "What Teenage Girls Say About Pregnancy," *Parents Parade*, February 2, 1997, 4-5.

[11] Leah Lefstein, *Portrait of Young Adolescents in the 1980s* (Chapel Hill: Center for Early Adolescence, University of North Carolina at Chapel Hill, 1986), 7.

[12] Jones, *How & When to Tell Your Kids About Sex*, 147.

[13] David Lewis and Carley Dodd, *National Adolescent Survey.* 1998 Youth & Family Ministry Conference, 80.

[14] Napier, *The Power of Abstinence*, 76-77.

[15] Barry and Carol St. Clair, *Talking With Your Kids About Love, Sex, and Dating* (San Bernardino: Here's Life Publishers, 1989), 100.

[16] Ronald L. Koteskey, *Understanding Adolescence* (Wheaton, IL: Victor Books, 1987), 101.

[17] Langford, *The Big Talk,* 135.

[18] Ibid., 135.

[19] Mary Pipher, *Reviving Ophelia* (New York: Ballantine Books, 1994), 219.

[20] Jones, *How & When to Tell Your Kids About Sex,* 242.

[21] Olson, *Counseling Teenagers,* 38.

[22] Medved, *Saving Childhood,* 171.

10
They're Almost Gone

Late Adolescence — Ages 16-19

Some of the topics discussed in the previous chapter anticipated future activities by teens. For example, you were encouraged to talk with early adolescents about dating in order to prepare them adequately in advance for the dating experience. When young people reach late adolescence, they begin in earnest to experience dating and many other potentially sexual activities. Also, most young people leave home during late adolescence, so this stage represents a parent's last opportunity for instruction while teens are still in a somewhat controlled environment. For this reason late adolescence is a very important time for both parent and teen. With older teens our role should shift from that of a manager to that of a consultant. As our teens mature through the later stages of adolescence, we will have less direct control, but we can have more opportunities to influence their thought process and behavioral standards by being available to offer wise advice and counsel. Our task during late adolescence is to help our teen sort out options, responsibilities, and consequences of their behavior in order to help them experience good decision making. Late adolescence generally involves the following characteristics: autonomy nearly secured, body image and gender role definition nearly secured, empathetic relationships, attainment of abstract thinking, defining of adult roles, transition to adult roles, greater intimacy skills, and sexual orientation nearly secured. We need to discuss several important subjects: sex versus intimacy, how far is too far, theology of sexuality, fathers, forgiveness, and several related topics.

Romance, Love, Sex, and Intimacy

Teenagers are greatly influenced by feelings and emotions, and often their decisions are based on these emotions and feelings. Because adolescents are so emotional they frequently cannot distinguish between romantic feelings, infatuation, and love. They often believe the romantic notion of a very special person who suddenly appears and sweeps them off their feet. This love-at-first-sight feeling then leads to a perfect relationship that lasts forever. Of course, this myth only works in the movies. In real life there is a big difference between infatuation and true, genuine love.

Intimate relationships are needed and craved by all humans. We desire relationships where understanding, caring, and sharing can take place. And teenagers, in particular, need close, intimate relationships. Unfortunately, the confusion between infatuation and real love generally occurs at the same time. Adolescents really want to know about love and often complain that no one really ever tells them about love. They want to know what love is and how it feels to be in love. They are very curious about all aspects of love. Parents often make the mistake of thinking that they are too young and immature to even be thinking about love and marriage. We often think that they are not capable of comprehending what love really is and that they must wait until they are older to experience love. Such an attitude robs our teens of the opportunity to begin learning about love and how to recognize and experience feelings of love. As our teens enter older adolescence, we should start asking them what they think love is and what they think is the difference between loving someone and being in love.[1] Such questions help older teens begin to see the difference between loving siblings and parents and being attracted to a special person. We need to help our teens understand that often feelings of attraction for someone begin with sexual feelings, but if it's really love it moves beyond that. Real love develops and deepens only when people spend hours getting to know each other, and when they begin to sense a deep concern for each other. Love involves a person beginning to want to give unselfishly of himself or herself to another person. This search for intimacy, coupled with an inability to differentiate between infatuation and real love, can lead to sexual involvement by teens. In many instances, sexual activity was not originally planned or desired. A relationship began, based on romantic feelings and infatuation, and continued because of a desire for intimacy. Many young couples who get involved in premarital sex are not really looking for sex; they are searching for intimacy and understanding. It is often very confusing for teens to understand that sex is not intimacy because we live in a world where sex and intimacy are frequently linked and thought of as one. We must help our teens understand that being intimate with someone doesn't just mean physical involvement. Intimacy means being with someone whom you feel very safe with, whom you can be yourself with, and with whom you can share your feelings and emotions. Our teens need to understand that they can be intimate with someone without having sex with them. They need to understand that intimacy involves sharing your thoughts, talking, laughing, and sharing time together. In fact, focusing on sex very often keeps couples from really getting to know each other. When a teenage romance becomes sexual, everything changes. Sex often becomes the major focus of the relationship. Every time the couple gets a chance to be together, they have sex. And as a result there is much less meaningful conversation and other relationship building activities. Teens often become consumed by the sexual relationship, and there is no time to really get to know the other person. When I counsel with teenagers who have become sexually involved, I always ask them what motivated or encouraged them to have sex. Very often at the root of the motivation is a desire for intimacy, affection, and love. Sex was not the primary goal. Most adults know that there are differences between sex and intimacy, and that love and sex do not necessarily mean the same thing. But, unfortunately, many teens do not see and perceive these differences.

As parents we have a two-fold task: to teach our children how to have intimate, non-sexual relationships and to teach them the difference between infatuation and real love, intimacy and sex. In his book *Dating*, Scott Kirby notes the differences between love and infatuation:

1. Infatuation is a feeling; real love involves a commitment also. In real love both the emotions and the will are involved.
2. A person "falls into" infatuation, but "grows into" real love.

3. Infatuation is basically selfish where real love is basically selfless (John 3:16).
4. Infatuation is weakened by time and separation where real love is strengthened by time and separation.[2]

Parents should discuss these differences with their teens in light of the Apostle Paul's definition of love in 1 Corinthians 13. Adolescents need to understand that real love and intimacy must continually be worked at and nurtured, and cannot simply be a romantic or sexual feeling.

Teaching our children how to have intimate relationships is a lifelong process and probably involves modeling more than teaching. Children need to see and understand that it is okay not only to have close intimate relationships, but it is also necessary for our emotional well-being. When intimacy has been taught and demonstrated throughout the life of a child, it will be easier during adolescence for the child to make distinctions between sex, love, and intimacy. Even when parental modeling and teaching concerning intimacy and love have occurred, there will continue to be a need to help adolescents clearly see and understand the difference between intimacy and sex. Adolescent girls particularly need to realize that sexual intimacy is not an indication of love. Many people have sexual intercourse, but love has nothing to do with it. Norman Wright, a noted family and child counselor, in his book *Dating, Waiting and Choosing A Mate*, has a chart that lists some differences between love and sex.

Differences Between Love and Sex[3]

LOVE ..	SEX ...
... is a process; you must go through it to understand what it is.	... is static; you have some idea of what it is like prior to going through it.
... is a learned operation; you must learn what to do through first having been loved and cared for by someone.	... is known naturally; you know instinctively what to do.
... requires constant attention.	... takes no effort.
... experiences slow growth — takes time to develop and evolve.	... is very fast — needs no time to develop.
... is deepened by creative thinking.	... is controlled mostly by feel — that is, responding to stimuli.
... is many small behavior changes that bring about good feelings.	... is one big feeling brought about by one big behavior.
... is an act of will with or without good feelings — sometimes "Don't feel like it."	... is an act of will — you feel like it.
... needs the respect of the person to develop.	... does not require the respect of the person.
... is lots of warm laughter.	... has little or no laughter.
... requires knowing how to thoughtfully interact, to talk, to develop interesting conversations.	... requires little or no talking.
... develops in depth to sustain the relationship, involves much effort, where eventually real happiness is to be found.	... promises permanent relationship but doesn't deliver, can't sustain relationship by itself, "forever" features are illusory.

Far too many teens are engaging in sexual activity in their search to be loved and understood. We must teach our teens that sex is not a three-letter word for love. Love that is real is a developing emotion that involves a willingness to invest time and effort in developing a lasting relationship.

As we teach about love, sex and intimacy and the many differences that are associated with these feelings and emotions, it is also an opportune time to teach adolescents that males and females have different views on these matters. For example, there is a large amount of research that indicates that women enjoy hugging, kissing, cuddling, closeness, and conversation as much as intercourse. Men, on the other hand usually associate these activities as merely a warm-up for intercourse. To women, such closeness is an end in itself; to men it is a means to an end. Therefore, intimacy, sex, and love can be, and usually are, viewed differently by males and females. An understanding of these differences will provide older teens with a more realistic view of intimacy and sex, and it will also begin preparing them for marriage.

How Far Is Too Far?

We talked about the importance of discussing dating prior to the actual dating experience. As adolescents begin the dating process, however, there is a need to reiterate the information concerning dating and to address additional dating problems and temptations. This is necessary because teens not only need repetition, but also because it is difficult to understand the nature of the problem or temptation apart from the context of experience. In other words, prior to dating, teens will not have a clear understanding of sexual pressures. When actual single dating begins, teens will have a suitable context in which to discuss certain problems and temptations. It is particularly important to reintroduce the issue of knowing when to draw the line. Such a discussion raises the question, how far is too far?

As was mentioned previously, it is impractical to assume that teenagers will not have any physical contact. There will be physical touching as teens go through the dating process. In the past, couples were warned to avoid petting or physical contact because it might motivate them to "lose control and go all the way." Unfortunately, many teenagers today view matters differently. They "go all the way" without going all the way. That is, they practice some form of mutual masturbation or mutual genital fondling so that an orgasm is reached and sexual gratification is achieved. At the same time, they pride themselves on having refrained from intercourse. Sexual experience is gained, but virginity is preserved. This kind of activity is so widespread that a new term has been coined by psychologists and counselors to describe the teens in this category–they are called "technical virgins." They have not technically engaged in sexual intercourse, but they have in fact participated in many sexual activities that result in orgasm. Biblically speaking, they are observing the letter of the law but not its spirit. Since the Bible only forbids sexual intercourse, anything but intercourse is considered fair game (in the teen's mind). It is true—Scripture does not give a direct answer to the question: How far is too far? Dating, as we know it today, did not exist in Bible times. Most marriages were arranged, and the people getting married were very close to the age of puberty. The issue of sexual desire for several years prior to marriage was unheard of in Bible times. Therefore, the Bible is silent on the specific issue of petting. The Bible does, however, emphasize purity instead of specific acts.

We need to communicate to our adolescents an understanding that being a Christian means obeying the spirit and intent of God's commandments. A quick reading of 1 Thessalonians 4:3-8 will add another dimension to the discussion. "It is God's will that you should be holy; that you should avoid sexual immorality, that each of you should learn to control his own body in a way that is holy and honorable, not in passionate lust like the heathens, who do not know God... For God did not call us to be impure, but to live a holy life." Teens need to understand that if God did not call us to impurity, he called us to purity. As Christians we are to control our body and our lust. Christians are called to "moral purity", which obviously includes more than refraining from intercourse.

From a practical standpoint, parents should advise teens how they can avoid going too far. Our goal is to empower our teen to firmly establish a sexual standard in advance — before the need arises. Our task is to help them plan ahead and avoid risky situations. We must also show them how to get out of situations that might arise. Parents can discuss with their teen several things that will help them set firm limits. First, we must acknowledge that sexual feelings and desires are normal and God-given, and it is natural to desire to express those feelings in a loving relationship. While this may be difficult for parents, teens need to be taught to expect such feelings and that these feelings are normal and God-given. Remember, we are not only teaching our children to avoid sex before marriage, but we also need to teach them a positive view of sexuality within marriage. Of course, they should be taught the reality that many sexual desires are not good and are simply selfish, insincere, and predatory. Our children need to understand that their sexual feelings are both a gift from God and a temptation. It is up to them to decide! Second, advise them to never violate their conscience. Any physical activity that breaches their beliefs or convictions is wrong and should be avoided. Of course, it is possible to train our conscience in such a way that almost anything is acceptable. But godly, spirit-filled teenagers generally know when they are violating their conscience.

Third, counsel them to abstain from any activity that causes sexual arousal. They need to be told that physical sexual activity is progressive. It is designed to progress, ultimately culminating in intercourse. We should give specific illustrations and information with regard to sexual activity and how to express affection without going too far. Let them know that hand-holding, quick hugs, and sitting close to each other are good ways to express how one feels without getting into trouble. However, kissing for long periods of time and French kissing can steam things up quickly. A good guide is — if you find yourself thinking and fantasizing about the next step, you have kissed too long. We should tell our teens to never lie down beside each other, especially when no one else is around or if they are wearing swimsuits (this would be a good time to reintroduce the topic of appropriate dress). Teenagers need to be told to avoid touching breasts and genitals. Such touching should not occur either outside or inside clothing. I am constantly amazed by the attitude of many teenagers that touching any body part is okay as long as the hands stay on the outside of clothing. The touching of breasts and genitals is extremely arousing and a thin layer of clothes will not diminish this arousal. All touching in these areas should be off limits. And finally, teens need to be told to not be alone with each other in their respective homes.

In sex education classes at my church, I draw this progression on a graph on the blackboard. I start with simply being together and hand holding and proceed through physical activity until reaching sexual intercourse. I explain that prolonged kissing is the beginning point for danger and that when they proceed to necking and petting genitals feelings become aroused. I then ask the students where they are positioned on the graph. I explain that, whether they agree or not, physical sexual relationships are progressive and that the younger they begin, the faster they will be tempted to progress to the end. Teach your teens that they must avoid arousing situations that will quicken the progression.

Fourth, teens need to be told that often the only way to avoid "going too far" is to end the relationship. This is especially true once sexual activity has taken place. One researcher "discovered that once a pattern of intense sexual relations is established, that pattern is seldom broken except through the termination of the relationship."[4] Christian teenagers who are seriously trying to avoid "going too far" might have to end the relationship.

The question "how far is too far?" is an age-old question that causes parents to shudder. It is really the wrong question because it seems to be really saying—"how much can I get away with?" The real question we should encourage our teens to ask is: "How can I show purity in my dating relationships?" or "What is best for me and the person I'm dating?"

We must encourage our teens to look at "going too far" in a totally different manner.

In earlier times it was assumed that girls would be less aggressive or would "draw the line" because they bore the brunt of the consequence. Today, however, this is not the case. I, like many others, believed such unaggressive behavior and line-drawing was instinctive. But it now appears that this was a learned or taught behavior. Girls were taught to "draw the line" sexually. As parents, we must teach our teenage girls and boys that they must "draw the line" in order to avoid "going too far." They must be taught that even though sexual feelings are very powerful, our God is more powerful, and that they must have a pre-determined plan in order to avoid "going too far."

The Gift

During my years of discussing sexual matters with teens, I have found a way to approach abstinence and "going too far" that seems to capture their attention. I ask them to imagine finding just the right person and being totally and completely in love with that person. Further they are to imagine that after an engagement the two of them decide to be married. It will be a marriage between two wonderful people who are very much in love. Next I ask them, "What would be the most precious gift you could give that special person? A gift more precious than anything money could buy — a unique gift that is valuable because it is part of yourself." Then I tell them that the most precious and valuable gift they could give their future loved one is their virginity. It is precious because it is a part of them and can only be given once. And when it has been given, it can never be given again. I explain to them that if they give their virginity to someone else before that special person comes along, they will always regret that this beautiful gift cannot be given to their spouse. This explanation of the specialness and uniqueness of their virginity seems to touch them. Several teens who grew up in our youth program have returned to tell me that this story concerning "The Gift" influenced their thinking with regard to premarital sex. During all my years of ministry to teens, I have never heard first-hand or seen research that suggested that waiting to have sex was detrimental to a subsequent marriage. Waiting to give "The Gift" is one of the best choices teens can make. Use illustrations, anecdotes, or anything that will help teens see the importance of their virginity.

Person or Object

In his book, *Growing Up In America – A Sociology of Youth Ministry*, Tony Campolo says:

Instead of looking at biblical texts that either condemn or affirm sexual activities, it may be more useful to explore how the Bible instructs young people to view those persons with whom they become romantically involved. [5]

Being sexually exploited – used for another person's pleasure – is one of life's saddest experiences. For many young people, it is a firsthand lesson in the pain of betrayal. In our use-it-and-throw-it-away society, people are often regarded as objects. If a person is viewed as an object, then that person can be used for personal satisfaction or gratification. But when a person is esteemed as valuable and created in the image of God, abuse is less likely. Teenagers need to be encouraged to understand the value and dignity of all people. They need to learn that by avoiding sexual activity, they are displaying respect for themselves and others. Parents should help teens see that as surely as their bodies are the "temple of the Holy Spirit", so also are the bodies of their boyfriends or girlfriends. In other words, parents need to begin at birth teaching the value and dignity of all people and that people are not to be used as objects. Teaching the value of personhood will have a profound affect on the way teenagers treat members of the opposite sex. Using or manipulating others for sexual gratification will be viewed in a much different light. Any activity that cheapens or diminishes the value, dignity and personhood of others should be avoided. Selfish use of others for personal gratification violates the basic message of Christianity.

Where's Daddy?

Throughout this book I have stressed the importance of the father/daughter relationship. Current research indicates a correlation between the father/daughter relationship and teenage pregnancy. Dr. Grace H. Ketterman, in her book *Ketterman on Kids: Answers to the Questions Parents Ask Most*, says: "In working with a great many teenage pregnancies, I found one of the common denominators of them was an emotional distance from their fathers. In fact, many studies indicate that estrangement from her father is a major factor in becoming intimate with a man."[6] Prior to adolescence the mother is generally the major influence in a child's life. But during the teenage years fathers become more powerful and influential.

Ideally, they offer protection and guidance and demonstrate responsibility. A father's approval and/ or disapproval are very powerful factors in a young person's life. He serves as a role model for his son to become a man, and for his daughter's choice of a future spouse. Daughters also gain confidence in themselves as women from experiencing the approval of their fathers. Dads need to spend time with their daughters during this sensitive time in their lives. Spending time with your daughter gives her a chance to understand herself and her relationship with a boyfriend, because many times a relationship with a boyfriend is symbolic of her relationship with you. It appears that many teenage girls turn to sexual relationships with boyfriends in an effort to find a substitute for their father's love and approval.

During a conversation concerning teenage pregnancy, I asked a caseworker at a home for unwed mothers whether she saw any recurring themes in the experiences of pregnant teens with whom she worked. She immediately responded that during her seven year period as a caseworker almost every teenage girl she questioned said: "I didn't have a very good relationship with my daddy."[7] She further said that a very high percentage of these pregnant girls expressed a strong desire to have spent time with their dads. This does not mean that fathers are completely responsible for their daughter's sexual activity, or that a poor father/ daughter relationship is totally the fault of the father. However, fathers need to understand their vital role as a major influence in the life of their teenage girls.

There are several ways fathers can strengthen relationships with their daughters and help prevent pregnancy. First, beginning in infancy, fathers should take an active role in the sex education of their children, including daughters. Many fathers are frightened by the prospect of talking about sex with their daughters, but children need perspectives from both parents, and mothers often resent the father's lack of involvement. Fathers should be one of the first and primary persons to discuss sex with their daughters.

Second, fathers should spend as much quality time as possible with their teenage daughters. Fathers who work or play all the time are just the same as gone or dead! Do not assume that your teenage daughter does not need as much of your time as she did as a young child. At this critical age she probably needs more.

Third, fathers should exemplify spiritual leadership. A father's modeling of a Spirit-led life will be a tremendous source of strength and security to a teenage daughter.

Fourth, fathers must be morally pure. I will never forget a conversation with a teenage girl in my youth group. This young lady had very suddenly become sexually active. She was not even attempting to hide her sexual escapades. I asked her to lunch in order to express my concern about the direction of her life. When I asked why she had suddenly turned to sexual activity, her reply was sobering. She said, "My father has been having an affair for two years now, and if he can live like that then so can I." Obviously the girl was deeply hurt and resentful. She chose to lash out and get even with her father by playing the same sexual game he was playing. Fathers who expect moral purity from their daughters must be willing to live by the same standards.

Obviously fathers play an important role with their teenage sons, and mothers influence their teenage daughters, but there is considerable evidence relating to the importance of the father/daughter relationship during the teen years and its effect on teenage pregnancy. Therefore, fathers must very carefully and prayerfully prepare themselves to nurture their daughters through these very difficult years.

What If Pregnancy Occurs?

Unfortunately, I have considerable experience with both parents and young people who must face pregnancy out of wedlock. Most of the time a teenage girl comes to me and asks me to help her tell her parents she is pregnant. Before accompanying her to tell her parents, I spend some time processing her feelings and attempting to assure and comfort her.

Almost always parents, especially Christian parents, react in much the same way as they would respond to a death in the family. They go through all the stages of grief. At first there is shock and denial — they are certain that a mistaken diagnosis has been made. Shock and denial are followed by anger. Often this anger is directed at the young man. During one of my experiences helping a teenage girl tell her parents about her pregnancy, the parents were convinced that their daughter was raped and started to call the police even though their daughter repeatedly admitted her compliance. Of course, anger is also directed at their child with responses like: "How could you?" Anger is followed by sadness and depression which generally leads to guilt. Parents often spend time blaming themselves and lamenting things they either did or did not do in rearing their child. As expected, parents experience strong negative emotions when a child becomes pregnant. In order to cope with these strong emotions and help a pregnant daughter, let me suggest several steps that you should taken in the event of pregnancy.

First, acknowledge your own mistakes and demonstrate unconditional love to your daughter. Express your hurt and disappointment, but continue to love and support your child through this difficult time. Your child will need love and support in order to handle the tough choices and decisions ahead. Second, get your daughter to a doctor. This is important because young mothers have more complications during and after pregnancy and because considerable time may have passed before pregnancy was admitted. Third, I strongly recommend that the entire family go to a counselor who is skilled in such issues. Dealing with everyone's emotions and feelings will require deep personal reflection and introspection and the assistance of a professional counselor will facilitate this process. The difficult choices that are ahead will require clear thinking and sound decision making. A good counselor can help with personal emotions and feeling, as well as assist in the discussions concerning options and choices.

Unfortunately, there are only four choices available: marriage, keeping the baby, adoption, and abortion. All of these choices have problems and difficulties, but I would strongly recommend that parents encourage their daughter **not** to choose abortion (more on this subject in the next chapter). In assisting your daughter in making a decision, carefully consider the future and what is best for everyone concerned. Seek the advice of people who have chosen all four options in similar circumstances.

Parents, do not forget your responsibility if your son has conceived a baby out of wedlock. Many of your feelings and emotions will be similar to those of the parents of the girl. Your son's needs will differ from those of the girl, but he must face his responsibility and be prepared to provide for his child. Let me assure parents that you can and will recover from all these painful feelings and emotions. When handled with love and prayer, I have seen many of these difficult situations restore peace and joy to the lives of all concerned.

Forgiveness

When counseling with Christian teenagers who are either pregnant or have become involved in sexual misconduct, the topic of forgiveness surfaces as a major issue. Premarital sex customarily produces a tremendous amount of guilt. And most Christian teens have difficulty forgiving themselves and receiving God's forgiveness. It has been my experience that the teens who are more easily and quickly able to accept and experience forgiveness have one thing in common — parental forgiveness.

Teens who have been reared in forgiving homes, and who experience genuine forgiveness from parents, heal and recover much more rapidly than teens reared in an unforgiving atmosphere. This point was emphasized to me by a case worker in a home for unwed mothers. This home housed pregnant teenage girls from many different churches and denominations. The case worker found that pregnant girls from churches or denominations characterized by a liberating, grace-oriented theology or doctrine, generally chose either adoption or keeping the child, while girls from churches characterized by a more legalistic or restricting theology or doctrine, usually chose abortion. During counseling and questioning the girls who opted for abortion expressed feeling terrified at the thought of talking to their parents about the pregnancy. They did not feel forgiveness was a real possibility.

The pregnancy of your daughter outside of marriage or the knowledge that your son is responsible for a pregnancy is one of the most emotionally painful events that can occur in a parent's life. This pain is most intense for Christian parents who, not only must deal with the realities of pregnancy, but who also feel guilt and doubt because their child has apparently rejected their faith and morals. Christian parents feel shame and embarrassment when pregnancy occurs. These factors cause some parents to be harsh and unforgiving. But the realities and consequences of pregnancy are so overwhelming and traumatic that the young people involved do not need the extra emotional stress of unforgiving parents. They need a tremendous amount of love and support. The first parental step toward helping and healing must be forgiveness. If teens are to choose realistic options and find genuine support, they must experience forgiveness. But in order for forgiveness to occur during such a highly emotional and stressful time, it must be a previously established, routine practice. Begin early in the lives of your children to create a communications system that encourages them to share their sins and failures, as well as their successes. When children are reared in an atmosphere of openness and forgiveness they will be better equipped to make difficult decisions, and to rationally determine which options and alternatives are best in a given situation. But unfortunately the opposite is also true—a perceived or real lack of forgiveness confuses teens and interferes with their ability to make intelligent choices.

There are several elements involved in creating an atmosphere of forgiveness. First, parents must forgive themselves. In the event of pregnancy or any other sinful or disappointing conduct by their teens, parents must fully accept the fact that they are sinful human beings who are fully capable of making mistakes, but who are also fully forgiven. If they have not already sought God's forgiveness for real and specific failures with their teenagers, they should ask forgiveness for busy schedules, overprotectivensss, ill-tempered behavior, or whatever seems to have contributed to a problem between themselves and their teens. Once this is done, the need to accept God's forgiveness and continue with the job of rearing their children. Accepting forgiveness removes parental guilt, freeing parents to act out of love and concern for their teens' welfare instead of responding on the basis of their own guilt. Parents need to accept the fact that they will make mistakes with their teens, that these mistakes can be forgiven, and that life can proceed. Modeling the confession of sins and acceptance of forgiveness teaches children valuable lessons.

Second, parents must build an atmosphere of forgiveness instead of condemnation. When children, especially teens, are constantly criticized and condemned they become excessively guilt-ridden. Children who fear criticism, guilt, or condemnation tend to avoid parents when they have problems or temptations, making it impossible for parents to help and support them.

One way parents display forgiveness and acceptance is by not over-correcting. In their desire to rear successful teenagers many parents spend most of their time and energy correcting. This often causes teens to feel unaccepted. Acceptance means allowing a teen to make mistakes and grow from the experience, and offering needed forgiveness.

Third, parents can greatly contribute to a forgiving atmosphere by simply saying, "I'm sorry, please forgive me." There is no better way for parents to teach forgiveness than to admit their own mistakes and shortcomings. Parents are sometimes cruel, harsh, forgetful, and insensitive. When such failures are openly acknowledged, parents communicate to their children that all people make mistakes and that the way toward healing is to admit mistakes and ask for forgiveness. The simple words, "I'm sorry, I blew it. Please forgive me," will teach more about forgiveness than a dozen lectures on the subject.

Fourth, parents must always communicate unconditional love. Children need to know that no action on their part will cause parents to stop loving them. Unconditional love does not mean that parents can or will remove the consequences of a child's behavior or that some form of discipline will not be necessary. When attempting to convey this concept to teenagers I ask them to imagine the worst sin they could possibly commit. Most often teens say that the sin that would hurt, anger, and disappoint their parents the most would be pregnancy or causing pregnancy.

I then say — "Okay, in the event of pregnancy how would your parents react?" I ask if their parents would throw a suitcase in the middle of the room and say, "Pack up and get out, you are no longer part of this family!" Most all teens admit that their parents would not behave so drastically.

I then ask if their parents could remove all the consequences of a pregnancy. I go on to explain that unconditional love means that they will always be a part of their family and that parents will support, help, and encourage as much as possible, but consequences must still be faced. The central theme of the Gospel is this: "While we were still sinners, Christ died for us." (Romans 5:8). God demonstrates unconditional love and grace. As parents we must copy God's example.

Expressing forgiveness to young people in this situation is extremely difficult, requiring parents to summon all their inner strength and emotional capabilities. But forgiveness is mandatory, both to heal the teen and to help them make intelligent, rational choices. Do not despair—forgiveness is a gift from God, and when it's needed he will provide the strength to forgive.

Characteristics of a Sexually Healthy Adolescent

During late adolescence parents should begin seeing the effects of their efforts to teach healthy, biblical sexual attitudes to their children. If we have lovingly taught and discussed sexual matters with our children during their entire lives, they will demonstrate certain characteristics with regard to sexuality. The following list of characteristics of a sexually healthy adolescent was compiled from several sources and my own experience and should serve as a checklist as your children pass through late adolescence.

Self

Appreciates own body:
- Understands pubertal changes
- Views pubertal changes as normal
- Practices godly behaviors, such as abstinence from alcohol and drugs

Takes responsibility for own body:
- Identifies own values based on God's word
- Decides what is "right" and acts on those values
- Understands consequences of actions
- Understands that media messages can create unrealistic expectations related to sexuality
- Is able to distinguish personal desires from that of the peer group

Is knowledgeable about sexuality issues:
- Views sexual feelings as God-given without acting upon them
- Understands the consequences of sexual behaviors
- Makes personal decisions about masturbation after prayer and Bible study
- Understands gender identity and sexual orientation
- Seeks further information about sexuality as needed
- Understands peer and cultural pressure to become sexually active

Relationships with Parents and Family Members

Communicates effectively with family about issues:

- Maintains appropriate balance between family roles and responsibilities and growing need for independence
- Is able to negotiate with family on boundaries
- Respects the rights of others
- Demonstrates respect for adults
- Asks questions of parents and other trusted adults about sexual issues
- Can accept trusted adults' guidance about sexuality

Peers

Interacts with both genders in appropriate and respectful ways:

- Communicates effectively with friends
- Has friendships with males and females
- Is able to form empathetic relationships
- Is able to identify and avoid exploitative relationships
- Understands and rejects sexually harassing behavior
- Understands pressures to be popular and accepted and makes decisions consistent with godly values
- Believes that boys and girls have equal rights and responsibilities for love and sexual relationships
- Communicates desire not to engage in sexual behavior prior to marriage
- Is able to distinguish between love and sexual attraction

- Talks with a date about sexual behaviors before they occur
- Is able to communicate and negotiate sexual limits

Almost Gone

She had really done it! Our daughter had actually gone off to college and left us. After the final good-byes as we left the dormitory parking lot, our minds were full of many unanswered questions. Had we taught her enough about life? Was she prepared for college existence? Had we taught and modeled our Christian faith effectively? Was she prepared to handle mature dating relationships? Could she manage money...and on and on. Our questions were endless. When our daughter left for college, I had just signed the contract for the first publication of this book. So I began to question my daughter's preparedness concerning sexual matters. What new or additional sexual temptations would she encounter in her new environment? Thoughts of this kind are especially scary to parents of college freshmen because for the first time our teens will be facing sexual temptations without the daily support of their parents and families. But when teens leave home, parents have a great opportunity to reiterate many important teachings and principles. They have one last shot to communicate their values and feelings on significant and weighty issues! It been my experience that because of their maturity and the traumatic occasion, teens are less defensive and better able to discuss important and controversial issues as they prepare to leave home. I would advise you to begin talking informally about important topics several months before your teen actually leaves home. The key word is "informally." You are not checking off one controversial issue after another, but rather engaging in easygoing conversations to reinforce your child's understanding of your values, beliefs, and feelings.

Since our topic is sex education, let me suggest some items that should be addressed before your teen leaves home for the first time.

First, your child should not leave home confused regarding your beliefs, values, and morals — especially with regard to sexual matters. They should know what you believe God's word says about sexual matters.

Second, as they leave home they should be told that in all likelihood sexual temptations will increase in intensity. Dating relationships after high school are more intense and serious for several reasons, including the increased maturity of teens, greater freedom from interruption and parental controls, and internal and societal pressures to marry. Teens should, therefore be warned that it will now take increased effort, dedication, and commitment to avoid sexual misconduct. They also need to understand that they must become increasingly motivated from within. Hopefully you began teaching responsibility and self-control during the growing up years, and your teen is now prepared to assume responsibility for controlling his own actions.

In addition to discussing increased sexual temptation and re-emphasizing parental values and beliefs, you may consider sharing the experience of your own college years. I am not suggesting you divulge potentially painful and emotionally damaging secrets or indiscretions, but that you perhaps share some of the struggles and temptations you faced during a similar time in your life. Such sharing will encourage and strengthen teens because they will begin to believe it is possible to defeat temptation, and that mistake are not fatal and can be overcome with God's help.

Fourth, as teens contemplate leaving home, you should initiate some discussions concerning qualities of a perspective mate. Ask them what specific qualities they are looking for in a mate. In fact, you should start asking this question as teens are entering the last year of high school. It is important for them to be thinking about what is important to them in a future mate, because every person they date is a potential mate. Discuss with your teen the popularly held myth that God has only one special person for them to marry and that if they don't marry that person then a happy marriage is impossible. A marriage involves commitment, hard work, and adherence to God's principles for marriage. Therefore, there are many people that could be married and the result would be a happy marriage. Helping teens see this fact frees them to see many possibilities concerning future mates. It also helps them to focus on the real qualities and characteristics of potential mates rather than concentrating on some romantic notion of "the only one."

Fifth, as your teens are leaving home, express confidence in their ability to overcome and triumph over temptation and sin. Your teens, like everyone else, will do much better if they feel others, especially their parents, believe in them.

Your teen will never be totally prepared to face the world, but do your best and take advantage of this one great opportunity to communicate your values, beliefs and feelings once again.

For Further Thought

1. Read 1 Corinthians 13:4-8. Create an opportunity with your teen to discuss the differences between real love and infatuation.
2. Do men and women disagree about what constitutes love and sex? If so, how?
3. Read 1 Thessalonians 4:3-8. How does verse 4 apply to the term technical virginity? Write a letter to your teen expressing your beliefs and feelings on this matter.
4. How much importance did you attach to marrying a virgin? Have you discussed your feelings regarding the importance of virginity with your teenager?
5. Fathers, when was the last time you had a "date" with your daughter? Make a "date" for this week.
6. Complete the following: When I think about my role as a parent, I have difficulty forgiving myself for…
7. When was the last time you said "I'm sorry" to your child? What behavior precipitated this statement?
8. If your teenager was leaving home today and you could only tell her three things—what would they be?

---

[1] Langford, *The Big Talk,* 218.

[2] Scott Kinby, *Dating* (Grand Rapids: Baker Book House, 1979), 34-36.

[3] Norman Wright and Marvin Inman, *Dating, Waiting and Choosing a Mate* (Irvine, CA: Harvest House, 1978), 145-146.

[4] Campolo, *Growing Up in America: A Sociology of Youth Ministry,* 84.

[5] Ibid, 85.

[6] Ketterman, *Ketterman on Kids,* 82.

[7] Charlene Walker, untitled lecture on teenage pregnancy, Abilene Christian University Graduate School, Abilene, TX, July 1, 1987.

11
Additional Difficult Topics

I have saved several topics until the end of this book. This does not mean I am inferring that these subjects should not be dealt with until after teens reach or pass older adolescence. Like most of the information in this book these topics should be discussed with children whenever they express an interest or need to know the information. As we have repeatedly stated, sex education is an ongoing, lifelong process, so you should be prepared to have frequent talks about all areas of human sexuality, especially about highly emotional and controversial topics such as sexually transmitted disease (STD), contraception and birth control, abortion, pornography, and homosexuality. It would be extremely difficult for parents to explain all of their beliefs and feelings on any of these subjects in one or two attempts. It is also very difficult in a book such as this to completely cover the numerous issues related to these sensitive subjects. Our focus will be on helping you present rational, biblical viewpoints to your teenagers. As was stated at the beginning of this book, the opinions of Christians differ on many of these sensitive issues. I will present all opinions and let you prayerfully decide how to discuss these matters with your children.

Sexually Transmitted Diseases (STDs)

Some subjects in life are so unpleasant or disgusting that many times we simply ignore or avoid even the mere mention of them. One such topic is sexually transmitted disease. This subject is so frightening and offensive that most people simply pretend it does not exist, and they are therefore woefully ignorant about this ugly area of human sexuality. Consider a few facts and statistics concerning sexually transmitted disease:

- There are more than 25 significant sexually transmitted diseases.
- STDs spread faster among teenagers than any other group.
- It is estimated that one in four sexually active teenage girls has an STD.[1]
- Three million teenagers get an STD each year (8,219 every day or one every 11 seconds).
- STDs accounted for 87 percent of all cases reported among the top 10 most frequently reported diseases in 1996 in the US.
- Eight new STDs have been identified since 1980.
- Approximately $10 billion is spent annually on STDs (If HIV is included the total is $17 billion).
- Seventy five percent of all new cases of STDs are in teens.[2]

A recent research summary reported that sexually active teenagers have a higher rate of contracting STDs than any other age group. There are two basic reasons. First, teenagers are more likely to have multiple sex partners. Second, they are less likely to use contraception. [3]

As the above statistics attest, sexually transmitted diseases have reached epidemic proportions in this country. There are several possible reasons for this epidemic: increased sexual promiscuity, ignorance, and professional and public apathy. Whatever the reasons, these statistics are shocking.

In spite of the fact that STDs account for a large percent of all cases of the most frequently reported diseases and numerous educational programs, most parents and teens remain ignorant concerning this area of human sexuality. There are many popularly held myths related to STDs:

- Having sex with one person at a time means not contracting a disease.
- One can detect by sight if someone has an STD.
- Everyone who has an STD has symptoms.
- STDs can only be transmitted by genital contact.
- Once a person contracts an STD, they know they have it.

Our object in this section of the book is to inform you about these diseases and help you pass this information to your teens. It is important to inform your early adolescents about sexually transmitted diseases and discuss the subject thoroughly. This type of informational discussion is not based on the assumption that teens will be sexually active. It is rather based on the belief that adequate knowledge will promote responsible behavior and encourage abstinence. When you provide this information during early adolescence, your teen will have additional facts on which to base decisions. Unfortunately, teenagers make mistakes and lose control of themselves. If sexual activity does occur, there is always the risk of STD. Ignorance of the facts concerning STD will only compound an already painful situation. So prepare your adolescents with regard to STD. Hopefully, they will never need the information personally, but if the need arises, adequate STD information may save their lives.

In general, adolescents need to know that some forms of STD are highly contagious and not curable. For example, the three most common STDs are chlamydia, herpes, and genital warts (HPV Human Papillomavirus). Chlamydia is the number one STD with 4 million new cases each year. Approximately 45 million Americans have herpes or one out of five people over 12 years of age! HPV is considered the fastest spreading STD in America with an estimated 24 million cases reported and over one million new cases each year. HPV has no known cure.

Teens also need to know that the term STD refers to infections that can be transmitted during intimate body contact other than sexual intercourse. In other words, STDs are diseases that are capable of being transmitted through contact with the genitals, the anus, the mouth and other body areas. You may be thinking that such information will unnecessarily scare your teenagers. There are two points I want to make in that regard. First, awareness of the dreadful consequences of sexually transmitted diseases may save their lives, so let them have some fear. And, secondly, if being scared of sexually transmitted diseases aids teenagers in avoiding sexual misconduct and in remaining pure, as God intended, then a little realistic fear has done its work.

Parents and teenagers should be aware of the following signs of STDs. (Unfortunately, several STDs have no noticeable symptoms—chlamydia, HPV, and often gonorrhea.)   In general, a woman should seek medical help if she has any of the following signs.

- Burning while urinating.
- A persistent sore throat.
- Pain or itchiness in or around the vagina.
- Any soreness or redness around the vulva or the anus.
- Any sores, warts or pimples in or near the vulva.
- A discharge that is yellow, green or otherwise discolored. (A normal discharge is usually clear or milky).
- A thick discharge that looks like cottage cheese.

In general, a man should seek medical help if he has any of the following signs:

- A persistent sore throat.
- Burning during and shortly after urination.
- Any sores, warts or pimples on or around the penis.
- Any unusual coloring of the urine, such as urine which is reddish or very dark.
- A milky or puslike discharge.
- Any soreness or redness around the anus.

For information concerning specific sexually transmitted diseases, consult a physician. Specific information can also be obtained from the Center for Disease Control and Prevention by calling (800) 227-8922 or on the Internet at www.cdc.gov/ nchstp/dstd/dstdp.

AIDS/HIV

By far the most frightening sexually transmitted disease is AIDS. AIDS (Acquired Immune Deficiency Syndrome) is the final and fatal stage of HIV (Human Immunodeficiency Virus). HIV attacks and destroys the body's immune system, making it impossible for the body to fight off other infections. As soon as HIV enters the body, it begins making thousands, millions, then billions of copies of itself. This process goes for many years and during this time, the victim looks and feels fine, and may have no idea he is sick. People with HIV usually develop AIDS, and other infections eventually kill them. There is no cure or vaccine for HIV/AIDS. About 30 million people worldwide and 1 million Americans are infected with HIV. That is equivalent to about one out of every 300 Americans over age 13.[4]

AIDS/HIV presents a rather bleak picture. Many people have questions regarding the origin of AIDS. Scientists have suspected for many years that HIV originated in African primates, but until recently the link was unproven. However, in early 1999, researchers from the University of Alabama at Birmingham said they have convincing proof that the virus has spread on at least three occasions from chimpanzees to people in Africa. After analyzing the genetic makeup of a similar virus that affects chimpanzees, scientists say that one subspecies of chimpanzee harbors a virus that gave rise to the current epidemic. Chimps have carried the virus for thousands of years with no apparent effects. The *Pan troglodytes troglodytes* subspecies of chimpanzee is often killed for meat in the same west central African region that has been the epicenter for the AIDS pandemic. [5] Hopefully, determining why chimps do not become sick from the virus will have implications for human medicine.

During the first few years of the AIDS epidemic most people associated AIDS with homosexuality. This simply isn't the case. In fact, the incidence of AIDS is increasing most dramatically among teenagers who have sex with members of the opposite sex. AIDS is now the number six killer of people age 15-24. However, many AIDS victims are from the following high-risk categories: sexually active homosexuals and bisexual males, intravenous drug users, people who receive blood transfusions, infected mothers, and sex partners of the above.

In light of the frightening and dangerous nature of AIDS/HIV, it is important that adolescents be thoroughly informed concerning this dreaded disease. I believe parents should furnish their adolescent children with factual and accurate information regarding all aspects of this disease. In transmitting these facts to your children, dispel the myths and make certain they understand the life-threatening possibilities of this disease. Parents should tell their adolescents the following about AIDS:

1. The AIDS virus is present, and can be transmitted through body fluids or discharges such as blood, semen, and vaginal secretions.

2. Rectal, oral and vaginal sex can transmit AIDS. It can be transmitted from a man to a woman, or a woman to a man during heterosexual intercourse.

3. It is easier for girls to catch AIDS. In 1987, 14 percent of teen HIV cases were girls. But by 1994, girls made up 43 percent of teen cases.[6]

4. As it relates to AIDS, sexual intercourse not only involves the current partner, but includes everyone with whom the partner had sex with for the past several years.

5. There have been no confirmed AIDS cases as a result of kissing, sneezing, coughing, hugging, sharing food, mosquito bites, toiletseats, or masturbation.

6. It is possible to contract AIDS from someone who is unaware they have the disease, because it is possible to have the disease, or be a carrier, without symptoms.
7. Condoms only reduce the risk of getting AIDS, they do not prevent risk. Condoms are only about eighty percent effective in preventing AIDS.
8. The best way to prevent AIDS is to remain sexually pure until marriage. Abstinence offers the only protection against AIDS.

Information concerning AIDS, as well as other STD's, should be furnished to teenagers. The purpose of sharing this information is to equip them with relevant, factual knowledge related to sexually transmitted diseases. This knowledge and information will assist them in making sound decisions. By sound decisions, I mean the total avoidance of sexual activity until marriage.

Birth Control — Contraception

A highly controversial aspect of sex education relates to teaching about birth control. This subject is especially emotional for Christian parents because sometimes parents cannot tolerate the idea that their own teenagers might have sexual relationships. Even Christian parents must realize that a high percentage of high school girls have sexual intercourse before graduation. This is an inescapable fact of the world in which we live. Therefore, the much debated question is, should adolescents be given information concerning birth control and contraception? In other words, if our goal is for our children to abstain from sexual intercourse, why would we ever consider telling them about contraception and birth control?

During many seminars and speaking engagements related to sex education, I am often asked whether it is right or wrong to teach our children about ways of preventing pregnancy and sexually transmitted diseases if they become sexually active. I will present both sides of the argument for your prayerful consideration.

First let us briefly clarify what is meant by the terms "birth control" and "contraception," because these terms are not synonymous. Birth control refers to anything that prevents a live birth from occurring and includes abortion. Contraception means literally to prevent conception from occurring. Disease prevention is not the same thing as birth control or contraception, however, we will include disease prevention in our discussion of contraception. Back to our original question — if it is not a good thing for our teens to conceive a child or get a sexually transmitted disease, should we inform them about contraception? What are the reasons for and against teaching our teens about contraception? Obviously, these questions are very controversial and there are no easy or correct answers, only opinions.

There are two schools of thought on this issue. Some people believe that by providing adolescents with information and knowledge concerning contraceptives and birth control, we are encouraging them, and even giving them permission, to have sexual intercourse. A leading proponent of this belief is Dr. James Dobson of *Focus on the Family*. Dr. Dobson voices utter opposition to teaching teens about contraceptives, especially condoms. He argues that our entire society underemphasizes abstinence (a point on which we can all agree). The core of his opposition to teaching kids about birth control or contraceptives is that instructing teens about contraceptive usage undermines their commitment to abstinence. This is a very powerful argument and many Christian leaders and parents agree with Dr. Dobson.

Other people believe that if contraceptive information is given by parents in the context of a strong set of moral values it will give the child the information needed without encouraging sexual activity. While it is true that Christian teenagers engage in sexual activity less than non-religious teens, when Christian teens do engage in sex, they are less likely than their non-Christian peers to use effective contraceptive and disease preventing methods. Thus, they are more likely to get pregnant when they have sex.[7]

Perhaps we should discuss why teens do not use contraceptives and birth control for several reasons. First, as I have mentioned several times, many teenagers suffer from a very low self-esteem. Girls in this situation often want to get pregnant. They feel alienated and unloved by the significant people in their lives, and they fantasize that a baby will fill the void and make them feel loved and useful. So, in order to fulfill this fantasy they do not use contraceptives. In younger adolescents, rebellion is a major reason for pregnancy. These young girls are using pregnancy as a way to rebel against their parents and assert control over their own lives. They want to get pregnant as a way of rebelling.

Another reason teenagers do not use contraceptives relates to what several adolescent experts refer to as the "personal fable." This fable is very prominent during adolescence and revolves around the teenager's belief that he or she is unique and special and as a result of this specialness is shielded by a cloak of invulnerability. In other words, they believe that bad life situations such as cancer, auto accidents, and even death, do not happen to them. This belief in a personal fable leads teens to conclude that pregnancy cannot happen to them. Therefore, they do not use contraceptives because, after all, their uniqueness protects them from life's problems.

Perhaps the primary reason teenagers, especially Christian teens, do not use birth control is that it would make sexual intercourse seem premeditated. In other words, the use of birth control would indicate a prior plan to sin or to go against God's laws. In the teen's mind, if sexual intercourse occurs during a highly passionate moment of uncontrolled emotions and feelings, the act does not produce as much guilt. But, on the other hand, if contraceptives are purchased and their use planned, more guilt is produced because it is impossible to blame unrestrained passion. So, they deny and do not accept the responsibility for becoming sexually active. They claim some innocence by saying, "It just happened."

Hopefully a lifetime of teaching children that they are sexual beings and that they need to control physical cravings will help prevent sexual activity from "just happening." From their earliest years children should be taught that actions have consequences, and that people take precautionary measures to avert damaging situations. A lifetime of such teaching will help avoid accidents.

People who believe that teens should be furnished information about contraception and birth control argue that we cannot always guarantee that our children will remain sexually pure, and we should give them information to encourage them not to compound their sexual sins. An additional argument for teaching our children about contraception is that they are going to hear about these things anyway. And it would be much better for them to hear it from their parents in a Christian home.

This birth control/contraception issue is so highly charged emotionally that people on each side of the question usually make false assumptions concerning those who hold differing opinions. For example, people who oppose teaching about birth control and contraception traditionally believe that the advocates of such teaching are opposed to teaching abstinence. And those people who propose teaching about birth control and contraception accuse the opponents of being unrealistic and shortsighted. But I believe it is possible to both teach about sex and promote abstinence, while at the same time maintaining a realistic view of teenage sexual conduct, and providing factual knowledge concerning birth control and contraception. I do not believe it must be an either/or proposition.

I would suggest that parents not dilute their own and God's view on sexual sins. Sex before marriage is a sin! Parents should clearly communicate this fact to their teens. A couple who has sex outside of marriage is committing sin. But if that couple fails to protect itself and others by using contraceptives, that magnifies the damage! We must not send mixed messages to our children or pretend to be morally neutral, but I really believe it is possible to provide information regarding birth control and contraceptives without compromising years of teaching about abstinence. Perhaps one way to handle the issue is to tell your teenage children about birth control and contraceptives couched in terms of marriage. In other words, tell them you are providing this information, so they will be prepared for marriage.

During the past several years I have interviewed many Christian psychologists and counselors. I have also researched the literary works of many professional psychologists, counselors, and sex therapists. I have been unable able to find much evidence that suggests that providing birth control and contraceptive information to teenagers encourages sexual activity. And many of these men have done extensive research on this subject. Dr. Ron Rose, a family therapist, stated:

> I have not seen any scientifically done research indicating that the giving of information and knowledge concerning birth control promotes sexual activity. In fact, most research indicates the opposite.[8]

My own experience, while not of a scientific nature, confirms these findings. For many years I have talked with teenagers in my church on this subject. During sex education classes and discussions I have said something like this: "Sex before marriage is damaging and sinful. It should be avoided at all costs. But if you choose to disobey God and your parents, then you should protect yourself and use some form of birth control or contraceptive." In subsequent private conferences I have asked numerous teenagers, including my own, if they interpreted my remarks as giving permission to have sex. I have yet to have one girl or boy answer yes! You see, for many years these teens have been taught by me that sex before marriage is wrong and a few informational remarks regarding birth control and contraception cannot possibly undo all previous teaching. It will be the same with your children. When your lifelong message is one of sexual abstinence before marriage, your children will not misinterpret your feelings and beliefs. And for those few teenagers who directly disobey God and parents, at least they will be spared additional problems.

I am not advocating the distribution of contraceptives, merely the giving of knowledge and information. I believe that we can inform our children about birth control and contraceptives, while at the same time telling them that we pray that they will not use this information until marriage.

Abortion

Abortion is one of today's most controversial and hotly contested social and political issues. Approximately 1.3 million women in the United States had an abortion in 1996 and 23 percent of those abortions were performed on teenagers. Forty percent of pregnant teens abort![9] Space does not permit an in-depth discussion of all the details and ramifications of this highly emotional and controversial subject. I am speaking from the position of a Bible-believing Christian, who opposes abortion. Unfortunately, I am also speaking as one who has considerable experience in counseling teenage girls who were considering abortion. Our discussion will focus on what our teenagers should be told about abortion and/or possible alternatives for dealing with teenage pregnancy.

Some parents believe abortion should not be discussed because to discuss the subject would be to admit the possibility of pregnancy. But a clear statement of biblical and parental beliefs concerning this important topic will help our teens make intelligent, godly decisions. Hopefully, our teens will avoid pregnancy altogether. But if not they need clear, accurate information regarding choices available to them.

A teenage girl has four choices when pregnancy occurs: give the baby up for adoption, marry the father of the child, raise the child alone, or have an abortion. Regardless of her choice, she will probably have to make it alone, since research indicates that more than 85 percent of boys who impregnate teenage girls will eventually abandon them. Abortion is often seen by the teenage couple as the most efficient and least troublesome choice. It requires no marriage and appears to allow all parties to resume normal lifestyles after a quick, simple, medical procedure. It sounds neat, clean and easy. To immature, troubled teens, abortion resolves the situation for the moment. However, teens need to he told about the terrible emotional problems abortion often causes in girls and women. The guilt often continues for years. One researcher found that long-term stress related to abortion continued for up to ten years after the abortion, with 56 percent of women experiencing guilt over the decision.[10] Post-abortion distress is real and symptoms can range from mild to extensive post-traumatic stress disorder.

All of the women I have talked to regarding their abortion have expressed deep regret or guilt. Several of these women have accepted God's forgiveness and resumed a productive Christian life. Others have been devastated by the abortion experience. Even the well-functioning women who have accepted forgiveness have some guilt and regret. They indicate that there will always be the burning question, "What would my child have been, or done?" Teenagers need to be told that abortion is not as simple or as easily and quickly forgotten as they might think. Guilt can be a devastating emotion, especially when spread over an entire lifetime.

During many years of youth work I have had several opportunities to minister to pregnant teenagers and their families. One surprising aspect of this ministry relates to abortion. I have been astonished at how quickly Christian parents view abortion as an alternative. This is especially true when parents first discover that their daughter is pregnant. One of my counseling tasks with these families is to convince them that abortion is not a good choice. It should be pointed out that I am referring to good Christian families who were totally and completely opposed to abortion before the pregnancy of their daughters. When abortion could be viewed as simply theory or a problem of others, then abortion was opposed. But when the theory became their reality, different viewpoints surfaced. I should also point out that, in most cases, I and others were able to persuade these families against abortion. My point is this—as it relates to abortion, other sexual matters, or life in general—children must see consistency between what parents say during the calm and what they do during the storm. I remember the day a teenage girl and her parents asked to speak with me concerning the daughter's pregnancy. As the counseling session unfolded it quickly became obvious that the parents were in disagreement concerning what the girl should do. One parent wanted me to talk the girl into getting an abortion and the other parent wanted me to talk her out of it. I felt great pain for this teenage girl who was caught between two parents with conflicting views. How was she ever going to make a wise, godly decision? When parents say one thing and then attempt to do something altogether different during life's difficulties, children receive double messages. Such double messages cause confusion in the minds of teens with regard to right and wrong.

I believe there are two attitudes that parents can begin teaching and demonstrating early in the life of their children that will create an atmosphere in the home that will greatly discourage abortion. First, parents should create and maintain a forgiving system with their children, one that encourages them to admit and share their sins, mistakes, and failures. We have talked about the importance of forgiveness and its relevance to many issues. Forgiveness is extremely important with regard to abortion. Many religious, church-going teens choose abortion because they conclude that forgiveness is impossible, and they opt for the quick fix. Children reared in homes where the forgiveness of Jesus is taught and modeled can better review all options and make decisions based upon the interests of the unborn baby instead of their own guilt. A forgiving atmosphere is vital in the prevention of abortion.

In addition to a forgiving atmosphere, children should be taught the sanctity of all life. Help your children understand that life is a gift from God and therefore very precious. Human life, especially, is holy because we are made in the image of God. We teach our children about the sanctity of life by valuing and respecting all people and by avoiding racism, sexism, and any other "-isms" that devalue or degrade human life. All people should be treated with dignity. This applies to the born as well as the unborn. Abortion violates the sanctity of life by killing the unborn, but as Christians we must also be concerned about the sacredness and dignity of the born as well. We must teach our children to show concern, compassion, and kindness to all human life — born and unborn — and exemplify the compassion of Jesus to all humans. When children have been taught to view all life as a precious gift of God and that, as such, it has sanctity and holiness, then they will be much less likely to view abortion as a viable alternative or solution.

Christians and churches alike must do more than condemn abortion. We must in compassion and love offer alternative solutions to the problem. For example: churches and other groups opposed to abortion must be prepared to extend practical help to both the unmarried woman who is pregnant, and the married woman who may be faced with the question of abortion. Merely to say to either one, "You should not have an abortion," without being ready to involve ourselves in the problem, is another way of being inhuman.

The unmarried woman may need a place to stay. Time should be taken to tell her about the many couples who cannot have babies who long to have a child to adopt. She will certainly need counsel about how to care for her child if she decides to keep the baby. Pleasant institutions should be available for unmarried women awaiting the birth of a baby, but each person who does not believe that abortion is right should personally be prepared to offer hospitality, financial aid, or other assistance.[11]

In communicating your beliefs concerning abortion to your teens, the procedure itself and its emotional trauma should be portrayed realistically. It is important that teens comprehend exactly what it means to have an abortion. In addition, you should help them explore all other options available to them.

Homosexuality

For Christians, few issues cause more intense emotional feelings and reactions than the topic of homosexuality. Fear is among the most common reactions to this behavior. Parents fear that their children might become homosexual, and teenage boys fear that they might be gay.

Simply defined, homosexuality means preferring or choosing to pursue sexual gratification with members of the same sex. However, in real life defining homosexuality can be far more complicated, and simplified definitions often cause problems. For example, many adolescent and pre-adolescent boys have numerous fears regarding homosexuality. They worry about being or becoming homosexual because of involvement in sex play or mutual sexual exploration. Some sex play and thoughts about the same sex are a normal part of adolescence and most fears regarding homosexuality are completely unfounded. You should relieve this anxiety for your adolescents by informing them that sexual thoughts and impulses regarding the same sex happen routinely and generally has no relationship to future sexual identity.

The cause or causes of homosexuality have been hotly debated in both Christian and secular circles for many years. Opinions and theories span the spectrum. The evidence concerning the cause of homosexuality is inconclusive. Some have argued that there may be genetic or biological factors that predispose some to become homosexual. However, studies indicating a genetic or biological link are few and have been largely discredited. The evidence is very mixed at best. Others believe homosexuality is primarily a learned behavior acquired as a result of a dysfunctional family. Attempts to understand homosexuality and its causes are difficult because of emotionalism, distortion, and debate regarding interpretation of scientific and psychological data. In addition, great disagreement exists between leading experts in the fields of science, medicine, psychology and religion.

A more detailed examination of causes of homosexuality will be helpful to parents. Following are the more frequently cited causes of homosexuality.

1. *Disrupted gender identification.* Many modern theorists believe that homosexuals at their core have a sense of being male or female, but that they lack confidence in being a man or woman. In other words, their gender identity is fragile. Several studies indicate that homosexuals report higher rates of being viewed as effeminate or as a sissy. Children who begin life without the proper understanding of their gender develop a more fragile identity and begin to act in ways that are not typical for their gender. In today's society many children have no role model in the home to assist with gender identification. Divorce contributes to this loss of role models in many homes, and children from single parent homes are believed by some to be at a higher risk regarding sexual identities. Compounding the problem of fragile gender identities is the loss of sexual role definitions in today's world. In times past there were clearly distinguishable differences between men and woman. The sexes looked, dressed, and acted in discernibly different ways. Often today, hair styles, fashions, jobs, attitudes and behavior are so similar that differences between males and females are blurred. In some ways this is good for society, but for children struggling with

gender identity, today's unisex habits can be extremely confusing.

2. *Disrupted relationships with the same-sex parent.* Many researchers and psychologists believe homosexuality is at least partially caused as a result of ineffective relationships with same-sex parents. Fathers who are unaccepting, detached, cruel, angry, or passive are more likely to produce children with homosexual tendencies. Mothers who are overprotective, threateningly powerful, dominant, possessive, permissive, and overly critical are likely to have the same results. The combination of a parent who acts powerful, dominant, and controlling, with one who acts passive, incompetent, and scared, creates a climate very conducive to developing homosexual tendencies in children. Ideally, children need to learn the qualities and characteristics of males and females from their parents in a noncompetitive atmosphere where parents accept, respect and love each other. Children especially need to spend much time with their same-sex parent. The opposite sex parent should encourage and approve such expenditures of time. Dads should be teaching sons, and mothers teaching their daughters. Of course, if parents are too busy to spend time modeling same-sex roles, children will not learn what it means to be a man or woman. Children who have disrupted relationships with same-sex parents are not only more likely to have homosexual tendencies, but they are also more likely to have trouble with heterosexual acting out!

3. *Non-normative childhood sexual abuse.* Many homosexual men have had sexual experiences with older boys or men before puberty. And many homosexual women have been victims of sexual abuse leading them to be suspicious and anxious

about males and male sexuality. Sexual molestation or abuse appears to be a bigger issue for homosexual women than men.

4. *Critical self-judgement.* Many homosexuals, especially males, are highly critical of themselves and have for years judged themselves to be less masculine than others. They often were reared either by absent fathers or fathers who expected perfection from them, and as a result, they grew up being overly critical and judgmental about themselves. They grew up never believing they were as masculine as other boys and this led to homosexual tendencies.

There are many additional theories concerning the causes of homosexuality but most professionals agree that there is no single cause of homosexuality; it is a multifaceted problem. However, there are things parents can do to reduce the likelihood of homosexuality becoming a preference of their children.

1. *Affirm gender and encourage gender specific behaviors and activities.* You must take every opportunity to positively affirm your children's gender. Children should regularly hear affirming statements about their gender ("I'm so glad God made you a girl"). You should use every opportunity to connect your children's behavior and development to their gender. Boys need to be encouraged to behave as males and do male activities and girls need to be encouraged to behave as females and do female activities. You must teach against chauvinism, sexism, and other negative attitudes toward the opposite gender. But children need healthy feelings concerning their masculinity or femininity. Encourage pride and acceptance in your child's gender. Both genders are uniquely designed by God, and children need proud, positive

attitudes regarding their own gender. You help promote such attitudes in children by accepting them and discouraging society's unisex attempts to remove distinctions between men and women. Men and women are truly equal, but they are also very different. Our children need to learn this lesson.

Negative, critical attitudes aimed at an entire sex can cause children to reject themselves as part of a whole gender. Parents of both sexes must accept maleness and femaleness and project positive attitudes toward both genders. Such acceptance helps children understand and accept his or her maleness or femaleness. Children reared in homes where positive attitudes toward both genders are taught and demonstrated have healthy sexual identities. You should use every occasion to remark and affirm your children's gender as a gift from God. Hopefully, this will cause them to fully accept their gender.

2. *Same-sex parents must be effective role models.* In order for parents to properly demonstrate how an adult of their sex acts, time must be generously spent with children. The reader must be thinking at this point that I have a one-track mind because over and over again I have advised and encouraged parents to spend time with their kids. But I know of no other way to effectively teach and train children apart from time invested in them. Little boys will only learn to be men by observing and doing. Girls become women by watching and engaging in activities with their mothers. To develop healthy gender identities children must spend time with same-sex parents. It is critically important that same-sex parents are available to spend time with their children during the first five years of their lives. It is also of great importance for early adolescent children

of both sexes to spend both quality and quantity time with their same-sex parents. Effective parental role modeling is crucial for the prevention of homosexuality.

3. *Protect young children.* Furnishing young children with gruesome details concerning homosexuality can confuse and frighten them. However, children must be protected from the many dangerous influences in today's world. We have talked about preventing molestation, and I gave several suggestions to help children avoid dangerous situations. If younger children have been properly trained to avoid unfamiliar situations and people, they will have no need for explicit information regarding homosexuals. Graphic descriptions of any kind of sexual abuse should be shunned. The pivotal issue in protecting young children is being aware of potentially harmful circumstances or situations. For example, parents should be well acquainted with babysitters, nursery attendants, neighborhood parents, and all other persons with whom their children might have unsupervised contact. If parents have any doubts or suspicious, keep your children away from the person in question. Unfortunately our world is not always a nice place, and the protection of our children demands high parental visibility.

4. *Encourage Teenagers to Avoid Certain Situations.* Teenagers should be helped to avoid situations where temptations may arise. As has been discussed earlier, many teens are easily confused when they have homosexual thoughts, impulses or engage in same-sex play. They fear the experimentation may cause them to become homosexual. In addition to relieving their fears, you should suggest ways for teens to avoid tempting situations. For example, when friends stay the night suggest that they not

sleep together. Also in parental discussions regarding masturbation, you should tell them that even if they occasionally feel the need to masturbate, under no circumstances should it be done in the presence of others. In addition, encourage teens to report immediately to you any time they are propositioned by someone of either sex. Temptations avoided are temptations defeated.

5. *Avoid overprotection.* Overprotection, especially with males, produces children who are uncertain and afraid and who begin to view themselves as sissies or as people who cannot do the things others of their gender can do. Mothers will often need the help of fathers in determining when they are being overprotective with their sons. Boys need to grow up taking a certain amount of healthy risk, so they can feel good about their manhood.

6. A*void critical judgmental attitudes with your children.* Children in this society have enough opportunities to view themselves in the negative light of self-criticism. They do not need parents who continually make derogatory and disapproving remarks and who display judgmental attitudes toward their behavior. We must be positive with our children, especially with regard to their gender and gender specific behavior.

Preventing homosexuality, like preventing other forms of sin, involves a lifetime of teaching and modeling. Hopefully you will find the suggestions I have given to be helpful and beneficial. But, please remember to seek God's guidance often when confronting these difficult parenting tasks.

Most people, including many Christians, have a strong aversion to homosexuals. This extreme repugnance causes many to develop what some psychologists and counselors are calling "homophobia" — fear of homosexuality. And unfortunately, many Christians do not attempt to help homosexuals, but instead completely reject them and view this sin as being the worst possible sin. Parents often reject their own children because of homophobia. Such intense feelings raise two very important questions: What specifically does the Bible say about homosexuality, and how should Christians treat homosexuals?

There are references to homosexuality in both the Old and New Testaments. (Genesis 19:1-10, Leviticus 18:22, 20:13, Romans 1:25-27, 1 Corinthians 6:9-11). While God's word does not dwell at length on homosexual behavior and does not seem to regard it as worse than heterosexual sins, the Bible does plainly judge homosexuality as sin. The Bible also clearly condemns heterosexual intercourse outside of marriage. So homosexual acts as well as heterosexual acts outside of marriage are both sin. But fleeting sexual thoughts of any kind are not sin unless dwelt on to the point of fantasy, at which time they become sin. All sexual lusts, fantasies, and acts are sinful when practiced outside of God's plan.

My point is simply this: practicing homosexuality is sin, but the homosexual should be treated as any other person who commits sin. Our response ought to be exactly the same as toward any other sinner. A Christian response to homosexuals should not be fear and critical judgment (homophobia). We should attempt through love and kindness to persuade homosexuals to accept redemption by the blood of Jesus. In 1 Corinthians 6:9-10, homosexuality is listed with a group of other sins, and it goes on to say that such people will not inherit the kingdom of God. But in verse 11 we read: "And that is what some of you were. But you were washed, you were sanctified, you were justified in the name of the Lord Jesus Christ." The homosexual's only hope rests in the grace, forgiveness, and lordship of Jesus. A cure will also involve good professional counseling, and a desire to be cured, but apart from the blood of Jesus there is no forgiveness of sins.

Parents must do all within their power to prevent homosexuality in their children. But you should also teach children that God loves and desires to redeem all sinners, including homosexuals. One of the most outstanding and obvious characteristics our Lord displayed while on earth was his compassion. I believe He wants us to teach our children to treat homosexuals much the same way as we are told he treated the woman caught in adultery in John, chapter eight. He understood that love, not judgement, has a greater likelihood of producing true repentance in people.

Much of the information in this section on homosexuality was obtained in a conversation with Chris Austin, Ph.D. Chris has authored a great book on counseling homosexuals (*Cleaning Out the Closet*) and has another in progress. Chris has had great success counseling with homosexuals and helping them turn their lives around. He is currently working out of the counseling center at the South MacArthur Church of Christ in Irving, Texas.

Single Parents and Sexuality

Single parenting is no doubt one of the most difficult and demanding tasks that a person can ever confront. A major concern for mothers raising sons alone is their boys' sexual development. The greatest fear many mothers have regarding their sons concerns homosexuality. These mothers fear that in homes where the father is absent there will be an increased likelihood of homosexuality. In her excellent book *Single Mothers Raising Sons,* Bobbie Reed states that after much research, she found no significant correlation between being raised by a single mom and being homosexual. [12] However, at least one study has shown that early adolescents in one-parent homes are more prone to engage in sexual activity.[13]

We have already discussed the complicated and controversial theories related to the causes of homosexuality, and while mothers cannot be blamed for their son's sexual orientation, there are some things mothers can do to encourage the development of a healthy sexual orientation. Here are a few suggestions:

1. *Confront your own emotions about your former spouse.* Divorced parents will have some powerful feelings concerning their former spouse. Do not make the mistake of thinking that you are concealing these negative emotions from your children. You should, however, not allow these feelings to cause you to over-generalize about all males or females. Attempt to confront your emotions and feelings and take measures to settle them; do not communicate them to your children.

2. *Provide good male role models for your son.* Moms need to work at finding good role models for their sons. The key here is good role models. Coaches and other males can, unfortunately, be negative role models. Strive to select positive male role models and use negative modeling situations as opportunities to teach. Mothers should not attempt to be both parents. It may also be helpful to

encourage a relationship with the same-sex parent.

3. *Avoid overprotecting your son.* Single mothers especially need to avoid overprotection because this practice tends to produce immature and overly dependent young men who lack confidence in their ability. This kind of dependence on the mother may contribute to a homosexual orientation.

4. *Avoid excessively dominant behavior.* Mothers raising sons alone often feel the need to become very dominant. They assume that boys need a firm hand and since the father is gone, they need to become tougher and more dominant. Single mothers certainly need to discipline their male children assertively, but extreme dominance should be avoided. One study of homosexuals found that 76 percent had dominating mothers.[14]

5. *Encourage your son to develop a healthy attitude toward both sexes.* Single mothers should not criticize and belittle men in general. Your sons need to know that all men are not bad or evil. If boys have been taught that men are evil creatures, how will they be able to accept their own manhood? Encourage your sons to have friends of both sexes, and to view both sexes as being capable of good and evil.

6. *Give emotionally to your child.* Single mothers sometimes consume all the energy and time of their sons, in an effort to meet their own emotional needs. Mothers must not move the child into the role of the spouse. Mothers must branch out and become involved in a variety of activities, thereby freeing their sons to develop healthy attitudes and activities.

So far we have confined our discussion of single parenting to mothers raising sons. Single parents, again mostly mothers, also must rear daughters. Most mothers, however, feel more confident in this role because they know from experience how girls should act and feel. But single mothers of daughters should also avoid certain pitfalls. For example, a mother should not overly criticize men, especially her daughter's father. In order for young girls to develop healthy attitudes toward men, they must not be exposed to constant negative criticism of males. The importance of a father figure for teenage girls has already been established. The single mother should encourage a good relationship between her daughter and the child's father. If such a relationship is not possible, then mothers must seek positive male substitutes (grandfather, uncles, youth ministers, etc.).

The subject of single parenting is much too complex to be totally discussed in this work. We are focusing on sex education and the promotion of healthy, godly sexual attitudes and orientations. In seeking to prevent premature sexual activity and to avoid homosexual orientation, it is of paramount importance for single parents to live sexually and morally pure lives. A wholesome example of godly attitudes and behavior will have more influence on children than any other single factor. When parents are striving to live according to God's will and plan, children will not fail to notice and emulate their attitude.

Single parents, like all parents, need to provide wholesome, godly, sex education for their children. The principles contained in this book can be taught and practiced by single parents. Your task will be more difficult because you will not have anyone with which to share the work and stress of sex education. But plunge ahead and when additional help is needed, find sources for such help. For example, do not hesitate to call upon ministers, counselors, relatives, or anyone who can teach and demonstrate healthy sexual attitudes to your children. Ask the Lord to provide help — He has promised to provide!

Pornography and the Internet

Our society is inundated with sex and eroticism. We are constantly bombarded many times each day with sexual images and references. These images and references intrude into our lives via television, movies, billboards, magazines, music, and general conversation. Sexually explicit language and messages are almost impossible to filter out of our lives. Unfortunately, no matter how hard we try to shelter or protect our children, they will hear and see a great deal of sexually explicit material. Many parents are very naïve concerning the kinds of sexual materials that are popular and available to children. For many parents the term "pornography" conjures memories of *Playboy* magazines viewed during their adolescence. However, the pornography available when most of us grew up is extremely mild compared with what our children are exposed to today. Our children can find much more sexual content channel surfing on television that we could in *Playboy*. In fact, the first center-fold model in *Playboy* magazine during the middle 1950s exposed less of her body than can be seen today on the cover of almost any modern woman's magazine. The availability of hard-core pornography is becoming one of the biggest threats to the healthy development of our children's sexual attitudes and behaviors. Pornography is especially alluring to young boys before and around the age of puberty because they are deeply impressed by any form of visual sexual stimuli. Dr. Archibald Hart in his book *The Sexual Man* found that 94 percent of all males surveyed reported exposure to pornography and that the first exposure to pornography in the majority of the sample occurred between the ages of 13 and 15.[15] A primary consumer group of pornography is adolescent males ages 12 to 17. Unfortunately, scores and scores of pubescent boys all over this country are learning to use pornography as a sexual outlet during the period from puberty until marriage. Such habitual use of pornography is proving both addictive and extremely destructive.

In this section of the book, we will examine the effects of pornography on our children and discuss the easy access to pornography provided by the Internet. We will also suggest specific things you can do to protect your children from this depraved menace.

In today's world it is probably as easy and as likely for your child to run onto hard-core pornography on the Internet as it was for you to chance onto a *Playboy* during your childhood. Parents must be particularly concerned these days with the widespread availability of pornography through the Internet. Consider the following facts:

- Adult entertainment on the Internet is the third largest sector of sales, surpassed only by computer products and travel. Just one World Wide Web site that offers pornographic materials reported receiving nearly 1.5 million visits, or "hits," per day.[16]
- According to the *Washington Post*, adult sites generate an estimated one billion dollars in revenue yearly.
- The *Playboy* web site has received 4.7 million hits in one seven-day period.[17]
- Most Internet service providers provide public access to hundreds of USENET

newsgroups that are specifically reserved for posting explicit and extreme categories of pornography (i.e., alt.sex.snuff.cannibalism, a l t . s e x . b e a s t i a l i t y , alt.binaries.pictures.erotica.teens, etc.). All these are as freely accessible to an intrepid ten-year-old as to an adult.[18]

Any child with a computer and modem can access pornographic material in seconds. In some instances children can click on picture files, and images appear on the screen–free of charge. Any computer literate child can view adult pornography from *Playboy* or *Penthouse*, as well as unthinkable obscenities such as people having sex with animals, men engaged in sex acts with children, and the rape and mutilation of women. Once such material has been seen, the images can never be erased from the mind. There is considerable evidence that children are being exposed to violent and sexually explicit material while online. Children can access such pornography unintentionally or intentionally.

Before we look at the harmful effects of pornography, let me assure you that every child who happens to view some pornography will not be traumatized. The effects of pornography are progressive and addictive, and just like every child who takes a drink will not become an alcoholic, every child who is exposed to pornography will not automatically begin to sexually act out or become a sexual deviant. However, since pornography is so prevalent in our society, it is important for us to examine the many negative effects of pornography and the ways that pornography can potentially harm our children.

The negative and harmful effects of pornography

1. *Pornography encourages sexual expression without responsibility.* Exposure to pornography often results in sexually transmitted diseases, unplanned pregnancies, and sexual addiction. As we have previously noted, STDs are rampant and teenage pregnancy rates are also very high. Pornography not only promotes sexual acting out, but it is self-perpetuating and addictive. Research indicates that males who are exposed to a great deal of erotica before the age of 14 are more sexually active and engage in more varied sexual behaviors.[19]

2. *Exposure to pornography threatens to make children victims of sexual violence.* Pedophiles and sexual predators are frequent users of all types of pornography. The more pornography these individuals are exposed to, the more the likelihood they will act on what they see and abuse children.

3. *Pornography almost universally presents a degrading and victimizing view of women.* Women are often presented as passive objects of men's sexual desire and women are not portrayed as having value or function apart from their bodies. Pornography often presents women as objects of violence, degradation, and torture. Pornography of this type is being linked with the victimization of women.

4. *Pornography presents human bodies in unrealistic ways that are likely to result in harmful comparisons with a married partner.* Pornography depicts ideal bodies doing fantasized acts under ideal conditions. Very often the pictures seen are of people under ideal conditions of make-up and lighting and the final images are "air brushed" to make everything look perfect. The problem is that a real person in a real

marriage under normal conditions of work, worry, stress, and child rearing, will never look like the perfect images portrayed in pornographic pictures. Such idealized comparisons can be devastating to a marital relationship.

5. *Extended exposure to pornography destroys normal libido or sexual urge.* Pornography is very often associated with masturbation, and when men repeatedly masturbate to the images of perfect, "air-brushed" women, a typical woman will not cause the same arousal. So it is possible over time to no longer be aroused by one's mate because she does not measure up to the altered images of pornography.

6. *Exposure to pornography interferes with a child's healthy sexual development and identity.* As we have discussed, sexual identity develops gradually through childhood and adolescence. As children grow and mature, they are especially susceptible to influences affecting their development. Exposure to healthy sexual norms and attitudes results in the child developing healthy sexual orientation. Pornography, on the other hand, distorts the normal developmental process and exposes the child prematurely to sexual deviance and misinformation. Such misinformation leaves the child confused and damaged. Pornography also interferes with the emotional and spiritual development of children.

7. *Pornography is progressive and addictive.* Dr. Victor Cline, a clinical psychologist at the University of Utah and a specialist in the area of sexual addiction, says in regard to the compulsive or addictive nature of pornography: "In over 26 years, I have treated approximately 350 males afflicted with sexual addictions. In 94 percent of the cases I have found that pornography was a contributor,

facilitator, or direct causal agent in the acquiring of these sexual illnesses."[20]

What should parents do?

The best way to reduce the damaging effects of pornography on our children is to prevent pornography from entering their lives. Gone are the days when finding a *Playboy* under our son's bed causes us to simply say, "Boys will be boys!" We must do everything in our power to reduce our children's exposure to pornography. Here are some suggestions to prevent exposure and reduce the damaging effects of pornography.

1. *Anticipate that your children will be exposed to pornography; prepare them.* We must begin from a very early age to precondition them with a positive view of sex so that if they are exposed to pornography, they will see its negative, grotesque, and dangerous depictions of sex as deviant. They will know that such images are not in-keeping with a godly, healthy view of sex. Prior to puberty (age 7-10), begin discussing the subject of pornography openly and make them aware of possible situations involving pornography. Your goal should be to keep the subject open and to look for opportunities to have discussions with them on this important topic.

2. *Control and filter your children's environment.* We have already discussed at length how to manage and control your children's access to TV. We must also control and filter their exposure to movies and other forms of media. If you have Internet access in your home, you should have some form of censoring software. Several elaborate screens and blocks have been developed to keep children away from Internet pornography. Some of the favorite ones are: Net

Nanny (http://www.netnanny.com), Surfwatch (http://www.surfwatch.com), and Cyberpatrol (http://microsys.com.). These three can be downloaded from the Internet. Bess, the Internet Retriever, is a blocking system from the Internet service provider N2H2. Yahooligans (http://www.yahooligans.com) is offered by the search engine company Yahoo. Many other providers offer their own brands of protection. Unfortunately, the problem with these software restraints is that they often do not work. Computer-literate children, especially teens, can often work around these restraints. In an effort to control and purify the environment, I suggest that children not be allowed to have televisions and computers in their rooms. Your home computer should be in a very public room of your house and children should not be allowed to use the Internet if parents are not at home. Internet pornography is not child's play; it is very dangerous, and we must make every effort to protect our children.

3. *Establish house rules governing the Internet.* Every family should draft its own Internet use policy. We must accept the preventive role of setting limits that keep our children safe from harmful material and predators. In her excellent book *Kids Online: Protecting Your Children in Cyberspace*, Donna Rice Hughes suggests that your house rules include concerns every parent should discuss with his or her children. She calls her list the "Top Ten Things to Tell Your Child."

- Never fill out questionnaires or any forms online or give out personal information about yourself or anyone else without Mom's or Dad's permission.

- Never agree to meet in person with anyone you have spoken to online without Mom's or Dad's presence.
- Never enter a chat room without Mom's or Dad's presence or supervision. Some "kids" you meet in chat rooms may not really be kids.
- Never tell anyone online where you will be or what you will be doing without Mom's or Dad's permission.
- Never respond to or send e-mail to new people you meet online.
- Never go into a new online area that is going to cost additional money without first getting Mom's or Dad's permission.
- Never send, without Mom's or Dad's permission, a picture over the Internet or via regular mail to anyone you've met on the Internet.
- Never buy or order products online or give out any credit card information online without Mom's or Dad's permission.
- Never respond to belligerent or suggestive contact or anything that makes you feel uncomfortable. End such an experience by logging off and telling your mom or dad as soon as possible.
- Always tell Mom or Dad about something you saw, intentionally or unintentionally, that is upsetting. (It is better for your child's mental health to be able to discuss exposure to pornography than for it to become a dark and confusing secret.)[21]

4. *Determine when your child is ready to go online.* Determining when your child is ready to go online

does not depend on her ability to use a computer. We must be sure our children are mature enough to follow the house rules and not accidentally become exposed to pornography. It is much better for our children to be older when they go online than to allow them to log on unsupervised and risk contact with pornography.

5. *Parents should avoid all forms of pornography themselves.* During the past year, I have counseled with several men that have a problem with pornography and all of these men are fathers. It is vital that parents keep themselves pure and avoid all forms of pornography. Our children need positive role models who practice purity.

6. *Monitor your children's exposure to the Internet at school and public libraries.* Do not assume that your children will be adequately supervised while using computers at school or the public library. The anti-pornography group Enough is Enough reports that the American Library Association's list of "50 Great Sites for Kids" provides unsupervised children in libraries with sites equipped with "hot links" only six clicks away from Internet pornography. [22] So far, libraries have resisted any Internet screening as an invasion of childrens' right to privacy. We must make sure our children are not being exposed to the Internet without proper supervision. We must make it our business to check out Internet access in schools, libraries, and friend's homes.

The subject of Internet pornography has far-reaching implications and a complete, in-depth examination is beyond our scope in this work. However, I highly recommend a book that looks at the subject of children, computers, the Internet, and pornography: *Kids Online: Protecting Your Children in Cyberspace*, by Donna Rice Hughes, published by

Fleming H. Revell (1998). This book, as well as other resources, will help parents protect their children from the damaging and harmful effects of pornography.

For Further Thought

1. What specific plans do you have to inform your daughter or son about STDs and AIDS/HIV?

2. In your opinion, should teenagers be provided with factual information regarding contraception and birth control? If your child, though having been taught that premarital sex is wrong, chose to engage in such activity, would you advise him to protect himself? Do you believe this sends a double message?

3. How does your child feel about contraception/birth control and "double messages?" How can you find out?

4. What are your attitudes and feelings regarding abortion? Is abortion an option in cases of rape or when the life of the mother is in danger?

5. Write a letter to your teenager explaining your feelings about abortion. Deliver the letter and use it as a discussion starter.

6. What prejudices prevent you from viewing life as sacred and dignified?

7. Ask your children to recall the last time you asked for their forgiveness.

8. Ask your child to define homosexuality (if he/she is old enough). What are the sources of his/her information?

9. Ask your son if he has ever worried about being homosexual. Ask why.

10. Discuss "homophobia" with your teenage children.

11. What activities do you do with your son/daughter that promote and foster positive gender identification?

12. If you are a single mother with one or more male children, make a list of possible male role models for your son.
13. Ask your child (adolescent or pre-adolescent) if you are overprotective. If he says yes, ask for an explanation.
14. Relate some of your fears as a single parent to your children. Discuss them.
15. What are your feelings and experiences with pornography?
16. What specific plans do you have to purify your children's TV and computer environment?
17. Make specific plans to discuss pornography with your age-appropriate children.
18. Read John 8:1-11 with your children. How does this episode relate to abortion, homosexuality, etc.?

---

[1] Pogany, *Sex Smart*, 157-158.

[2] Centers for Disease Control and Prevention, Division of STD/HIV Prevention, Atlanta, 1996.

[3] Jones, *How & When to Tell Your Kids About Sex*, 17.

[4] J. M. Karon, et al., "Prevalence of HIV infection in the U.S. 1984-1992," *Journal of the American Medical Association*, July 1996, 276 (2): 126-131.

[5] " Test Trace Origin of HIV to Chimps," *Dallas Morning News*, Monday, Feb. 1, 1999.

[6] Pogany, *Sex Smart*, 178.

[7] Jones, *How & When to Tell Your Kids About Sex*, 233.

[8] Ron Rose, telephone interview, Nov. 11, 1987.

[9] David Lewis and Carley Dodd, *National Adolescent Survey.* 1998 Youth & Family Ministry Conference.

[10] Hart, et. al., *Secrets of Eve*, 191.

[11] Francis A. Schaeffer and C. Everett Koop, *Whatever Happened to the Human Race?* (Old Tappan: Fleming H. Revell, 1979), 113.

[12] Reed, *Single Mothers Raising Sons*, 133.

[13] Rainy, *Parenting Today's Adolescent*, 99.

[14] Lush, *Mothers and Sons*, 106.

[15] Hart , *Sexual Man,* 89.

[16] John Simons, " The Web's Dirty Secret," *U. S. News and World Report* , August 19, 1996, 51-52.

[17] Donna Rice Hughes, *Kids Online* (Grand Rapids: Fleming H. Revell, 1998), 53.

[18] Randall E. Stross, " The Cyber View Squad," *U. S. News and World Report,* March 17, 1997, 45.

[19] Hart, *Sexual Man* , 90.

[20] Hughes, *Kids Online,* 94.

[21] Ibid, 107-108.

[22] Medved, *Saving Childhood,* 91.

12
Final Thoughts

Being able to provide honest, accurate, and helpful sexual information in an atmosphere of openness and caring represents the ideal goal of sex education. However, in the real world the ideal often does not happen. Many parents have the desire to provide sex education for their children but lack the skills or resources necessary to do a thorough job. Other parents are simply not comfortable discussing sexual matters. I believe that parents can do an effective job of teaching their children healthy, godly sexual attitudes and behaviors when the desire and the resources are available. Hopefully, this book will provide some of the resources. There are many other good books to assist you. However, the greatest resource available to you should be provided by the church.

The Church's Role

Our churches must begin to become actively involved in the sex education of our children. Most parents object to sex education taught by the public schools because such teaching generally ignores the moral and spiritual aspects of sexuality. Therefore, logically, churches should help provide sex education resources to families. Providing sexual resources and help for parents during the coming millennium will be one of the church's greatest challenges. It could also be one of the church's greatest legacies. Churches can assist families with regard to sexual matters in several ways. Here are a few.

1. *Provide sex education classes for families.* Ideally, trained ministers and counselors would teach parents how to provide sex education in the home and should help parents create the open environment so vital to sex education. Churches should have regular, ongoing classes designed to equip parents with the necessary skills to teach effectively on all sexual matters. Churches should also have sex education courses specifically designed for children of all ages, especially adolescents. Sex education taught by trained church personnel should complement what is being taught in the home. Children should be receiving moral and spiritual teaching on human sexuality at church, and then have such teaching reinforced at home by additional teaching and demonstration. Such repetition of godly teaching is necessary to offset the constant bombardment of sexual material heaped on children by the media.

Many issues would need to be negotiated and settled before a church could begin a program of sex education. At what age do the classes begin? At what age do the sexes attend the same class? How do you handle the more controversial issues? There are many other topics, as well, that should be carefully discussed before any church embarks on such a program. But offering such classes to families should be a high priority for churches. Of course parental involvement would be necessary from the beginning. It has been my experience that when parents are involved and communicated with, they will support such a program.

A youth minister friend of mine organized sex education classes for junior high students in an effective and non-threatening manner. On Sunday night the class material would be presented to the parents. The parents had an opportunity to hear, experience, and discuss all the issues that were to be presented to their children. Then on the following Wednesday evening the material was taught to the junior high students. This schedule encouraged parental participation and involvement, while at the same time providing needed sex education to the students. Church leaders and parents cooperated for the benefit of their children. There are some excellent, biblically-based curriculum resources available from several major Christian distributors (Youth Specialties, Group, Josh McDowell, etc.). You must insist on such help from your church. And if help is not forthcoming, you may have to find another church that will assist you in providing biblical sex education for your children.

2. *Provide a library of resources.* Churches should maintain a library of helpful books, periodicals, audio and video tapes, and other resource material. There are many helpful books available on the subject of sex education. Many parents will check out and use helpful resources when available. When sex education classes are being offered it helps to have the material available for parental inspection. After examining curriculum, parents feel more at ease and will probably be more supportive. Most books and other resources are relatively inexpensive, and it would not be difficult to begin a library of beneficial sexual information resources.

3. *Provide opportunities for teens to be exposed to real life situations.* Teens and pre-teens need to be informed about the many negative consequences of

sex, but rather than simply telling them, we should help them see these consequences. For example, have several unwed mothers speak to your youth group; have someone in his or her twenties or thirties talk about his or her infertility as the result of a sexually transmitted disease. In my church several women have come forward and revealed painful experiences of abortion, stating they would be willing to talk privately with any girl struggling with pregnancy choices. I once invited a college student, who had not been sexually abstinent, to speak to our girls about how she would have been better off if she had remained a virgin. The opportunities are limitless! Teenagers are much more affected by clear presentations of negative consequences of sexual experimentation by real people than by dry, boring lectures from adults.

4. *Provide parental support groups.* Churches should encourage and organize parental support groups on a variety of issues. When functioning properly, the church is a supporting community of believers who sustain and serve one another. Support groups consist of small numbers of parents who are either presently experiencing, or have experienced similar situations and circumstances. Such groups meet regularly to encourage, serve, support and love one another. Hurting parents benefit greatly by being part of a group that understands and listens.

The sexual sins of a child usually produce a tremendous amount of guilt in Christian parents. As a result of this guilt and accompanying embarrassment, parents will probably not voluntarily join a support group advertised as being for parents with sexually active children. Church leaders must be creative and subtle in providing help for hurting parents. For example, for years in my church we had regular, general parental support group meetings called H.E.L.P. (Help, Encouragement, and Learning for Parents). At these meetings a pre-arranged topic encourages participation by all parents of adolescents. These parental meetings have two purposes: to provide help, encouragement, and peer support for parents in a non-threatening and general environment, and to encourage parents with specific adolescent problems to seek help from the appropriate group.

In other words, when parents begin attending the H.E.L.P. meetings and the staff discovers, or the parents admit, specific problems, then they can be directed to functioning support groups designed to deal with their particular concern. When handled sensitively, this procedure integrates hurting parents with others who have had similar experiences, and it also avoids public embarrassment. Most churches are full of parents who have experienced painful problems with their children. Some of the parents have successfully solved these problems and others have learned from their mistakes. Many are very willing to encourage and help others who are having similar struggles. Such sharing, encouraging, listening and supporting helps parents survive difficult struggles with their children. As Christians we are to "bear... one another's burdens" (Gal. 6:2). Hurting parents are provided much support and encouragement by receiving help from others who have been through similar situations.

If your church is not large enough or does not have trained staff to assist with support groups, perhaps you might join with other churches in your area to furnish this needed help. In addition, there are parachurch organizations in many cities that provide parental support groups. You can obtain information about parental support groups by calling youth ministers, counselors, preachers, and other church leaders. Hopefully, your church already has a support group helping parents cope with sexual as well as other adolescent problems, but if not, perhaps you can help start such a program. The benefits of parents helping parents are great, and parental support groups should be a high priority of churches.

5. *Provide professional counseling.* Many churches have trained counselors as part of their regular ministerial staff. These skilled professionals can provide much-needed counseling during times of crisis. Hurting families receive many benefits when churches offer this service. Churches that lack the means to furnish staff counselors can help families with adolescent problems in at least two ways. First, the church staff could contain a qualified youth minister. Most youth ministers have some training in counseling and can deal effectively with most typical adolescent problems. Often the most beneficial counseling resource youth ministers can provide involves helping parents determine when professional counseling assistance is needed. A qualified youth minister should be able to differentiate between normal transitional adolescent problems and deviant behavior that requires the services of a professional counselor.

Churches can also help families with adolescent problems by developing a working relationship with several Christian counselors in their area. Pastors, youth ministers, and other church leaders should know and be familiar with local counselors and psychologists. This contact will help church leaders direct families to the appropriate professional for their particular problem. Good Christian counselors who combine professional training with adherence to God's principles are valuable assets to parents struggling with major adolescent problems.

6. *Provide an active, effective youth program.* The general conclusion of much research is that personal religious devotion is a strong protective influence against sexual experimentation. Youth programs can help teenagers remain sexually pure by surrounding them with a positive peer support group, and by offering programs and experiences that minimize sexual opportunities and encourage group activities. Teens handle sexual pressure much more effectively in a peer context than with parents or adults. Teens who are part of a loving, active, and serving Christian youth group have an easier time resisting sexual temptation.

Youth ministry programs can assist teens in avoiding sexual misconduct in at least two ways. First, the program must emphasize sound biblical teaching on sexual issues. Biblical teaching on sexual matters should be integrated into Sunday school curriculum on a regular basis and can be very effective as a part of a retreat or camp program. This kind of teaching will help negate the onslaught of sexual stimulus teens receive from society.

A second way that the youth program can help teens avoid sexual problems relates to specific activities within the program. For example, youth activities that promote one-on-one boy/girl relationships, especially with young adolescents, should be discouraged. Instead, activities should be structured around groups of boys and girls. Activities must also attempt to avoid pushing young boys and girls together before they are old enough for such relationships.

I mentioned the situation that arose at our summer camp, where somehow the tradition of taking "dates" to our final evening hike and devotional began with the older campers. Before long, through pressure and example, we had third- and fourth-grade girls devastated because they did not have a date to the bonfire, or because they had a date with the wrong person. No one on our staff encouraged or anticipated this problem. Youth ministers must not only plan activities that avoid boy/girl relationships for those too young, but they must also actively organize and promote activities that stress group dating.

Churches also need to find ways to provide their young people with positive peer pressure. Christian teens need to function as support groups, helping each other stand up against the enormous sexual pressures of today's society. The church can, and must be, the special place where our children learn about sexuality, and where they receive protection and help as they learn to cope with their sexuality.

Fear Versus Lordship

Many of the wonderful books available today on the subject of teenage sexuality or sex education contain large sections devoted to the reasons teenagers have sex, and reasons they should not have sex. These books, and the particular sections that concentrate on causes and prevention, are excellent resources. I have, however, deliberately chosen not to focus on such lists in this work. Many of the causes of teenage promiscuity are obvious, others controversial. There is perhaps some benefit derived from examining causes, but in order to effectively help teens avoid premarital sexual involvement, parents must begin early, teaching and demonstrating wholesome, godly sexual values and attitudes. When Christian values and accurate information are provided in an atmosphere of openness and love, children will be much less likely to succumb to sexual temptations. Our energy should be concentrated on providing positive, on-going sex education for our children.

This book was written as a resource designed to help you as you attempt to help your children avoid sexual sin. Hopefully, the principles stressed here will help you teach about human sexuality from a Christian perspective. Unfortunately, too many parents fail to provide early sexual training to their children, and later, when the children reach adolescence, the parents attempt to use scare tactics and fear to prevent sexual activity. The use of fear becomes a substitute for continual and accurate sex education.

I am not saying that teenagers should not be warned about the possible consequences of sexual sins. They need to know that if they engage in sexual intercourse devastating consequences are a possibility. They need to know that even though God forgives sin, he does not remove the consequences of sin. God will forgive sexual sins, but if pregnancy occurs, there will be a baby nine months later. There are terrible consequences to sexual sins. But after many years of working directly with teens and pre-teens, and helping rear two teens of my own, I am convinced there is only one sure antidote for sexual promiscuity: the lordship of Jesus Christ.

It is appropriate to use a certain amount of healthy fear to help your teens avoid sexual involvement. In fact, in the 1998 survey conducted by the Center for Adolescent Studies at Abilene

Christian University, the first three reasons teens listed as the reasons they abstained from sexual activity were fear of AIDS, fear of other STDs, and fear of pregnancy.[1] It is certainly a good idea to tell teens that if they are sexually active, possible consequences might involve pregnancy, AIDS, sexually transmitted diseases, and other physical and emotional problems. However, avoid the temptation to use fear as the only or primary teaching method. This distorts the biblical message of true sexuality. Begin early in the life of your children to teach the concept of the Lordship of Jesus. Christian teens need to be taught to avoid sexual sins because they have given their lives to Jesus. The apostle Paul says in 1 Corinthians 6:18-20:

> Flee from sexual immorality. All other sins a man commits are outside his body, but he who sins sexually sins against his own body. Do you not know that your body is a temple of the Holy Spirit, who is in you, whom you have received from God? You are not your own; you were bought at a price. Therefore honor God with your body.

Teenagers need to be taught to avoid sexual activity because they have been "bought at a price." Their bodies have been purchased and house the Holy Spirit of God. They flee sexual sins because of the tremendous hurt such activity causes their Lord.

Teens need to also understand that sex is much more than a physical experience. Sex has tremendous spiritual dimensions and implications. Let me explain with a letter my wife was asked to write to the teenage girls in our church.

A Spiritual Act

"James and I broke up last night. He said he didn't want to be with me anymore."

I listened to the story which has the same plot (with name changes) that I have heard hundreds of times. She just knew they were in love; in fact, they were going to look at promise rings not long ago. What had happened? How could he be so cruel?

As a teacher who makes no secret of her beliefs about chastity and sexual purity, I often have students confess their sexual sins to me. I have come to believe that they choose me from their circle of adults as a test—to see if I will still love them after finding out that they have sinned. I do. But I sometimes wish that my love for them gave me a special language to communicate the things about sex that **I know** to be true.

I know that sex is more than a physical act. Sex cannot be compared to hunger. You feel hunger pangs; you naturally seek to relieve those pangs by eating. The world will tell you that sexual longing, like hunger, should be relieved by gratifying your sexual need. Don't listen—it's a lie.

Sex involves more than your body. In fact, the principal component of sex is spiritual rather than physical. Consider this: Why did God forbid the Israelites to intermarry with pagans? Why was Jesus' first miracle performed at a wedding? Why does Paul compare the relationship between married people to the relationship that Christ has with the church? While I do not presume to know the mind of God, I believe it is safe to say that God intends for us to recognize that when we give our bodies to someone through the sexual act, we have also committed to them a part of our spirit.

When you give your body to someone sexually, you allow yourself to be totally vulnerable. Sexual gratification involves the abandonment of self. Similar to the way that you physically expose your body, your psyche is exposed to your partner. I have been married for over thirty years, and the only way that I know to describe the mystery of marital sex is to compare it to when I accepted the Lordship of Christ. When Paul discusses the relationships of man and wife and the relationship of Lord Jesus and his disciples in Ephesians, he refers to it as a "profound mystery." When I accepted Christ as Lord, I **exposed** myself with all my imperfections. By becoming completely vulnerable (by confession) I became **one** with Christ. I abandoned myself and my will to the entity and will of Christ. I strive in my daily life to become **one** with Christ. I **became** one with my husband when we were married. In my mind the analogy of sex and spiritual commitment is obvious.

I often wonder if my students would give their chastity away so casually if they knew how easily this sexual act could be compared to idolatry. Very few of my students would knowingly bow down in front of a figure of Baal. I do not know of a single student (present or past) who would consciously say, " I choose to thumb my nose at God!" Most of my students really want to be pleasing to God. They just fail to recognize sex as a spiritual act. God knew when he forbade the Israelites to intermarry with the pagans, that the pagans, through the intimacy gained through the sexual act, would lead the Israelites into idolatry. Jesus recognized and sanctioned the spiritual nature of marriage by blessing the ceremony with his first miracle. Paul recognized the suitableness of comparing marriage (and inferentially the sexual act) to the acceptance of Christ as Lord by using the comparison in Ephesians. Why do we twentieth-century humans have such difficulty recognizing idolatry in the form of sexual gratification? It's because we have bought the lie. We believe that sex is only a **physical** act. I am here to testify that sex is **more** than a physical act. Sex is also a spiritual act. As with all spiritual acts, treat it with reverence.

Romans 12:1-2: Therefore, I urge you, brothers, in view of God's mercy, to offer your bodies as living sacrifices, holy and pleasing to God — this is your spiritual act of worship. Do not conform any longer to the pattern of this world, but be transformed by the renewing of your mind. Then you will be able to test and approve what God's will is — his good, pleasing and perfect will.

My experience as a parent and a youth minister tells me that adolescents can understand and relate to this message when it is lovingly and continually taught and demonstrated to them.

Providing children with accurate and honest sexual information is of critical importance in today's society. We live in a time of great sexual awareness, and a time of almost total absence of societal restraints and morals. Frances Schaeffer in his book *Whatever Happened to the Human Race,* says,

> Aldous Huxley said it clearly in his brilliant little novel *Brave New World.* In it he pictures a society which has reversed the morality of the present, especially in the area of sexual relationships. Faithfulness within a unique love relationship becomes evil; promiscuity becomes good.[2]

Providing honest, accurate, sexual information within the framework of an open, caring family proves to be one of the most important parental responsibilities of this age. And the payoff is enormous.

> Extensive research demonstrates that parental involvement is the single most critical factor predicting teen sexual behavior. In one study, girls whose parents had a close relationship with them, which included supervising their activities and homework, were 42 percent less likely to become pregnant teens.[3]

It is my prayer that God will help you teach your children about his beautiful gift of sex, and that you will pray for each of your children to develop godly attitudes and behaviors regarding sexuality.

---

[1] David Lewis and Carley Dodd, *National Adolescent Survey,* 1998 Youth & Family Ministry Conference.

[2] Schaeffer, *Whatever Happened to the Human Race,* 136.

[3] Napier, *The Power of Abstinence,* 200.

GLOSSARY

A

Abdomen — The lower part of the trunk of the body (belly).

Abortion — The expulsion of a human fetus (unborn baby). An abortion may result from natural body function (miscarriage) or it may be done intentionally by a doctor at the mother's request.

Adolescence — From the Latin "to grow up." The state or process of growing from childhood to adulthood. Generally the years between 12-19.

Adrenal — One of a pair of glands located above the kidneys. They help produce hormones which control body metabolism.

Amnion — The sac in which the baby is contained inside the uterus.

Anus — The opening at the lower end of the alimentary canal, at the base of the buttocks, through which solid waste passes.

Areola — A ring of dark color around the nipple of a female breast.

B

Bisexual — One who is sexually responsive to or aroused by both sexes.

Bladder — A sac or organ in the region of the pelvis for the storage of urine.

C

Caesarian section — A method of delivery by surgical procedure in which a baby is taken through an incision through the abdomen and uterus. This procedure is done when the mother cannot have a normal vaginal delivery.

Cervix — The neck or constricted lower end of the uterus which leads to the vagina.

Chromosome — Small protein substances that are found in a cell nucleus, and carry the genes in a linear order.

Circumcision — The procedure of removing the loose skin (foreskin) from the end of the penis.

Climax — The high point of excitement in sexual intercourse (orgasm).

Clitoris — A small, sensitive organ located just beneath the lower edge of the pubic bone where the inner folds of the vulva meet. With stimulation it becomes rigid and erect and causes muscular contraction extending to the vagina. When stimulated it is extremely pleasurable to the female. It is similar to a tiny penis.

Coitus — The act of sexual intercourse between two human beings.

Conception — The beginning or fertilization of the organism that grows into a baby. This happens when a sperm attaches to the ovum.

Condom — A thin rubber sheath worn over the penis during sexual intercourse to prevent conception or venereal disease.

Contraception—The prevention of conception by either averting the sperm and ovum from meeting, or by destroying their ability to fertilize. Birth control.

Copulation—Sexual union or intercourse.

D

Douche—The process of cleansing or washing the vagina with water or disinfectants

E

Ejaculate (Ejaculation)—The discharge of semen from the penis.

Embryo—An organism in the earlier stages of its development. In humans it refers to the fertilized egg during the first eight weeks of growth in the uterus.

Epididymis—An elongated tube on the back of the testis (testicle) where the sperm are stored until they travel into the body.

Erection—The condition in which the penis stiffens and becomes rigid. This happens as blood fills tissue during sexual arousal. The penis in this condition is ready for sexual intercourse.

Estrogen—The primary female sex hormone that is partly responsible for breast development and other feminine traits.

F

Fallopian tubes—A pair of slender, hollow tubes connecting the womb with the ovaries. The egg is released by the ovary and through gentle movement of the tube the egg travels to the uterus.

Fertilize or *Fertilization* — To make pregnant. The union of the male sperm and female ovum.

Fetus — In humans, the developing baby from the beginning of the third month until birth.

Foreplay — Sexual stimulation, usually by hugging, petting, kissing, caressing, or rubbing, intended to create sexual arousal and lead to sexual intercourse.

Foreskin — Loose skin covering the head of the penis. It can be removed by circumcision.

Frigidity — The inability of a person, usually a female, to enjoy or respond to sexual stimulation.

G

Gene — Complex part of a chromosome that determines a person's uniqueness. Genes are responsible for color of eyes and hair, facial features, and other traits.

Genital — Pertaining to or noting the sexual organs.

Gland — A cell, group of cells, or organ that produce a secretion. Some glands eliminate waste (sweat gland), others secrete substances which affect growth and development (pituitary, adrenal, thyroid, ovaries, and testes).

Glans penis — The head of the penis.

Gonads — The sex glands (ovaries and testicles).

H

Homosexual — A person who is sexually aroused by or who satisfies sexual desires with a person of the same sex.

Hormone — A chemical substance or compound produced by a group of glands. They interact with each other to stimulate and regulate the activity of various parts of the body.

Hymen — A fold of tissue which partially closes the entrance to the vagina.

I

Impotence — The inability of a male to achieve an erection or an ejaculation. Incapable of functioning sexually.

Incest — Sexual intercourse between relatives or family members.

Intercourse — Sexual coupling (coitus). Intimate physical closeness between a husband and wife. The husband inserts his erect penis in the wife's vagina and through thrusting movements a climax or orgasm is reached. The husband ejects semen and unless preventive measures are taken, pregnancy may result.

L

Labia (labium) — A lip-like fold of skin bordering and protecting the vagina. Sometimes called the outer lips.

Labor — The contraction of the walls of the uterus as the baby is slowly pushed through the

cervix and through the vagina. Labor may
last from a few hours to an entire day.
Lesbian — A female homosexual.

M

Masochism — A perversion in which sexual
gratification depends on suffering physical
pain and humiliation.
Masturbation — Sexual stimulation or
manipulation of one's own genital organs,
often to the point of orgasm. Sexual self-
gratification.
Menarche — The beginning of a female's menstrual
cycle. It generally occurs approximately one
year after the appearance of body and
pubic hair.
Menopause — The period of permanent stoppage
of menstruation in women, usually
occurring between the ages of 45 and 50.
Ovulation stops and pregnancy is no longer
possible.
Menses — The periodic flow of blood and tissues
from the uterus.
Menstruation — The monthly discharge of blood
and tissue from the uterus, occurring
approximately monthly from puberty to
menopause. This fluid lines the womb in
preparation for the growth of a baby, and
when conception does not take place it is
discharged.
Miscarriage — The expulsion or birth of a baby
(fetus) before it is mature. Usually occurs
between the third and seventh month.

N

Navel — A depression or low area in the middle of the abdomen at the point where the umbilical cord was attached to the placenta.

Nocturnal emissions (wet dreams) — The passing or automatic discharge of semen and sperm from the male during sleep. It is experienced by most adolescent boys as a normal way of releasing sexual tension.

O

Orgasm — The climax or peak of sexual intercourse, accomplished by high excitement and followed by a sense of relaxation. In males the ejection of semen occurs with orgasm.

Ovaries — Two reproductive sex glands of a woman. Located in the lower abdominal region. These glands produce tiny eggs (ova) and sex hormones.

Ovulation — The formation and discharge of mature eggs from the ovary to the fallopian tube. Generally occurs every 25-30 days.

Ovum — The female reproductive cell (egg) located in the ovary. The singular form of "ova."

P

Penis — The male genital or sex organ through which urine and semen pass out of the body. A penis is normally about five to seven inches in length and one-and-a-half inches in diameter.

Pituitary — A small, oval gland attached to the base of the brain. It secretes hormones, regulating growth and maturity of the body.

Placenta — The organ formed in the lining of the uterus by the union of the uterine mucous membrane with the membranes of the fetus. It serves to feed the baby and to dispose of waste. The umbilical cord connects to the placenta and the baby.

Pregnant — The condition of having a baby developing in the body. The nurture and growth of a fertilized ovum in the uterus; generally the process takes nine months (280 days).

Prepuce — The fold of skin that covers the head of the penis (foreskin).

Prostitute — A person, usually a woman, who engages in sexual intercourse for money.

Prostate gland — A gland at the base of the bladder, surrounding the urethra, which secretes a fluid that becomes part of the semen.

Puberty — The age at which a person begins rapid physical development and becomes capable of reproduction. It generally occurs between 13 and 16 in boys and between 11 and 14 in girls.

Pubic — Related to the lower part of the body near the pelvis, where hair grows.

R

Rape — The act of physically forcing a person to have sexual intercourse against his or her will.

Rectum — The lower end of terminal section of the large intestine, ending or extending to the anus.

S

Sadism — A perversion in which sexual gratification is gained through causing physical pain or humiliation.

Scrotum — The external sac of skin and muscle fibers in which the testicles hang; located between the legs of males.

Semen — The thick, whitish fluid produced in the male reproductive organs, containing sperm and discharged through the penis. It is produced in the testicles for fertilizing the female ovum.

Seminal vesicle — Two small storage sacs near the urinary bladder and prostate. The sperm cells and seminal fluid are stored here after production.

Smegma — A thick secretion that collects beneath the foreskin or around the clitoris.

Sperm (spermatozoa) — The male sex cell that fertilizes the female ovum (egg) and is produced in the testicles. It is about the size of a pinpoint and is shaped like a tadpole, with a head and tail. It contains genes and chromosomes that are needed to create human life.

Sterile — Incapable of producing offspring.

Sterilization — A process whereby a man or woman is made sterile, or unable to produce children.

T

Testis (pl.,testes) — The male reproductive gland (gonad) suspended in a sac between the legs. These glands produce sperm.

Testosterone — The predominantly male sex hormone secreted by the testicles; stimulates masculine characteristics.

Testicle — One of the two male reproductive glands. They produce sperm.

Thyroid — A gland located in the neck. Its secretion regulates the rates of metabolism and body growth.

U

Umbilical cord — The cord which connects the baby to the placenta within the uterus and through which the baby is fed.

Urethra — The membranous tube through which the urine passes from the bladder to the exterior. In males it also carries the discharge of semen.

Uterus — A muscular, hollow organ of the female reproductive system in which the fertilized ovum implants itself and develops into a baby. During the growth of the baby the uterus stretches and expands.

V

Vagina — The passage leading to or connecting the uterus with the outside of the body.

Vas deferens — The duct or tube that transports the sperm from the testicles to the penis.

Virgin — A person who has never had sexual intercourse.

Vulva — The folds of skin, flesh and other structures which protect the opening of the vagina.